*Secret Weavers*

# Secret Weavers

## Stories of the Fantastic
by Women Writers of Argentina and Chile

Editor
## Marjorie Agosin

Assistant Editor
Celeste Kostopulos-Cooperman

WHITE PINE PRESS

Publication of this book was made possible, in part by grants from the National Endowment for the Arts and the New York State Council on the Arts.

The artwork used on the cover, *Harmony*, 1956, is by Spanish artist Remedios Varo and is used by gracious permission of the Museum of Latin American Art, Washington, D.C.

Grateful acknowledgement is made to the following for permission to reprint previously published material:

"Country Carnival" and "The Legend of the Self-Sufficient Child" by Luisa Valenzuela appeared in *Open Door*. San Francisco: North Point Press, 1988.

"Two Words" by Isabel Allende appeared in *The Stories of Eva Luna*. New York: Macmillan, 1991.

WHITE PINE PRESS
76 Center Street
Fredonia, New York 14063

# Acknowledgements

This anthology has been made possible by a research grant from the Fulbright Commission that allowed me to travel to Buenos Aires and study the fantastic tradition of Argentine women writers. I especially want to thank Rolando Costa Picazo for his encouragement in this project, his inspiring conversations and his kindness. Also, special thanks to Rosemary Lyon. In Buenos Aires, I met many of the writers of this anthology. Their generous spirit allowed me to understand and feel the paradoxes, the beauty and the sense of wonder found in Argentine fantastic literature.

My special recognition to Marcela Solá, Elvira Orpheé, Ana María Shua, Angélica Gorodischer, Liliana Hecker, Alina Diaconú, Luisa Valenzuela, Adolfo Bioy Casares and to Osvaldo Sabino, who encouraged me from the very beginning with this project and introduced me to many of the writers that appear in this anthology.

The translators of this collection have been the true heroes and heroines of this project. Their sensitivity and unselfish work, as well as their talent in rendering the pieces into English, have made this project a powerful and rewarding experience.

I wish to thank in a special way my colleague and friend Celeste Kostopulos-Cooperman for her support throughout this entire project as well as for the many hours of lively discussion we had regarding the introduction. Also, Lorraine Roses deserves special recognition for her collaboration on this book as well as for the kindness she has shown me in the ten years I have been working with her at Wellesley College. The presence of Irene Kestembaum in the Wellesley College department of Spanish has been an inspiring force.

Since I began working with editor Dennis Maloney of White Pine Press, ideas, projects and books have become a reality. His vision and encouragement have been a real inspiration to me, allowing me to have a sense of continuity in the wide scope of Latin American letters. I thank him for his presence, wisdom, and belief in my work.

My husband, John Wiggins, and my son, Joseph, are the sources of joy and wonder in my life and in my writing. I thank them for just being around, for not letting me take my literature too seriously, and for the capacity of laughter and amazement.

*To my mother, Frida Agosín, a secret weaver, a nurturer of words.*

# Contents

Reflections on the Fantastic—Marjorie Agosin / 13

**Compulsive Dreamers**
The Compulsive Dreamer—Silvina Ocampo / 27
Things—Silvina Ocampo / 36
The Velvet Dress—Silvina Ocampo / 40
The House of Sugar—Silvina Ocampo / 44
Thus Were Their Faces—Silvina Ocampo / 53
The Story of María Griselda—María Luisa Bombal / 60
The Little Island—Luisa Mercedes Levinson / 81
The Boy Who Saw God's Tears—Luisa Mercedes Levinson / 85

**And The Wheel Still Spins**
An Eternal Fear—Elvira Orpheé / 93
I Will Return, Mommy—Elvira Orpheé / 100
How the Little Crocodiles Cry!—Elvira Orpheé / 104
For Friends and Enemies—Olga Orozco / 108
And the Wheel Still Spins—Olga Orozco / 117

**The Wild Mirrors**
The Mirror of Melancholy—Alejandra Pizarnik / 133
Blood Baths—Alejandra Pizarnik / 136

Severe Measures—Alejandra Piznarik / 138
Excerpts from *The Wild Papers*—Marosa Di Giorgio / 141
Excerpts from *Dream Time*—Ana María Shua / 144
Other/Other—Ana María Shua / 146
Fishing Days—Ana María Shua / 157
The Man in the Araucaria—Sara Gallardo / 164
The Blue Stone Emperor's Thirty Wives—Sara Gallardo / 166

**Invisible Embroidery**
The Condemned Dress in White—Marcela Solá / 181
Happiness—Marcela Solá / 186
Invisible Embroidery—Marcela Solá / 190
The Storm—Alina Diaconú / 194
Welcome to Albany—Alina Diaconú / 199
The Widower—Alina Diaconú / 203
Country Carnival—Luisa Valenzuela / 210
Legend of the Self-Sufficient Child—Luisa Valenzuela / 216
Viennese Waltz—Alicia Steimberg / 221
Garcia's Thousandth Day—Alicia Steimberg / 227
Segismundo's Better World—Alicia Steimberg / 230

**Letters**
The Perfect Married Woman—Angélica Gorodischer / 243
Letters From an English Lady—Angélica Gorodischer / 248
Under the Flowering Juleps—Angélica Gorodischer / 259
The Resurrection of the Flesh—Angélica Gorodischer / 281

**Annunciations**
When Everything Shines—Liliana Hecker / 287
The Annunciation—Cristina Peri Rossi / 296
Selections from *Silendra*—Elizabeth Subercaseaux
 Tapihue / 311
 Enedina / 312
 Juana / 313
 Silendra / 315
 Francisco / 317
Two Words—Isabel Allende / 320

The Authors / 328
The Translators / 337

# Secret Weavers

# Reflections on the Fantastic

Fantastic literature from early times to the present has seduced, intrigued, disconcerted and impassioned not only its authors but also its many readers. To talk and dream about the fantastic already implies an indefinite territory filled with unlimited possibilities, unknown landscapes and new frontiers. Perhaps the passion for and continuous interest in fantastic literature can be found both in its resistance to classification and its break with conventions that are present in literature of a more realistic type. More than anything, fantastic literature offers territories and spaces for subversion, disorder and illegality by using the only code possible: the imaginary.

The fantastic, whatever genre it occupies, has the option or, better said, the desire to act through what has been culturally defined as forbidden and marginal. By talking and writing about the forbidden, about zones of silence, fantastic literature resides in the area of the *always possible*.

Throughout history women have occupied a prominent position in texts pertaining to the fantastic, texts filled with the mythical worlds of legends and fables. These tales were told by mothers and by grandmothers and their beauty resided in their poetic imaginations, where women, under the disguise of the fantastic, dared to enter worlds filled with subversion. This type of literature approaches a threshold of open possibilities in order to imagine and to penetrate a territory of intuition, magic and the beginnings of language.

Women writers, who have been considered marginal and thus underrated and obliged to exercise a sense of self-censorship in their writing whether in Europe, Latin America or Africa, have had to invent strategies to survive, ways to tell, narrate and be free. It is appropriate to remember the famous story of Sheherezade who, in order to survive, had to invent a new story every night. In the panorama of Latin American literary culture and imagination, we find an endless number of Sheherezades who are very clever and skilled at telling and singing stories, in weaving colorful tapestries that speak through the images that they convey. Although she is still considered a traitor by many, during the period of the conquest of Spanish America, Doña Marina (or Malinche, as the Mexican lover-interpreter of Cortés is known) was the one who translated and told stories, the one who communicated to the enemy the history of her Aztec people and invented in order to save herself from Spanish dominion. In a similar fashion, women writers have had to write coded stories of self-censorship where fantasy and subversion lie hidden within a seemingly ordered narrative voice.

Latin America is full of women who tell stories as they collect water in clay pitchers or as they prepare for combat and recite fantastic narratives told by their female ancestors. In this very act of affirmation and courage, they create new ways of writing by inverting, deforming and exaggerating reality. The fantastic literature that they write is both a refutation as well as an acceptance of what is considered real. It is also part of a totally imaginary world where one can say what cannot be said, where meaning can be disguised, where the structure of authority can be broken, and language can be constantly renewed.

The texts in this collection are joined by several common threads and have elements of fantasy that are related to the everyday experiences of women, to the almost utopian visions of new realities and to the psychological component inherent in science fiction. These elements form a unit of subversive texts whose great magic and inspiration lie within their transgression against and escape from all classification.

Here assembled is a group of women writers from the Southern Cone (a geographical region including Chile, Argentina, and Uruguay) who encompass diverse chronological epochs. They share a common literary tradition which involves the use of the fantastic to articulate not only the meaning of their existence but also that of an entire region besieged by a sense of magical understanding of history. It is not possible to establish particular definitions of rigid structures for the use of language in these stories because these would violate the nature of the fantastic. However, it is possible to state that these stories operate in different historical and social contexts that derive from elements associated with the marvelous and science fiction, as well as with uses of the fantastic linked to the political repression of the Southern Cone.

It is extremely difficult to find a theoretical model to establish categories of the fantastic. There is no abstract entity known as fantastic literature and the numerous studies that have attempted to articulate this experience have done so by dislodging it from its social context. Among these are the investigations of Tzvetan Todorov and his famous book, *An Introduction to Fantastic Literature*. Perhaps we can establish that the fantastic coincides with the elaboration of an open language without codes of definition, conclusions or morals, that it operates in stories where reality is transcended and becomes an imaginary space full of possibilities.

Both Italo Calvino and Jorge Luis Borges have contributed greatly to our understanding of the fantastic. Calvino in his book, *The Uses of Literature* says,

> I leave the critics the task of placing my novels and short stories within or outside of some classification of Fantasy. For me, the main thing in a narrative is not the explanation of an extraordinary event, but the order of things that this extraordinary event

produces in itself and around it; the patterns of symmetry, the network of images deposited around it as in the formation of a crystal. (Italo Calvino, *The Uses of Literature*, New York: Norton, 1979, p. 73)

For Borges, on the other hand, the key to the fantastic resides within the articulation of a new language. His allegories, fictions, poems and essays make a distinction between what language represents and what it wants to represent. Within the border space of that which is spoken and that which is not, arises the space that we would call the fantastic, where the unusual does and does not astonish and where magic is also reality.

For the majority of readers, Latin American fantastic literature operates under the tutelage of the great masters: Jorge Luis Borges, Adolfo Bioy Casares, Julio Cortázar and Gabriel García Márquez. However, although few are acquainted with their works, many women began experimenting with this genre well before their male counterparts and were the true precursors of the form, though their names remained on the shelves of oblivion, without the recognition that they deserved. María Luisa Bombal, for example, wrote the fantastic nouvelle, *House of Mist* (1937) before the famous *Ficciones* (1944) of Borges, and the Mexican, Elena Garro, wrote *Remembrance of Things to Come* (1962) before the publication of García Márquez' *One Hundred Years of Solitude* (1967).

In mid-nineteenth century Argentina, one can find a very interesting figure by the name of Juana Manuela Gorriti, an inexhaustible traveller between Buenos Aires, La Paz and Lima, as well as a writer of fantastic narratives and tales and of stories from Incan mythology. In her novel *Journeys of a Sad Soul* (1876), a young woman protagonist recounts stories from her adolescence, together with all the adventures that occur on her trip. Gorriti's novel and her descriptive travel tales allude to an almost magical reality that is part of the literature and landscape of Latin America, and part of the real world, without overflowing in exotic references and stereotyped landscapes.

Critics say that Gorriti was one of the first writers to actually begin writing fantastic literature by interweaving fiction with history, as portrayed in her essays and tales in the book *Panorama of Life*, in which she gathers together a series of brief stories, ghost tales and vignettes, among them the narration of the execution of Camila O'Gorman. This fusion of the imaginary with fiction and of fiction as an inseparable part of history constitutes perhaps the most important and essential aspect of the legacy of fantastic literature by women in the countries of the Southern Cone.

Beyond the Andean mountain range in the city of Valparaíso, another Anglo-Chilean writer, María Graham, wrote her only book, *A History of My Residence in Chile* (1883), where she mixed typical settings and stories about her experiences as a foreigner in strange lands with her relationship to the earth and all the magical and telluric elements of its legends. Simultaneously, in nearby Perú, Flora Tristán, one of the leading French feminists of the nineteenth century, was traveling alone through Perú and recording fascinating aspects of her journey that also border between the fantastic and the real.

In the late nineteenth century and early twentieth, works by the Argentinians Macedonio Fernández and Jorge Luis Borges and the Uruguayans Leopoldo Lugones, Horacio Quiroga and Felisberto Hernández prepared the groundwork for the development of narratives that later would reflect fantastic tendencies. However, it was not until 1937 that Argentine fantastic literature would experience its greatest achievements. The creative trio of Silvina Ocampo, Jorge Luis Borges and Adolfo Bioy Casares, good friends in Buenos Aires, met to publish their first anthology of fantastic literature; it would include such varied writers as Kipling, Chesterton, Sinclair and Rabelais, as well as the Latin Americans Quiroga, Cortázar, Borges and Macedonio Fernández.

In the postscript of the most recent edition, Adolfo Bioy Casares writes the following:

> We have not departed from the original intention of that eve-
> ning of 1937 to publish an anthology. We spoke about fantastic
> literature and we discussed the stories that seemed the best; one
> of us said that if we were to collect them based upon the notes
> that we had gathered together in our notebooks, that we would

have a good book. We put together this anthology of fantastic literature in 1939. (Jorge Luis Borges, Adolfo Bioy Casares and Silvina Ocampo, *Anthology of Fantastic Literature*, Buenos Aires: Editorial Sudamericana, 1939)

Since we have only included writers from the Southern Cone, our anthology does not pretend to be all-inclusive. Clearly a rich tradition of fantastic literature can also be found in other Latin American countries, as well as within the Hispanic communities that have emerged within the U.S.A. This anthology represents, rather, a selection of powerful precursory voices that began to form strong alliances and traditions in the thirties. We have also included stories of younger, more contemporary, writers from the Southern Cone who continue creating at a vertiginous speed.

The pioneer women writers of this anthology who began writing around the thirties and were part of this Argentine literary scene are represented by the voices of María Luisa Bombal, Silvina Ocampo, and Luisa Mercedes Levinson. Both Levinson and Ocampo were initiated into the enormous challenges of fantastic literature in the city of Buenos Aires, where they collaborated with Borges and participated in his literary circles. Bombal, in spite of having been born and raised in Chile, also formed part of the famous legacy of the journal, *Sur*, directed by Ocampo's sister, Victoria, where the most interesting voices of Latin American and European literature met. Bombal also wrote under the guidance of Borges, who not only discussed but also reviewed and praised the plot of her second novel, *The Shrouded Woman* (1938).

These three women knew each other quite well; they went to the same places and wrote stories of magic and desire. The unifying thread between them is a language in which images of fantasy and disorder prevail.

The stories of Levinson, like "The Whisper of Time" or "The Violated Dream," border on a mythical fantasy where the emphasis is above all on a dream world. In the universe of Ocampo, the city with its bourgeoise structures forms a type of reserved slavery and fantasy and becomes a way to alter the order of things and subvert them to perhaps reach a state of fulfillment. For each author, closed spaces like houses and neighborhoods are places to tie up and punish the cruel destiny of characters who submit to lives of boredom and of cruel existences.

In the universe of María Luisa Bombal, the fantastic functions within a lyrical space where the fable, like many variations of fairy tales that are transformed and distorted, creates a new vision not only of things and of time but also of the feminine condition. Just as Ocampo uses the metaphor of closed spaces to create a horrific dimension of female existence, Bombal, in "The Story of María Griselda," uses images of confinement for her female protagonist and turns beauty into a symbol of punishment.

These three women, who lived in the effervescent city of Buenos Aires of the forties, occupy without a doubt, a privileged place within the rich world of Argentine fantastic literature. In remembering her mother, Luisa Mercedes Levinson, Luisa Valenzuela in the introduction to her recent collection of stories says:

> . . . for those discoveries and much more I want to dedicate this freshly minted collection to the memory of Luisa Mercedes Levinson, my mother, and to the memory of her joy with literature and the way she and Borges used to laugh while writing a short story in collaboration with the memory of those wonderful writers who were often visiting Conrado Nale Roxlo and his alter ego Chamico—humor being the most precious tool of this extended family. (*Open Doors*, Berkeley, California: North Point, 1989, p. 2)

Following these three primary figures, the next generation of writers belongs to the decade of the sixties: Elvira Orpheé, Marcela Solá and Alicia Steimberg. Elvira Orpheé is clearly a writer of fantastic stories as profiled in her two collections, *The Beguiling Old Ladies* and *My Favorite Demons*. Orpheé also skillfully recreates the provincial world of anger and jealousy in her native city, Tucumán. Marcela Solá is also an heir to the legacy of Silvina Ocampo, for her stories possess the ability to transgress order and to make us see the invisible, as occurs in "Invisible Embroidery" and "The Condemned Dress in White," tales where the strange and the anomalous acquire the rhythms and the dimensions of the rites of death and life.

Alicia Steimberg likewise recovers the almost hidden magic of objects that appear and that are transformed in her stories of life as occurs in "Viennese Waltz" or "Segismundo's Better World."

Similarly, the works of Liliana Hecker and Alina Diaconú belong to a generation of writers very active in today's Argentina who are the inheritors of the magical as well as the lyrical world of Ocampo and Orpheé. Alina Diaconú, through an extreme economy of language, explores the psychological dimensions of fantasy through dreams, apparitions and the unexpected linked to the everyday as in her story, "Welcome to Albany." Liliana Hecker's "When Everything Shines" shares Ocampo's preoccupation with the subjugation of women, yet her voice is lyrical, her landscape often rural and her female protagonist submerged in an almost demential magic.

Ana María Shua, Marosa Di Giorgio, Alejandra Pizarnik, Olga Orozco and Sara Gallardo together exemplify how the fantastic does not obey the laws of any genre. Sleep would seem to be composed of unforgettable fragments of nightmares, visions and poems, as portrayed in Shua's "Dream Time," whose reading produces a new understanding of reality and of the zones of the imaginary. Such occurs in the lyrical as well as disturbing world of Marosa Di Giorgio. Her collection, *The Wild Papers*, demonstrates, in hybrid form, the diverse possibilities of fantastic literature and its link to the fairy tale, a phenomenon similar to that used by Sara Gallardo and Alejandra Pizarnik and by Olga Orozco, one of the most distinguished contemporary Argentine poets, who also writes stories in which she postulates an adventure of being, a metaphysics of knowledge as well as a return to identity.

Within this same generation, Luisa Valenzuela and Cristina Peri Rossi use language as a mask, an allegory to express the forbidden and to refer to a silent and closed world that can only be escaped through words and their subversion. In the stories "Country Carnival" by Valenzuela and "Annunciation" by Peri Rossi, the political and the forbidden are disguised beneath the terrain of the unusual as well as the marvelous.

# WHITE PINE PRESS

WHITE PINE PRESS is a non-profit literary publisher established in 1973. We publish fiction, poetry, essays, and literature in translation from a wide variety of languages and cultures including Asian, European, and Latin American. To join our mailing list and receive a copy of our free catalog, please return this card.

Name _____

Address _____

City _____

State _____ Zip _____

WHITE PINE PRESS

76 Center Street

Fredonia, New York 14063

The section "Letters" is occupied by Angélica Gorodischer, perhaps the most important writer of science fiction in Latin America. For Gorodischer the writing of science fiction has nothing to do with wars and intergalactic stars. Science fiction, instead, is a territory that offers a better possibility for being, seeing and speaking. In her rather long story "Under the Flowering Juleps," words also function as a mask that disguises what can and cannot be articulated and where the frontiers of a futuristic utopia merge with the reality of the present.

The other stories of Gorodischer contain a profound feminist message that is disguised in fantasy and fable, as in "The Resurrection of the Flesh" and "The Perfect Married Woman." Here Gorodischer combines irony and fantasy with the marginal role of women.

Stories by two Chilean writers, the internationally-known Isabel Allende and Elizabeth Subercaseaux occupy the last section of this book. Most of Subercaseaux's stories, like those of Bombal, take place in either rural settings, the homes of the bourgeoisie or the estates of Southern Chile. In her *Silendra* the action unfolds in the rural countryside of abandoned peasants where the haunting voices of wise women appear to weave silence with their words, and in Allende's "Two Words," the final story of this collection, the silences, themselves, speak eloquently of the power of language and of women's ability to transform by giving voice to words previously unspoken.

Throughout this introduction I have spoken of the "mask," which perhaps is the most significant way of envisioning these stories together as well as of understanding what these women create. Michael Batkin, in his famous text, *Problems of Dostoevsky*, postulates that in the carnival it is possible to speak with the dead, to hallucinate and to embark on eccentric journeys and separate the borders between reality, dream and desire. Michael Batkin also theorizes that it is possible to violate the acceptable and established:

> It was a genre which did not claim to be definitive of knowing. Lacking finality, it interrogated authoritative truths and replaced them with something less certain. As Batkin puts it the fantas-

tic serves here not in the positive embodiment of truth but in
the search after the truth, its provocation and most important
it's interest. (Rosemary Jackson, *Fantasy: Literature of Subversion*,
New York: Methuen, p.20)

The stories in this collection assume the disorder that is characteristic of the carnival of masks by negating all that is stereo-typical
of Latin America. They also challenge the genre of magical real-
ism, a term coined by Latin American criticism to define the mythical and magical world associated with the presence of the marvelous within the American continent. In 1955 this term was first
used by critics to characterize Latin American writers who were
not subscribing to the naturalism of the period. It is important
to point out, however, that the term was first used by the German
critic Franz Roh to designate the pictorial production of the Post-
Expressionist period.

This anthology includes writers who subvert codes and pre-
established styles in order to transgress the forbidden. Alejandra
Pizarnik, as a result, bases her story on a nefarious woman, the
bloody countess Erzebet Bathory, who assassinated young girls,
devoured them and bathed herself in their blood as a way of steal-
ing youth. Through legend, Pizarnik creates a tale in which she
can address violence, criminality and forbidden desires as well.

The women in this anthology can allow themselves to be open
and excessive in their metaphorical representations of language.
Perhaps this is how these women, like witches and fairies, can really
be free to escape from their destinies as reserved, subjugated writers.
This is perhaps why Liliana Hecker uses the forms as well as the
variations of the fantastic to speak about female obsessions with
order.

These writers are part of a fantastic legacy composed of history
and myth. The voices represented in this book are also the voices
of Latin America because there is nothing more fantastic than a
nation that transports the body of a dead woman for more than
20 years, as in the case of Evita Perón. If we examine carefully these
countries of the Southern Cone, we will discover that they are
immersed in a culture that encompasses fascinating doses of magic

and creativity. As the Cuban novelist Alejo Carpentier has observed, the marvelous does not violate the laws of reality but is instead very much a part of this world, a world that was described as magical in the early chronicles of the conquest.

This anthology reveals that the women of the Southern Cone are not united by countries or geography. They are women rooted in a faith, a vision of the world where language has defined their work and their unlimited imagination. This is not, however, a fantastic world in the surrealistic sense. For Luisa Valenzuela, it is erroneous to associate Latin American fiction with the French surrealist movement and with oneiric representations of reality. According to her, Latin American surrealist literature does not exist.

> ...although this fiction we are here concerned with is described as surrealistic or surrealist as usually happens with non-Latin American readers, it is absolutely realistic literature as you well know, but from another point of view, which could be semantic; for is this thing called reality always scoping explicable limitations or could it be philosophical or metaphysical even pataphysical? In the supplementary reality to the one we were taught to perceive, there is a cosmoginy, a world vision shared with native Americans; nothing must escape your notice but you must also learn to look again with your eyes at the very edge of what is visible. You must learn to look at the world twice. (From an unpublished text by Luisa Valenzuela)

The secret weavers of this anthology, from the balconies of their imaginations, from Buenos Aires to Santiago, and from the mysterious waters of Mar del Plata, invent stories that seem to dance within their minds as well as within those of their readers. Many of them have never been translated into English before. These are writers with unique imaginations that are not from the tropics but rather from the silent and austere regions of the Southern Cone, confined by seas and mountain ranges where the only possible escape is through the privileged frontier of the word.

—Marjorie Agosín

Translated and edited by Celeste Kostopulos-Cooperman.

*Compulsive Dreamers*

# The Compulsive Dreamer

## Silvina Ocampo

There were a million glances in my eyes, and for that reason I thought that by a miracle I had been born in a place where there were rocks and limitless sea. I thought many things which didn't bring me any nearer to the truth, and tired now, I stopped looking and resolved to give myself over to magic without fear and pangs of guilt. There was a deck of cards in our house; I took it and hid it under my coat. No one ever saw me play with cards, or taught me any games... A woman worked in the house who knew how to weave and unweave and who maintained that weavings were just like magic and that any weaving could enable me to tell the future without any difficulty. I accepted the idea, and that's how my fortunetelling career began. I dreamed all the things I'm telling here, or almost all, before I lived them.

I keep the deck of cards under the carpet in my room. If my mother finds it, she'll punish me. I don't do any harm in telling the future. Other times, when I left for school, a very pretty lady I had dreamed about came up to me and, stroking my hair, said to me:

"I've been told you're a fortuneteller; is it true?"

"It's true, but Mother won't let me be one. She says the world is very immoral, and I have no business finding out what adults do. What am I going to find out? If I tell the future, I tell the future, and nobody tells me anything. I find out everything in my dreams, and dreams are no sin."

Smiling, the lady looked at me.

"Those are grownup matters," she said. "If you weren't your mother's daughter, she wouldn't have told you those things. Maybe she's afraid you might find out some family secrets or those of her friends. I think it's very natural. I agree with you, and I think you're going to be a very important person because people from all over the world are going to consult you. Are you going to school now?"

"Yes. I have to hurry. It's eight o'clock." I looked at my wristwatch and saw that it was five minutes to eight. "I've got to run."

The lady bent down and said to me:

"My name is Lila. You won't forget me, will you? Do you like flowers? Then you'll think of me when you think of lilacs. And what's your name?"

"My name's Luz. And since you see light all the time you'll remember me, won't you?"

The lady kissed me and I was off like a shot. When I got to school, I thought it was late. I excused myself with a fib. I said I had fallen, and so it would look as though I had, I tied a handkerchief round my knee, like in my dreams. When it came to history and geography, my fortune telling powers didn't work. In math either. I needed something human, passionate and quite complicated. I didn't like to study. When I got back home, my mother was waiting for me at the door. She asked me to show her my notebooks.

"How sloppy," she told me. "No one would think this notebook belonged to an eleven-year-old girl. I don't understand why you can't follow our way of keeping everything in order."

I listened to her talk while thinking about something else. I thought of the lady that had been so nice to me on the street and who admired me for my knowledge. My mother frowned and said:

"If you keep on like this, I'm going to have to punish you. For your age you think you're a very important person. Don't you know that pride is the worst sin of all?"

I answered her:

"Why is it the worst? Concupiscence is worse, and coitus."

"Don't talk of things you know nothing about."

During this conversation I absentmindedly—because I'm very absentmended—pulled up the little rug in my room with my toe, the place where the decks of cards were hidden. My mother looked aghast.

"Why have you hidden those cards? Those are fortunetelling cards. Fortunetellers use them. You've hidden them for some purpose. You don't do things for no reason."

I knelt down to gather the cards, with the Queen of Hearts peeping out, just like in my dreams. My mother said:

"Give me the cards right now."

"I can't give them to you because a girl from school lent them to me."

"Give them to me immediately."

"Do you want me to behave badly towards her? I promised to give them back to her and not to give them to anyone."

"Your promises don't matter to me. What's the girl's name?"

"Rufina Gomez."

"You never told me that girl was a friend of yours."

"Do I have to ask your permission to have a friend?"

"Permission no, but you don't have to hide it either."

"I tell you I'm not hiding anything. If you can't guess, it's not my fault. You were nicer in my dream."

"Where did you learn to talk with so much arrogance?"

"Right here. You're the only arrogant one."

"This ridiculous dialogue has to end. Give me the cards."

I gave her the cards. They're beautiful cards. Rufina Gomez almost never plays with them; she never even learned to tell fortunes with the cards. Besides, it's terribly easy because every card has written on it in French what's going to happen to the person whose card it is. You really don't know anything; you just shuffle a few times, lay them out one by one on the table, and after counting them one by one, the card that belongs to the person consulting comes up. It's lots of fun. But I no longer have these cards, and I could get along with any cards at all. Basically, fortune-telling is a very easy thing; the people who consult you simply tell you everything that's going to happen, the personality they have, age, illnesses, dangers which threaten them, everything. The client knows everything, and he tells you when he asks, "Do you think I'm going to be unlucky?" or "Do you think I'm going to be very happy?" or "Do you think I'm going to fall in love?" or "Do you think they're going to be unfaithful to me?" Everything is already foretold. You don't have to make any effort at all.

That night I went to bed upset. Not because I was feeling guilty, I admit. I felt that my mother was so out of touch with me that she didn't even know she had offended me. I am eleven years old. How could someone possibly talk to me like that? In this day and age, children are respected as much as grownups. What right did she have to speak to me that way? If I tell my mother that my profession is fortune telling, I think she'll yell at me. I'll try to tell her in my dream. I don't know how long it'll take me to become a respectable person, but I think I can wait patiently. I'll look for some out of the way place to set up my consulting room and everyone will come to ask me advice and I'll use the normal decks of cards so that they won't say I'm doing it for fun. I turn out the light. I want to sleep and I can't.

I can only think about the guy who spoke to me in the street the other day. Before I saw him in person, I saw him in a dream. He was blonde, tall, but that wasn't what I liked best: it was the color of his blue-green-violet eyes. I'll never know what color his eyes were. Maybe if I knew, I wouldn't like them as well; but his voice was unique, too, that strange inflection when he said, "Hi, how are you?" or "Do you want me to take you to the movies? No, because you're too young. They won't let you."

"And you, how old are you?" I asked him.

He answered, "Me? Seventeen. What do you think of that?"

"Nothing. What do you want me to say?"

After this conversation, we didn't see each other again. I will have to find out his name. I'll consult the cards. I shuffled the deck and laid them onto the table. Mother had gone out. I shut my eyes and opened my hands. What might be his name? I thought, but no name came to me. I tried to dream. If I can do it this time, I'm a fortuneteller. I thought of all the names there are until I came to one particular one: Narcissus. It's not that I like it. Only this one satisfied me. I don't understand why. I searched among all the names around until I found the one I was looking for. I finally sat down in an easy chair and thought that his name was Armindo. Why Armindo? I realized that there was no reason to doubt my intuition. The next day when I came out of school, I saw him coming towards me. He said to me:

"Long time no see. Do you know that I miss you?"

"I don't miss you, Armindo?"

"How do you know my name's Armindo?"

"A dream told me. Armindo's a common name. Anyone could be named Armindo."

"I'm not just anyone."

"Me either."

We separated without looking at each other and with no hope of seeing each other again. I locked myself in my room, and Mother asked me:

"Why do you lock yourself in?"

"Because I like to be locked in. There are so many people in this house. I prefer absolute silence."

"But you're not old enough to impose your wishes."

"Is there an age for that?"

"I don't know, but in any case, I think a girl of your age doesn't have the right to do it."

I got up from my seat and ran out of the room because the conversation didn't interest me. It choked me. Things weren't going well at school. I told Mother I didn't like studying and she answered me as snottily as ever.

"You'll keep right on studying until you graduate."

That's the day I had a strange dream. I dreamed about a dog that followed me everywhere. I adopted him. He was gorgeous—

white and black spots—and he talked to me. He told me about his life, just like a grownup. All day long I missed him until all of a sudden, just like magic, when someone left the front door open, he appeared. He came over to me and lay down at my feet. He had a leather collar with studs on it and his name in gold: Clavel. "Clavel," I said to him and kissed him, not on the mouth because Mother doesn't let me, and petted him until bedtime. I made him a bed with a big pillow and a little sheet.

My mother said:

"Where'd you get the dog? Did somebody give him to you?"

"No, Mother. Nobody gave him to me."

"Then... What's his name?"

"Clavel," I told her. "He's mine and I'll never forget him."

This event brought my mother and me together. We would never fight again. She let the dog sleep with me. And it's strange to imagine, but for some reason my mother began to believe in my power to see the future. When someone got sick she would ask me:

"What's wrong with that person? What remedy should I give him?"

I advised strange remedies I had heard mentioned, and she would use them instantly and successfully and be grateful to me. One day she introduced me to the family. I don't know if it was a joke or whether she was serious.

"Let me introduce our little fortuneteller to you. Consult her. She knows everything that's going to happen."

This is how I openly became a fortune teller and a few years later was written up in the paper with Clavel. The headline said in big letters: THE COMPULSIVE FORTUNETELLER.

But I have to tell about the enormous experiments in my life. You know that I had beautiful curly hair and such mysterious eyes that everyone who looked at them never forgot them.

My mother had a boutique where she sold fake, and sometimes real, antiques. I worked for her, and I remember that my inventions were very successful. An angel I made out of cardboard and pigeon feathers was a big hit. I was respected not only as a fortuneteller but as an artist. We made a lot of money. An American family commissioned a number of items I made with my own hands. I invented decks of cards to tell fortunes, and all of these were especially educational.

One afternoon Armindo showed up at the boutique where I helped my mother sell things, just like in my dreams. He came directly over to me. Suddenly he said:

"What are you doing here? I waited for you for several days on the corner where you live, thinking you hadn't forgotten about me. I waited for you at school, too. Do you think because you're some run-of-the-mill kid I'm going to let you get away with the kinds of things you're pulling? I don't like your style, like I don't care for your hairdo or your eyes or this stuff they call antiques in your mother's boutique. I don't like anything about you."

I went over to him with my hands over my ears. Where was the attractiveness I had seen in him the first day I saw him? I told him in a voice difficult to recognize:

"You get out of here right now," and seeing that he refused to obey my orders, I called Clavel and told him in German *fass*, which means "get him."

Clavel came out from under the piano where he was sleeping and jumped Armindo. He bit his arm until blood came out. Hurt by the dog, Armindo left, screaming:

"You're gonna pay for this, you goddamn bitch."

He left the boutique. No one wanted to get involved in the stupid argument and Clavel went back to his place under the piano. Luckily my mother didn't hear the word "bitch" because she doesn't like it. I don't either.

That night I had a warning dream. I was quietly sleeping in my bed when Armindo came in with the intention of raping me. Did he have a knife in his coat? Would I hear him? If Clavel barked at him, would Armindo kill him? None of this happened. My dreams already knew I didn't obey them. Armindo came over to my bed, took out the knife and stuck it in my heart, the only way to kill me, but he didn't kill me and I felt no pain. I laughed at him until the tears were running down my cheeks. When I woke up, life went on, and it was only after many days during which

I couldn't sleep at night that I reached the conclusion that Armindo loved me uncontrollably and that I was a *fortuneteller* who fought against her dreams.

I dreamed that I went up to the attic with a basket full of bottles. The stairs were very steep, and, in the darkness, I lost my footing; I fell from the fifth floor to the fourth, to the third, to the second and kept falling without any floors into the darkness. It wasn't a dream; it was a nightmare. As I was falling, I heard the noise of the elevator; the cables banged against each other, wrapped themselves around me, crushed me. I thought I'd never wake up. Then I seemed to be in church. When I woke up, I had no idea where I was. I got out of bed shaking. Then I firmly decided to go against my dreams.

I never used to go up to the attic. The following day, I decided to go up with a basket, just like in my dream. When I got up there, I felt better. Nothing had happened to me. A couple of days later, I went up again with books, a hundred books and magazines. I went up very, very carefully. Day after day I went up the attic stairs barefoot taking different things up, and each time I did it more quickly, feeling the relief of disobeying my dream. I was killing my dreams. I was killing my power to tell the future so that I'd never die. Clavel followed me. Armindo came looking for me several times in my dreams. Later, when I woke up, I refused to see him. I dreamed I was getting married. The dream of my wedding was photographed and hung on the walls of my bedroom. I closed my eyes. I only kept a beautiful dress that I had on and a bracelet of real gold.

What fortuneteller has a photograph in advance of a lover with blue-green-violet eyes that she uses as a night light? What fortuneteller has managed to have her photographed dreams hanging on the walls of her bedroom? I am a very special fortuneteller, no doubt about it. And in spite of going against my dreams, I am still, poor me, a fortuneteller.

In school they called me the "extraterrestrial." My personality had changed. I didn't care about anything. I was very daring, and I remember that in the playgrounds where there were swings I hurled myself into the air as though I had wings. My dreams began to change. I didn't dream about Armindo or about my friends; everything looked like what I saw in the movies or on TV. I thought I could make up a story that would awaken everybody's interest, but I had to live it because telling it wasn't enough.

It was just about then that I won a prize in one of those TV contests for girls, and I won a trip to Barriloche, along with a pair of skates so I could skate in the snow.

In my dream, on the other hand, the heat was awful. You had to swim in the waters of Rio de Janeiro. I didn't want to live that dream. A knitted suit was part of the prize. My mother gave me a lovely suitcase, which I still have. That's where I put my woolens, the cap and the gloves. The night before I was to receive the prize I couldn't sleep. We were supposed to take the tour bus at seven in the morning. I was already set at five, but the other girls got there late. And as I didn't depend on my dreams to orient me, I visited Constitucion, the place where the trains come in. I had a very hot coffee, and even though they say coffee makes you nervous, I calmed down. I hadn't said good bye to my mother, but this didn't bother me, so that when I got on the bus I felt as light as a feather and so happy that my friends envied me. "Envy me? What does it matter that someone envies you?" I thought it was very funny, and it was part of my adventure. I forgot my house, my garden, all the flowers; I was going to get to know a new world, other faces. If people saw each other every day maybe they'd never get to love each other. You should see different people all the time.

Translated by Nina M. Scott.

# Things

## Silvina Ocampo

The day Camila Ersky turned twenty, someone gave her a gold bracelet with a ruby rose. It was a family heirloom. She liked the bracelet and only wore it on special occasions, like going to a party or to the theatre or a gala event. Still, when she lost it, she didn't share the sadness at its loss with the rest of the family. As valuable as they were, things could be replaced. She valued only people, the canaries that adorned her house, and dogs. During her entire life, I think she was only upset about the disappearance of a silver chain with a medal of the Virgin of Luján set in gold, which one of her admirers had given her. The idea of losing things, those things that we inevitably lose, didn't bother her the way it did the rest of her family or her friends, who were all so vain. She had shed no tears when she saw her birthplace despoiled—once by a fire, another by impoverishment, which was just as searing as fire—of its most valuable adornments (paintings, tables, bureaus, screens, pitchers, bronze statues, fans, marble statues of children, porcelain ballerinas, radish-shaped perfume bottles, entire glass cases of miniature figurines covered with ringlets and beards), just dreadful at times, but valuable. I suspect that her resignation was not a sign of indifference and that she foresaw with a certain unease that some-day these things would take something very precious to her child-hood away from her. She probably liked them better than some of the people who lamented ever losing them. At times she saw them. They began to call on her like people, in lines, especially at night when she was about to fall asleep, when she travelled by train or car or simply when she took her accustomed route to work. Many times they annoyed her like insects; she wanted to shoo them away, think about other things. Many times, for lack of imagina-tion, she would describe them to her children in the stories she told them for amusement while they ate. They didn't care about polish, or beauty, or mystery; it didn't matter.

One winter afternoon she was returning from doing some errands in the city streets, and when she crossed a plaza she stopped to rest on a bench. (Why does it have to be Buenos Aires? There are other cities with plazas.) An evening light bathed the branches, the streets, the houses which surrounded her—the kind of light that sometimes heightens the perception of happiness. For a long time, she looked at the sky, stroking her spotted kid gloves; then, attracted by something that shone on the ground, she lowered her eyes and after a few moments saw the bracelet she had lost over fifteen years ago. With the same emotion that saints must have felt at their first miracle, she picked the thing up. Night fell before she decided to put the bracelet on her left wrist as she used to do.

When she got home, after having looked at her arm to make sure the bracelet had not disappeared, she told her children, who didn't interrupt their playing, and her husband, who looked at her suspiciously and didn't stop reading the paper. For many days, in spite of the indifference of the children and the distrust of her husband, she was awakened by the joy of having found the brace-let. The only people who would have been properly surprised had died.

She began to remember with greater precision the things that had inhabited her life; she recalled them with nostalgia, with an unknown anxiety. As in an inventory, following reverse chronological order, there appeared in memory the rock crystal dove with the broken beak and wing, the piano-shaped candy dish, the bronze statue holding a torch with little light bulbs; the marble pillow with sky blue stripes and tassels, the opera glass with a mother-of-pearl handle, the engraved cup and the ivory monkeys with little baskets full of baby monkeys.

In the most natural way for her and the most incredible for us, little by little she began recovering the things that for so long had dwelt only in her memory.

Simultaneously, she noticed that the happiness she had felt in the beginning was changing to unease, to fear, to concern.

She scarcely looked at the things, for fear of discovering that some object was missing.

While Camila grew nervous, attempting to think of other things—in markets, stores, hotels, anywhere at all—the things appeared, from the bronze statue with the torch that illuminated the entrance of the house to the charm with the heart pierced by an arrow. The gypsy doll and the kaleidoscope were the last ones. Where did she find those toys which were part of her childhood? I'm ashamed to tell you because you, dear readers, will think that I'm only after the surprise effect and am not telling the truth. You'll be thinking that the toys were ones like the originals but not the same ones, that naturally more than one gypsy doll and one kaleidoscope exist. Luck would have it that the doll's arm was tatooed with a butterfly in India ink and that the kaleidoscope had the name "Camila Ersky" engraved on the copper barrel.

If it were not so touching, this story might be boring. If it doesn't seem touching to you, dear readers, it's at least short and telling it will be good practice for me.

In the dressing rooms of the theatres Camila regularly attended, she found the toys, which, through a series of coincidences, belonged to the daughter of a ballerina who insisted on swapping them for a mechanical bear and a circus of some plastic material. She went home with the old toys wrapped in newspaper. When she was on her way home, she tried several times to leave the package on a stair landing or on the threshold of some door.

There was no one at home. She opened the window wide and breathed in the afternoon air. Then she saw the things lined up along the wall of her room, just the way she had dreamt she would see them. She knelt down to caress them. She ignored everything. She saw that the things had faces, those horrible faces things take on when we have looked at them for a very long time.

By means of a sum total of joys, Camila Ersky had finally entered hell.

Translated by Nina M. Scott.

# The Velvet Dress

## Silvina Ocampo

Perspiring, wiping our foreheads with our handkerchiefs, which we had wet down in the Recoleta fountain, we got to the house with the garden on Ayacucho Street. How funny!

We went up in the elevator to the fourth floor. I was in a bad mood, as I didn't want to go out because my dress was dirty, and I had planned to spend the afternoon washing and ironing the bedspread of my little bed. We rang the bell; the door was opened for us, and we went into the house, Casilda and I, with the package. Casilda is a seamstress. We live in Burzaco and the trips into the city make her ill, above all when we have to go to the nothern quarter, which is so out of the way. Casilda right away asked the maid for a glass of water to take the aspirin she had in her wallet. The aspirin fell on the floor along with the glass and the wallet. How funny!

We went up a carpeted staircase (it smelled of mothballs) with the maid going first, who then showed us into Señora Cornelia Catalpina's bedroom; her name was terribly hard for me to remember. The bedroom was red all over, with white drapes and mirrors with gold frames. We waited a long time for the lady to come in from an adjoining room, where we could hear her gargling and talking to different voices. We could smell her perfume, and a little while later she came in wearing a different perfume. She was complaining when she said hello to us:

"How lucky you are to live outside of Buenos Aires! At least there's no soot there. There might be rabid dogs and burning garbage... Look at my bedspread. So you think it's gray? No. It's white. A flake of snow." She took my chin in her hand, "You don't have to worry about those things. What a happy age! You're eight, aren't you?" And turning to Casilda, she added, "Why don't you put a rock on her head so she won't grow? Our own youth depends on the ages of our children."

Everybody thought my friend Casilda was my mother. How funny!

"Señora, do you want to try it on?" asked Casilda, opening the package which was fastened with pins. She told me, "Reach me the pins out of my purse."

"Try it on! That's torture for me! If someone could try my clothes on for me, how happy I'd be! It tires me out so."

The lady got undressed and Casilda tried to put the velvet dress on her.

"When are you leaving, Señora?" she asked to get her mind on other things.

The lady couldn't answer. The dress would not go over her head: something was caught at her neck. How funny!

"Velvet sticks a lot, Señora, and today it's hot. Let's put a little talcum on you."

"Get it off me, I'm suffocating," exclaimed the lady.

Casilda removed the dress and the lady sat down in an easy chair, on the point of fainting.

"When are you leaving, Señora?" Casilda asked her again to distract her.

"Any time now. Today, what with planes, you can go whenever you want. The dress has to be ready. Just imagine that there's snow there. Everything is white, clean and shining."

"You're going to Paris, aren't you?"

"I'm going to Italy as well."

"Can you try the dress on again, Señora? We'll be through in a minute."

The lady agreed with a sigh.

"Raise your arms so that we can get the sleeves over them first," said Casilda, taking up the dress and putting it back on her.

For a few seconds, Casilda tried unsuccessfully to pull down the skirt, so that it would slide down over the lady's hips. I helped her the best I could. Finally she got the dress on her. For a few moments, the lady rested, exhausted, in the chair, then stood up to look at herself in the mirror. The dress was beautiful and very ornate! A dragon embroidered in black sequins glittered on the left side of the gown. Casilda knelt down, looking at her in the mirror and adjusted the hem of the skirt. Then she stood up and began to put pins into the seams of the gown, on the neck, on the sleeves. I touched the velvet; it was rough when I ran my hand one way and soft when I ran it the other. The contact with the nap set my teeth on edge. The pins dropped onto the wooden floor, and I picked them up religiously one by one. How funny!

"What a dress! I don't think there's another as lovely in all of Buenos Aires," said Casilda, letting a pin she'd been holding between her teeth fall. "Don't you like it, Señora?"

"Very much. Velvet is the material I like the best. And materials are like flowers; you have your favorites. I think velvet is like tuberoses."

"Do you like tuberoses? They're so sad," Casilda protested.

"Tuberoses are my favorite flower, but they're not good for me. When I smell their scent I get disturbed. Velvet sets my teeth on edge, gives me goosebumps the way linen gloves would when I was little, and yet for me, no material in the world can compare. To feel its softness in my hand attracts me even though at times it repels me. What better dressed woman is there than the one who wears black velvet! It needs no lace collar, no pearl necklace; anything would be superfluous.

When she stopped speaking, the lady was breathing with difficulty. The dragon, too. Casilda took a newspaper that lay on a table and began to fan over her with it, but the lady stopped her, asking her not to blow air on her because air was not good for her. How funny!

On the street, I heard the cries of street vendors. What were they selling? Fruit, ice-cream, maybe? The whistle of the man who sharpens knives, the bell of the ice-cream cone man also reverberated up and down the street. I didn't run to the window to find out, like other times. I could not get enough of watching the fitting of this dress with the sequin dragon. The lady stood up again and stood in front of the mirror, tottering. The sequin dragon tottered as well. The dress was practically perfect now, except for an almost imperceptible gather under her two arms. Casilda reached for her pins again to stick them dangerously into the extra folds of the that supernatural material.

"When you've grown up," the lady said to me, "you'll want to wear a velvet dress, won't you?"

"Yes," I answered, and felt how the velvet of that dress was strangling me with gloved hands. How funny!

"Now I'm going to take the dress off," said the lady.

Casilda helped her remove it, taking the full skirt in her hands. She struggled vainly for a few seconds, and then let the dress fall.

"I'll have to sleep in it," the lady said, as she stood in front of the mirror and looked at her pale face and at the dragon quivering over her beating heart. "Velvet is marvelous, but it's heavy," and she put her hand to her forehead. "It's a prison. How do you get out? They should make dresses out of immaterial cloth, like air, light or water."

"I recommended natural silk," Casilda protested.

The lady fell to the floor and the dragon writhed. Casilda bent over her body until the dragon lay still. Again I stroked the velvet, which felt like an animal. Casilda said sadly, "She's dead. And it was such a job for me to make this dress! Such a job!"

How funny!

Translated by Nina M. Scott.

# The House of Sugar

## Silvina Ocampo

Superstitions wouldn't let Cristina live. A coin with a worn design, an inkspot, the moon seen through two panes of glass, the initials of her name casually carved on a tree trunk made her mad with fear. When we met, she was wearing a green dress that she kept on wearing until it was in tatters because she told me it brought her luck and as soon as she would put on a blue one, which suited her better, we would never see each other again. I tried to combat these absurd obsessions. I pointed out to her that she had a broken mirror in her room, and even though I insisted on the wisdom of throwing broken mirrors into the water on a moonlit night to get rid of the bad luck, she kept it; she was never afraid that the lights in the house would suddenly go out, and in spite of the fact that it was a sure way to invite death, she calmly lit any number of candles; she always left her hat on her bed, a mistake no one would ever make. Her fears were of a personal nature. She imposed real privations on herself; for example, she could not buy strawberries in the month of December, nor hear certain music, nor decorate the house with red fish, which she liked so very much.

There were certain streets we could not cross, certain people, certain movie theatres we could not visit. At the beginning of our relationship, these superstitions seemed charming to me, but later on they began to irritate and, seriously, to worry me. When we got engaged, we had to look for a new apartment because, according to her beliefs, the fate of the previous tenants would influence her life (she never at any time mentioned mine, as though the danger were only to her and our lives were not joined by love). We went through every neighborhood in the city; we got to the farthest suburbs in search of an apartment in which no one had ever lived. Every one was either rented or sold. At last I found a small house in Montes de Oca Street that looked as though it were made of sugar. Its whiteness shone with an extraordinary glow. It had a phone and a tiny garden out front. I thought the house had been recently built, but I found out a family had lived in it in 1930 and that later, in order to rent it, the owner had fixed it up a little. I had to make Cristina believe that no one had lived in the house and that it was the perfect place: the house of our dreams. When Cristina saw it she exclaimed:

"What a difference from the apartments we've looked at! Here everything smells of cleanliness. Nothing can influence our lives and stain them with thoughts that contaminate the air."

A few days later, we got married and moved in. My in-laws gave us the bedroom furniture, and my parents things for the dining room. The rest of the house we furnished little by little. I was afraid that Cristina might find out about my lie from the neighbors, but luckily she always shopped outside the neighborhood and never spoke to them. We were happy, so happy that at times I got frightened. It seemed that our peace would never be shattered in that house of sugar, until a phone call destroyed my illusion. Luckily that time Cristina did not answer the telephone, but perhaps she would on another occasion. The person who called asked for someone named Violeta; undoubtedly it was the previous tenant. If Cristina found out that I had deceived her, our happiness would surely be over: she'd never speak to me again, would ask for a divorce, and at the very least we'd have to leave the house to go and live in Villa Urquiza or perhaps Quilmes, tenants in one of those houses where they'd promise to give us a place in which to build—with what? with garbage, because our money wouldn't be enough for better materials—one room and a kitchen. During the night, I took care to disconnect the receiver, so that no unexpected phone call would wake us. I put a mailbox on the door of the house; I was the one who had the key and who gave out the letters.

Early one morning there was a knock on the door and someone left a package. From my room, I heard my wife arguing; then I heard the sound of crumpled paper. I went down the stairs and found Cristina with a velvet dress in her arms.

"They've just brought me this dress," she said to me happily.

She ran upstairs and put on the dress, which was very low cut.

"When did you have it made?"

"A while ago. Does it suit me? I'll put it on when we go to the theatre, don't you think?"

"How did you pay for it?"

"Mother gave me a little money."

That seemed strange to me, but I didn't say anything, so as not to hurt her feelings.

We were madly in love. But my uneasiness grew, even when I was holding Cristina in my arms at night. I noticed that her character had changed: from happy to sad, from expansive to reserved, from calm to nervous. She had no appetite. She no longer prepared those rich, somewhat heavy desserts I liked, the ones made with whipped cream and chocolate, nor did she periodically decorate the house with nylon ruffles on the toilet seat, the dining room shelves, the wardrobes, all over the place, the way she used to. She no longer waited for me with ladyfinger cookies at teatime, nor wanted to go to the theatre or the movies in the evening, not even when we were given tickets. One afternoon a dog came into the garden and lay down by the front door, howling. Cristina, who gave him meat and something to drink, then a bath, which changed the color of his fur; she said that she would give him a home and would call him LOVE because he had come to our house at a time of true love. The roof of the dog's mouth was black, an indication that he was a purebred.

One afternoon I came home unexpectedly. I stopped at the entrance because I saw a bicycle parked in the garden. I went in quietly, hid behind a door and heard Cristina's voice.

"What do you want?" she repeated twice.

"I've come to get my dog," said a young woman's voice. "He's gone by this house so often that he's come to love it. This house looks like it's made of sugar. Ever since it was painted people have noticed it. But I liked it better before, with that romantic pink color old houses have. This house was very mysterious for me. I liked everything about it: the fountain where the birds came to drink; the flowering vines, like yellow bugles; the orange tree. Ever since I was eight years old, I've wanted to meet you, ever since the day we talked on the phone, remember? You promised you would give me a kite."

"Kites are for boys."

"Toys don't have gender. I liked kites because they're like huge birds; I used to imagine flying on their wings. For you it was a game to promise me that kite; I couldn't go to sleep that night. We met in the bakery; you had your back to me, and I couldn't see your face. From that day on I have thought of nothing else except you, about your face, your soul, your lying ways. You never gave me that kite. The trees spoke to me of your lies. Later we went to live in Moron, with my parents. Now I've been back for a week."

"I've only lived in this house for three months, and before that I never came to this neighborhood. You must be mistaken."

"I imagined you exactly as you are. I imagined you so many times! And to top it all off, my husband used to be your boyfriend."

"I've never had a boyfriend except for my husband. What's the dog's name?"

"Brute."

"Take it away, please, before I get too attached to it."

"Listen, Violeta. If I take the dog home, he'll die. I can't take care of it. We live in a very small apartment. My husband and I work, and there's nobody to take him out for walks."

"My name isn't Violeta. How old is he?"

"Brute? Two. Do you want to keep him? I'd come to see him every now and then because I like him a lot."

"My husband doesn't want strangers coming into the house, nor for me to accept a dog as a gift."

"Don't tell him, then. I'll wait for you every Monday at seven p.m. in the Plaza Colombia. Do you know where it is? In front of St. Felicitas church. Or if you'd prefer, I'll meet you wherever and whenever you want: like Constitution bridge or Lezama Park. I'll be happy just to look at Brute's eyes. Will you do me the favor of keeping him?"

"All right. I'll keep him."

"Thanks, Violeta."

"My name isn't Violeta."

"Did you change your name? For us you're Violeta. Always the same mysterious Violeta."

I heard the click of the door and Cristina's heels going up the stairs. I waited a while before leaving my hiding place and pretended I had just arrived. In spite of having witnessed the fact that the conversation was totally innocent, a silent distrust began to eat at me. I felt I had been at a theatre performance and that reality was somewhere else. I didn't tell Cristina that I had been there during the young woman's visit. I waited for things to happen, always fearful that Cristina would discover my lie, regretting that we had moved to this neighborhood. Every afternoon, I crossed the plaza in front of St. Felicitas church to see if Cristina had kept her appointment. Cristina seemed not to notice my unease. At times, I thought I had dreamed the whole thing. Hugging the dog, one day Cristina asked me:

"Would you like my name to be Violeta?"

"I don't like names of flowers."

"But Violeta is pretty. It's a color."

"I prefer your name."

One Saturday, in the late afternoon, I found her on Constitution bridge, leaning on the iron railing. I came up to her, and she was not startled.

"What are you doing here?"

"I'm looking around. I like to look at the rails from above."

"It's a very depressing place, and I don't like you to be walking around alone."

"I don't think it's that depressing. And why can't I go around alone?"

"Do you like the black smoke from the engines?"

"I like means of transportation. To dream about trips. Leave without leaving. 'To go and to stay and by staying to leave.' "

We went back home. Mad with jealousy (Jealous of what? Of everything.), during the trip home, I barely spoke to her.

"We might buy some little house in San Isidro or Olivos; this neighborhood is so unpleasant," I told her, pretending that it would even be feasible for me to get a house in those places.

"Don't feel that way. We have Lezama park very close to here."

"It's a mess. The statues are broken, the fountains have no water, the trees stink. Beggars, old men and cripples go around with bags, either to dump stuff or go through the garbage."

"I don't notice those things."

"Before you didn't even want to sit down on a bench where someone had eaten an orange or left some bread."

"I've changed a lot."

"No matter how much you've changed, you can't like a park like that. I know it has a museum with marble lions that guard the entrance and you used to play there when you were little, but that doesn't mean anything."

"I don't understand you," Cristina answered me. And I felt that she despised me, with a scorn that could lead to hate.

For days that seemed years to me, I watched her, attempting to hide my anxiety. Every afternoon, I went by the plaza in front of the church and on Saturdays to that awful black Constitution bridge. One day I dared to say to Cristina:

"If you were to find out that this house was once lived in by other people, what would you do? Would you leave?"

"If anyone had lived in this house, that person would have to be like the little statues of sugar that they put on desserts or on birthday cakes: a person as sweet as sugar. This house gives me confidence. Could it be the little garden out front that gives me peace? I don't know! I wouldn't leave here for all the money in the world. Besides, we'd have nowhere to go. You told me so yourself a while back."

I didn't insist because I knew I was going to lose. To feel better, I figured that time would take care of things.

One morning the front doorbell rang. I was shaving and heard Cristina's voice. When I was finished shaving, my wife was already talking to the intruder. I watched them through the crack in the door. The woman had such a serious voice and such huge feet that I burst out laughing.

"If you see Daniel again you're really going to pay for it, Violeta."

"I don't know any Daniel, and my name isn't Violeta," my wife answered.

"You're lying."

"I'm not in the habit of lying. I don't have anything to do with Daniel."

"I want you to know how things are."

"I don't want to listen to you."

Cristina put her hands over her ears. I went into the room and told the woman to leave. I looked closely at her feet, hands and face. Then I realized that it was a man dressed as a woman. I didn't have time to think about what I should do; he disappeared like lightning, leaving the door ajar behind him.

Cristina and I didn't discuss the episode; I will never understand why not. It was as though our lips were sealed for anything apart from nervous, unsatisfying kisses or futile words.

During that time that was so sad for me, Cristina began to sing. She had a nice voice, but it exasperated me because it was part of that secret world that distanced her from me. Why, when she had never sung before, did she now sing night and day, while getting dressed or taking a bath or cooking or pulling down the shades!

One day I heard Cristina say with an enigmatic air:

"I suspect I'm inheriting someone else's life, the ups and downs, the mistakes and the successes. I'm bewitched." I pretended not to hear that tormenting sentence. Nevertheless, I began to inquire in the neighborhood who Violeta was, where she lived, all sorts of details about her life.

Half a block from our house was a store where they sold postcards, paper, notebooks, pencils, erasers and toys. The proprietess of that store seemed the best person for my investigation; she was talkative and curious and liked to be flattered. Under pretext of buying a notebook and pencils, I went one afternoon to talk to her. I said nice things about her eyes, hands and hair. I didn't dare utter the name Violeta. I explained to here that we were neighbors. Finally I asked her who had lived in our house. I asked her shyly:

"Wasn't there someone called Violeta?"

She answered some very vague things, which only upset me more. The next day, I tried to find out more details in the grocery store. They told me that Violeta was in a mental hospital and gave me the address.

"I sing with a voice that isn't mine," Cristina told me, once again assuming her mysterious air. "Before it would have upset me, but now I love it. I'm someone else, perhaps happier than I am."

Again I pretended not to hear her. I was reading the paper.

I was so wrapped up in finding out things about Violeta's life, I admit I was neglecting Cristina.

I went to the asylum, which was in Flores. There I asked for Violeta and they gave me the address of Arsenia Lopez, her singing teacher.

I had to take the train at the Retiro station, so it would take me to Olivos. During the ride, I got something in my eye, so when I got to Arsenia Lopez's house my eyes were watering as though I had been crying. From the front door, I could hear women's voices singing scales, accompanied by a piano that sounded more like a hurdy-gurdy.

Tall, thin, frightening, Arsenia Lopez appeared at the end of a corridor with a pencil in her hand. I told her shyly that I had come to find out about Violeta.

"Are you the husband?"

"No, I'm a relative," I answered, drying my eyes with a hand-kerchief.

"You must be one of her innumerable admirers," she told me, half-closing her eyes and taking my hand. "You've come to find out what they all want to know—how were Violeta's last days? Sit down. There's no reason to think that a dead person necessarily has to be pure, faithful, good."

"You want to make me feel better," I told her.

Squeezing my hand with her own damp one, she answered:

"Yes. I want to make you feel better. Violeta wasn't only my student but my close friend. If she got angry at me, it was perhaps because she had told me too many things about herself and could no longer deceive me. The last days I saw her, she complained bitterly about her fate. She died of envy. She kept saying 'Someone has stolen my life, but she'll pay for it. I won't have my velvet dress anymore—she'll have it; Brute will belong to her; men will dress up as women to come into her house instead of mine; I'll lose my voice, which I will place in her undeserving throat; we won't put our arms around Daniel on Constitution bridge, dreaming of an impossible love, leaning on the iron railing the way we used to, watching the trains leave.' "

Arsenia Lopez looked me in the eye and told me:

"Don't be upset. You'll find a lot more faithful women. We already know she was beautiful, but is beauty the only thing in the world?"

Mute, horrified, I left that house without revealing my name to Arsenia Lopez who, when she said good-bye to me, attempted to give me a hug to show her sympathy.

From that day on, Cristina, at least for me, became Violeta. I tried to follow her all the time, to surprise her in her lovers' arms. I distanced myself so far from her that I saw her as a total stranger. One winter night, she fled. I looked for her until dawn.

I don't know who is whose victim in this house of sugar, which now stands empty.

Translated by Nina M. Scott.

# Thus Were Their Faces

## Silvina Ocampo

*Thus were their faces and their wings
were stretched upward; each had two wings,
each of which touched the wing of another.*
—Ezekiel 1:11

How did the little kids come to find out? There'll never be an explanation. Besides, you have to explain just what they came to find out and if the grownups didn't already know it. Nevertheless one assumes that it was a real event and not a fantasy, and only people who didn't know them and who didn't know the school and the women teachers could deny it without feeling any scruples.

During the hour at which they rang the bell—uselessly, as always, just to maintain a custom—that announced the milk, or a little later, during recess, when the children ran to the back patio, or maybe—and this is more likely—unconsciously, slowly, on a daily basis, with no order of age or gender, they came to find out, and I say *came to*, because it was noticed in many ways that up to this moment they were hoping for something that would permit them to hope again and definitively for something very important. We know for a fact that from this moment on, which I mention in an imprecise way, but about which many conjectures have been

made, without losing that apparent innocence that is so characteristic of childhood, the children thought about nothing else.

After thinking about it, everything leads one to suppose that
the children found out simultaneously. In the bedrooms, while falling asleep; in the dining hall, while eating; in chapel, while pray-
ing; on the playground, while playing tag or "London Bridge is
Falling Down," or sitting at their desks doing homework or serv-
ing detention; in the plaza, while swinging in hammocks; or in
the bathrooms, attending to their personal hygiene (important
moments, because while they last you can forget about your problems), with the same sullen and distracted look, their minds, like
little machines, spun the plot of one and the same thought, the
same desire, the same expectation.

The people who saw them go by all dressed up, clean and nicely
groomed on church or state holidays or on any given Sunday, said:

"Those children all belong to the same family or to some mysterious brotherhood. They're identical. The poor parents! They'll
never recognize their own child! In these modern times, one and
the same pair of scissors cuts out all children (the girls look like
boys and the boys like girls); times with no spiritual dimension
are so cruel."

In truth, their faces resembled each other very closely and were
just as devoid of expression as the centers of the rosettes or the
face of the Virgin of Lujan on the medallions they wore on their
chests.

But all of them, in the beginning, felt alone, as though they were
covered by an iron framework that isolated them and made them
hard. The pain felt by each one was an individual and terrible pain;
happiness, too, was painful and for the same reason. Humiliated,
they imagined themselves different, one from another, like dogs
with their very diverse breeds, or like the prehistoric monsters in
the illustrations. They thought that the secret, which at that very
time was breaking up into forty secrets, was not shared and would
never be. But an angel came, the angel that sometimes ministers
to the multitudes; he came, holding his shining mirror on high
like the poster of a candidate, a hero or a dictator carried by demon-

strators and showed them the identity of their faces. Forty faces were the same face; forty consciences were the same conscience, in spite of differences of age and of family.

As horrible as a secret may be, when it is shared it stops being horrible because its horror gives pleasure: the pleasure of unceasing communication.

But whoever supposes that it was horrible is getting ahead of events. Actually no one knew if it was horrible and became beautiful or was beautiful and became horrible.

When they felt surer of themselves, they wrote each other letters on different-colored stationery, with festoons of lace or little pasted-on figures. In the beginning, the letters were laconic, later on, longer and more confused. They chose strategic places that they used as post offices so that the others could collect the letters.

Because they were happy accomplices, the habitual inconveniences of life no longer bothered them.

If any one of them thought about making a decision, all the others immediately decided to do the same thing.

As though they had wanted to look alike, the little ones walked on tiptoe to appear taller; the older ones stooped in order to look shorter. One could say that the redheads toned down their fiery hair and the dark ones moderated the darkness of a passionately swarthy skin. They all had the same brown or gray lines characteristic of light eyes. Not one of them bit his nails any more, and the only one who sucked his thumb stopped.

They were also united by the violence of their gestures, by their simultaneous laughter, by a noisy and then suddenly sad solidarity which was hidden in their eyes. They were so indivisibly united that they could have defeated an army, a pack of hungry wolves, a plague, hunger, thirst, or the zealous lethargy which does away with civilizations.

At the top of a slide, not because of malice but because of frenzy, they were on the point of killing a little boy who had gotten into their midst. On a street, under the admiring enthusiasm of them all, a street flower vendor narrowly avoided being annihilated along with his merchandise.

At night, in the closets, the pleated navy skirts, the pants, the blouses, the stiff white underwear, the handkerchiefs, all squeezed together in the darkness with the same life that their owners had transmitted to them during the day. The lined-up shoes, ever closer together, formed an energetic and organized army; they walked just as much at night without their owners as during the day with them. A spiritual clay stuck to their soles. Shoes are pathetic enough when they are alone! The soap that went from hand to hand, mouth to mouth, chest to chest, took on the shape of their souls. Bars of soap lost among the toothpaste and the nailbrushes! All identical!

"The voice goes out to those who speak. Those who don't speak transmit their strength to the things around them," said Fabia Hernandez, one of the teachers; but neither she, nor Lelia Isnaga nor Albina Romarin, her colleagues, could penetrate the closed world that at times dwells in the heart of a single man (who defends and surrenders himself to his misfortune or his bliss). That same closed world dwelt in the hearts of forty children! The teachers, for love of their work and with utmost dedication, wanted to discover the secret. They knew that a secret can be poisonous to a soul. Mothers fear it for their children's sake; as beautiful as a secret might be, they think, who knows what demons lurk there!

The teachers wanted to surprise the children. They would suddenly put out the lights in the bedrooms under pretext of examining the roof where some pipes had burst or of catching the mice that had invaded the main storerooms; under pretext of imposing silence they interrupted recess, saying that the noise bothered a sick neighbor or the ceremony of some wake; under pretext of observing their religious conduct, the teachers came into the chapel, where excessive mysticism might allow for the articulation of disjointed yet clamorous and difficult words in the throes of divine love, before the flames of the tapers that lit their hermetic faces.

Like fluttering birds, the children would burst into the movies or theatres or some charity function, as they had the opportunity of being amused by picturesque forms of entertainment. Their heads would swivel from right to left and left to right all at the same time, revealing the full extent of their similarity.

Miss Fabia Hernandez was the first to notice that the children had the same dreams, that they made the same mistakes in their notebooks, and when she scolded them for having no character, they smiled gently, something they did not usually do.

Not one of them minded being punished for the mischief done by a classmate. Not one minded having another be praised before the others for work done by him.

On various occasions, the teachers accused one or two of them of doing the homework for the rest of the class, as there was no other explanation for the similarity of their handwriting and the sentences they used in their compositions. The teachers found out that they were mistaken.

In art class, when the teacher tried to stimulate their imaginations by telling them to draw any object they wished, during an alarming time they all drew wings, whose shapes and sizes showed an infinite number of variations without, according to her, taking away anything from the similarity of the whole. When they were reproached for always drawing the same thing, they grumbled and at last wrote on the blackboard: *We feel wings, Miss.*

Without falling into a disrespectful error, could one claim that they were happy? Within the scope of how children, with their limitations, can be happy, there is every indication that they were, except in the summer. The summer heat weighed on the teachers. Just when the children liked to run around, climb trees, wrestle on the lawn or roll down hills, naps, the dreaded custom of naps, took the place of outings. Crickets sang, but they didn't hear this song, which intensifies the feeling of heat. Radios blared, but they didn't hear this noise, which makes summer, with its sticky asphalt, so unbearable.

They wasted many hours waiting around for the teachers with screens to diminish the sun for the heat, and when they were left alone played unintentional tricks like calling to a dog from the balcony, who, upon seeing so many possible simultaneous masters gave a delirious leap towards them, or, by thumbing their noses at her, provoking the ire of a lady, who would then ring the bell and complain of such insolence.

An unexpected windfall allowed them to spend the summer at the seashore. The girls sewed themselves modest bathing suits; the boys bought theirs at a discount store whose merchandise smelled of castor oil, but the suits were of a stylish design, the kind that looks good on anyone.

To highlight the fact that they were going on summer holiday for the very first time, the teachers used a pointer to show on the map the blue dot by the Atlantic Ocean where they were going.

They all dreamt the same dream of the Atlantic and of the sand.

When the train pulled out of the station, handkerchiefs waved from the windows like a flock of doves; this is in a photograph that came out in the papers.

When they reached the sea, they barely looked at it; they kept on seeing the imaginary ocean before they saw the real one. When they got used to the new landscape, it was difficult to hold them back. They ran after the foam that formed shapes similar to snow. But happiness did not let them forget the secret, and gravely they returned to their rooms, where communication among them was more pleasurable. Even though love was not at stake, something very akin to love united them, made them happy and excited. The older ones, influenced by the younger ones, blushed when the teachers asked them tricky questions and replied with rapid head movements. The grave younger ones seemed like unflappable adults. Most of them were named for flowers, like Hyacinth, Dahlia, Marguerite, Jasmin, Violet, Lila, Lily, Narcissus, Hortense, Camilo, affectionate terms chosen by their parents. They carved them into tree trunks with nails as hard as tiger claws, wrote them on the walls with chewed pencils and in the moist sand with their fingers.

With joyous hearts, they began their trip home to the city, for on this leg they were to travel by plane. Just that day, a film festival began, and they were able to see elusive movie stars at the airport. Their throats hurt from laughing so much. Their eyes turned red from looking so hard.

An article appeared in the papers; I have one excerpt here:

> The plane, on which forty pupils of a school for deaf-mute children were travelling back from their first summer holi-

day, had an unforseen accident. The catastrophe was produced by a small door that opened during the flight. Only the teachers, the pilot and the crew were saved. Miss Fabia Hernandez, who was interviewed, maintained that the children, who were falling into the abyss, had wings. She wanted to stop the last one, but he tore himself out of her grasp to follow the others like an angel. She was so dazzled by the intense beauty of the scene that at first she did not call it a catastrophe but a heavenly vision she would never forget. She still doesn't believe in the children's disappearance.

"God would play a dirty trick on us if he showed us Heaven in order to hurl us into Hell," Miss Lelia Isnaga declared. "I don't believe in the accident."

Albinal Romarin said:

"It was all a dream the children had; they wanted to impress us, like they used to on the swings in the square. Nothing can persuade me that they've disappeared."

Fabia Hernandez is not discouraged either by the red sign which says that the building where the school used to be is for rent, nor by the shuttered windows. With her colleagues, to whom she feels as close as the children used to be to each other, she goes to visit the old building and looks at the names the children wrote on the walls (for which the teachers used to scold them) and several wings drawn with childish skill, which attest to the miracle.

Translated by Nina M. Scott.

# The Story of María Griselda

## María Luisa Bombal

She remembers that no one had come to meet her and that she alone had to open the gate while the coachman held back the horses and in an attempt to console her suggested:

"Perhaps they didn't phone from the town that you were coming, as you had advised."

For every reply, she had sighed deeply, debilitated by thinking about how much she still had to endure in order to arrive at that country estate lost in the forest.

The train. Dawn in a dismal station. And another train. And another station. And finally, the town. But straightaway, all morning and half of the afternoon in that horrible rented coach...

A flash of lightning had torn through the sky and shivered lividly in the space of a second. It was followed by a mute blow. A thunderclap. And once again a thickening silence.

She then looked around her and quickly noticed that it was almost winter.

A thunderclap. A single thunderclap. Like a stroke of a bell, like a sign! From the height of the mountain range, the equinox announced that it had begun to stir the sleeping winds, to hurry the waters and to prepare the snowfalls. And she remembers that the echo of that brief thunderclap reverberated deep within her being for a long time, penetrating her with chills and with a peculiar anxiety, as if it alone had announced the beginning of something pernicious in her life...

On the last step of the front stairs, a frog lifted its tremulous little head toward her.

"It is in love with María Griselda. Every afternoon it comes out here to wait for her and to see her when she returns from her ride on horseback," explained her son Fred as he passed by and delicately brushed it aside with his foot.

"Where is Alberto?" she asked as soon as she was in the house and verified with her gaze the disorder and abandonment of the rooms: a detached curtain, dry flowers in the vases, a dead hearth filled with parched newspapers.

"He is in town. I think he has to return this afternoon."

"It's a shame that here where you seem to know and repeat everything in a flash, you did not tell him about my arrival! I could have come with him."

A series of veiled allusions trembled in Fred's voice, who, from the moment that he had come out to open the door of the house for her, stubbornly avoided looking at his mother in the face.

"Light a fire, Fred. I am cold. How is this possible! Isn't there any wood at hand? What does Alberto's wife do? Does she think that it is perhaps harmful to her beauty to be the mistress of the house?"

"Oh no, this disorder is not María Griselda's fault. It's just that there are so many of us and... Mamma! he suddenly shouted, as he used to when he was a child and would run to her because he had hurt himself or because he was afraid. But this time he didn't wrap his arms around her neck as he would do then. On the contrary, by repressing his impulses brusquely, he escaped to the other extreme of the hall, where he let himself fall shame- fully on the armchair.

She approached him and placing both hands on his shoulders

asked sweetly, "What's wrong Fred? What is happening to all of you? Why do you stay in this house that isn't yours?"

"Oh, Mother, Silvia is the one who wants to stay. I want to leave! Remember, Mother, remember that it was also Silvia who was obstinate about coming."

Yes. She remembered the project that Fred's fiancée confided to her a few days before their marriage, that absurd marriage of Fred who, without having received his law degree, decided to marry the most foolish and beautiful debutante of the year!

"I have told Fred that I want us to go and spend our honeymoon at the country estate in the south."

"Silvia!"

"Dear God, señora! Don't get angry. I am aware that you and the rest of the family have not wanted me to meet Alberto's wife…, but I am dying to meet her. María Griselda! They say that she is the most beautiful woman that has ever been seen. I want Fred to see her and to say: It is a lie, a lie, Silvia is the prettiest!"

Yes, she remembered everything as Fred fervently continued speaking to her.

"Oh, Mother, it is sheer luck that you have come! Perhaps you will succeed in convincing Silvia that it is necessary for us to leave. Imagine that it has occurred to her that I am in love with María Griselda, and that I find her to be more beautiful than she… And she stubbornly insists that we stay so that I might reflect, so that I might compare her with María Griselda and so that I might choose…and how should I know. She is completely crazy. I want to leave. I need to leave. My studies…"

His voice, his trembling like an animal being hunted who wants to flee, sensing an imminent danger.

Yes, as a woman she now understood Silvia. She understood her desire to measure herself with María Griselda and to risk losing everything so that she would be the one and only in everything before the eyes of her husband.

"Fred, Silvia will never leave if you ask her in that way, as if you were afraid…"

"Fear!…Yes, Mother, that's what it is! I am afraid. If only you saw her! If you had seen her this morning! She was dressed in white and was wearing a yellow dahlia at the nape of her neck."

"Who?"

Fred suddenly threw his arms around his mother's waist, leaned his forehead against her fragile hip and shut his eyes.

"María Griselda," he finally sighed. "Oh, mother! Do you see her? Do you see her with her pale complexion and her black hair, with her little swan-like head and her majestic and melancholy presence, do you see her dressed in white and with a yellow dahlia at the nape of her neck?"

And it was here that as an accessory to her son, she clearly saw live and move in her mind, the delicate and lofty creature of the portrait that Alberto had sent her.

"Oh, Mother, every day a new image, every day a new feeling of admiration toward her to combat! No, I cannot stay here one more day. . . because I cannot stop admiring María Griselda more each day. . . admiring her more than Silvia, yes! And Silvia who doesn't want to leave! Talk to her mother, try to convince her, please. . ."

The tick-tock of the clock echoed everywhere as if it were the very heart of the house. She, in turn, strained her ears trying to locate the exact place where that clock was probably situated. "It's new. I wonder where they got it?" she asked herself, involuntarily distracted by that trivial thing as she wandered through hallways and solitary stairways.

Zoila's room was vacant. Nevertheless, it was Zoila who had persuaded her to pass through the threshold of that notorious house. Hadn't she refused up until then to recognize the existence of María Griselda, that unknown girl whom her elder son would marry one day without the knowledge of family and friends?

The letter that Zoila, her old wet-nurse, sent her, however, had made her overcome all of her reservations.

"Señora, come here immediately. . .," Zoila wrote. Ever since she got married, Zoila called her señora, but quickly forgetting to maintain distances, she would often address her in the familiar again, as if she were a child.

"Don't think that I am exaggerating if I tell you that very strange things are happening here. Your daughter, Anita, always gets her way; however, it seems that this time things will be different and that she made a big mistake in coming here to look for Don Rodolfo. If he stopped writing to her, it must have been for a reason! It is my opinion that she should have enough pride to forget him. That is what I told her the same day it occurred to her to come here for him. But she doesn't listen to me... And you obliged me to accompany her to this mountainous country."

"Well, the truth is that despite the fact that Don Rodolfo and Anita have been sweethearts ever since they were children, he no longer loves her because he is in love with señora Griselda."

"I don't know if you remember that when you told me that Don Alberto had employed Don Rodolfo at the estate in order to help him—since the poor guy was good for nothing—I told you that I thought Alberto had made a big mistake, but no one ever listens to me ..."

She was never able to explain during her life, how or why she guided her steps toward Rodolfo's room and pushed open the door... Now she knows that in moments such as those, it is our destiny that drags us implacably and against all logic to the sadness that it has arranged for us.

Alone, lying on Rodolfo's bed with her face buried in the pillows, is how she had found her daughter Anita.

Oh, that timidity that always hampered her before Anita! Fred, on the other hand, defended himself but would always end up yielding to her. And after breaking his silence, tight-lipped Alberto would always share with her outbursts of confidence and sudden tenderness.

However, Anita, haughty Anita, never condescended to let her penetrate her privacy. Ever since she was a little girl, she used to call her Ana María, delighting in the fact that she would respond without seeming to notice the lack of respect that was being shown by an adolescent daughter who had addressed her mother by her first name.

And much later after her studies, she always looked at her from above with such pious arrogance.

"This girl has a privileged mind," was what everyone said of her, ever since Anita was a child and could understand. She had always felt proud of that extraordinary daughter, before whom she lived, nevertheless, in a state of eternal intimidation.

"Anita!" When she finally called her, the girl raised her half-astonished and joyful face toward her and had already initiated a look of affectionate welcome. When animated by that unexpected reception, she declared quickly and foolishly:

"Anita, I have come looking for you. We are leaving tomorrow right away."

But then, Anita repressed her impulse and went back to being Anita.

"You forget that I am beyond the age at which they bring and carry one around like an object."

Already disturbed by her daughter's first response and sensing a battle that would be too severe for her sensibility, she quickly began to implore, to try to persuade...

"Anita, to debase yourself and grieve over such an insignificant young man... You, who have your whole life before you, you, who can pick the husband of your dreams, you, who are so proud, so intelligent!"

"I don't want to be intelligent, I don't want to be proud and I don't want anyone but Rodolfo as my husband. I want him just as he is, insignificant and all..."

"But if he no longer loves you!"

"And what does that matter to me! I love him, and that is enough for me."

"Anita, Anita, you spoiled little girl... Do you think that your will is what matters in this case? No, Anita, believe me. A woman never gets anything from a man who has stopped loving her. Come with me, Anita. Don't run the risk of worse things happening."

"What things?"

"Since you have not returned his ring, Rodolfo is capable of asking you for it one of these days."

"No, he no longer can."

"And why not?" she had asked ingenuously.

"Because he no longer can, that is, if he is a man and a gentleman."

"Anita!" She had looked at her daughter while a wave of blood burned her face. What are you trying to tell me?

"That! Exactly what you just thought."

"No!" she had shouted, and the other woman that was in her, the one that had to do with her children, had rebelled with tremendous anger.

"Oh, the scoundrel! The scoundrel!... He has dared!... Your father, yes, your father will kill him...and I...I... Oh, that coward!"

"Calm down mother, Rodolfo is not to blame. He didn't want to. I am the one who wanted. No, he didn't want, he didn't want to." Her voice had broken into a sob, and burying her face into Rodolfo's pillow again, haughty Anita had stretched out to cry like a child.

"He didn't want to! I looked for him until... It was the only way that he wouldn't leave me...the only way to force him to get married. Because now...now you must help me...you must tell him that you know everything...force him to get married tomorrow at once...because he pretends to be waiting...and I am afraid, I don't want to wait...because I adore him, I adore him..."

Anita cried. She, in turn, had covered her face with her hands but could not manage to weep.

How long had she been that way, mute, motionless, disenheartened? She doesn't remember. She only remembers that as she slipped toward the end of the room, that invisible clock began to sound its deafening tick-tock again...as if it were emerging all of a sudden next to her from the icy waters of a painful period of inertia.

Descending to the first floor, she impulsively opened the door that belonged to Alberto's room, which was totally transformed by a delicate and graceful hand. As she considered it with surprise, she heard some steps in the hallway.

It is *she*, she thought, quickly stirred.

But no, it wasn't María Griselda. It was Zoila.

"My God, señora, they just informed me that you arrived. I was going through the laundry. . .! Imagine, no one there to greet you."

"You are so pale! Don't you feel well?"

"I am tired. What is that. . .? What are those faces sticking to the windows?"

"Now they have gone. . .Who is trying to look inside?"

"They are the children of the countryside who always come to leave flowers for señora Griselda there at the foot of the window. They think she is so beautiful! They say that she is prettier than the Virgin Mary herself. . ."

"Where is Alberto?" she interrupted dryly.

Zoila looked away from her.

"I suppose he is in town. . ." she replied after a brief pause, and her voice trembled with the same reticence that had disquieted her in Fred's voice.

"But, what is going on? What is going on?" she shouted, suddenly overcome by excessive anger. "Since when does one speak in riddles in this house? Where is Alberto? Answer me clearly, I order you!"

Zoila would respond to the obstinancy and the outbursts of her bosses with an exaggerated and caustic complacency.

"Is my mistress ordering me to tell her where Alberto is?" she asked her mildly.

"Yes, of course."

"Well. . .he must be *drinking* somewhere or other. And in case you want to know more, I will tell you that Don Alberto spends his time drinking now. . .he who would not even sample wine with his meals."

"Oh, that woman! That damned woman!" she burst out impulsively.

"Always rash to judge others, señora. Nothing can be said against Doña Griselda. She is very good and spends the whole day closed up here in this room when she doesn't go out to walk alone, the poor thing! I have found her crying many times. . .because Don Alberto seems to hate her by virtue of loving her so much. My

God! I am beginning to think that being so beautiful is like any other misfortune!"

When she entered the room, after knocking several times without getting a reply, she saw Silvia sitting before the mirror, wrapped in a long sheer dressing gown.

"How are you Silvia?"

However, the girl didn't appear surprised at her ill-timed arrival, and barely greeted her because she was so absorbed in the contemplation of her own image.

"How pretty you look Silvia!" she then said, as much from habit as from a desire to break the disquieting situation... There was Silvia, looking at herself in the mirror attentively and obstinately as if she had never seen herself and Ana María, on foot, contemplating her daughter-in-law.

"Pretty! Me? No, no!... I thought I was until seeing María Griselda, who certainly is pretty!"

Her voice suddenly shattered and like an invalid who falls back debilitated on the pillows of her bed, Silvia immersed herself again in the depths of her mirror.

The panes of the window, stuck to the gray afternoon, doubled the multiple lamps that were lighted on the dressing table. In the nearby tree a chunco* incessantly chirped its little mysterious and soft cry.

"Silvia, Fred just told me how much he loves you.." she began, but the girl emitted a bitter laugh.

"But what do you think he says to me when I ask him who is prettier, María Griselda or me?"

"Naturally he tells you that you are prettier."

"No, he answers by saying 'You are so different!' "

"Which means that he thinks that you are more beautiful."

"No. What it means is that he thinks María Griselda is prettier and he doesn't dare tell me this."

"Even if it were so, what can it matter to you? Aren't you the only woman that he loves."

"Yes, yes, but I don't know.... I don't understand what is happening to me... Oh, señora, help me. I don't know what to do.

I feel so unfortunate."

And this is when the girl began to explain her miserable anguish:

Why that feeling of inferiority that always overcame her when in the presence of María Griselda?

It was strange. They were both the same age, but María Griselda intimidated her.

And it wasn't because she was arrogant; no, on the contrary, she was sweet and polite and very frequently would come knocking at the door of her room to speak with her.

Why did she intimidate her? Perhaps by her gestures, by her gestures that were so harmonious and stable. None of them fell disorderly like hers, none of them held back in suspense... No, she wasn't jealous of her. Didn't Fred tell her: "You are blonder than the wheat; your skin is as golden and as smooth as a ripened peach; you are tiny and graceful like a squirrel; and so many other things?"

But she wanted to know why, for what reason didn't she like her own blue eyes, pure and open like the stars whenever she saw María Griselda and whenever she encountered her narrow and misty green eyes? Why also did it seem vain to her to have to spend hours before the mirror, and why did she consider ridiculous the much extolled smile with which she enjoyed showing her marvelous, tiny white teeth?

While Silvia talked and talked, she repeated and repeated the same argument: Fred loves you. Fred loves you... In the nearby tree, the chunco continued emitting its short insidious and regular cry.

She remembers now how suddenly, upon leaving Silvia, she felt that irresistible urge that takes hold of the body in moments when the spirit is suffocating: to go out into the open air and walk.

And this was how she approached the gate and met Rodolfo, leaning against one of the posts and smoking in an attitude of expectation.

Rodolfo! She had seen him come into the world and grow; he was a frivolous and good boy who was sometimes more affectionate with her than were her own children. And here she was accepting the kiss with which he hastened to greet her, surprised that upon seeing him, she didn't feel any of the sentiments that she thought she would feel. She felt neither anger nor indignation, only the same embarrassing anxiety that paralyzed her before Anita.

"Were you waiting for Alberto?" she finally asked, just to say something.

"No, María Griselda. She should have returned an hour ago. I can't explain why she has taken such a long walk this afternoon... Come, let's look for her," he suddenly invited her, taking her arrogantly by the hand. And this was how, like hunters behind a fleeing gazelle, they began to follow María Griselda's tracks through the woods. Going through the narrow path that their horse opened among the brambles, they went as far as the edge of the slope that descended to the river. By separating the thorny branches of some of the trees, they stopped for a second over the crevice that opened at their feet.

A thick, orderly and implacable horde of trees descended through the fern studded slope until it sank its first tiers into the mist that was packed below, between the thick, strong walls of the ravine. And from the depths of that sinister crevice arose a strong and moist odor, an odor of a woodland beast: the smell of the Malleco River indefatigably rolling its tumultuous back. Quickly they began to ride downhill. Heavy branches of hazelnuts and of frozen lilies struck them in the forehead as they passed by... and Rodolfo told her that with the brushwood that she always carried in her hand, María Griselda often would amuse herself by disturbing the trunks of certain trees, so that she would discover the creatures crouching beneath their bark, the crickets that fled carrying drops of dew, the timid earth- colored moths and pairs of copulating frogs.

They descended the steep slope until they penetrated deep within the mist that was stagnating in the deepest part of the crevice, there, where there were no birds, where the livid light thickened, where the clamor of the water roared like a sustained and permanent thunderclap. One more step and they would have found themselves in the depths of the ravine, right before the monster!

The vegetation stopped at the edge of a narrow shore of smooth, round pebbles, opaque and hard as coal. Poorly resigned in its bed, the river ran in a torrent, furiously smashing the water disturbed by whirlpools and black bubbles.

The Malleco! Rodolfo explained to her that María Griselda did not fear it, and he showed her, there, erect in the middle of the current, the crag where she was in the habit of stretching out at full length, dropping into the waters her long braids and the heavy Amazonian pleats of her long gown. He also told her how, upon sitting up, she would rummage through her dripping hair laughing, in order to extract from it, like a forgotten hairpin, a silvery fish that the Malleco offered her as a gift.

Because even the Malleco was in love with María Griselda.

"María Griselda!" they called until the shadow of dusk began to fill the bottom of the ravine. Then, discouraged, they decided to return and to climb the slope through which the silence of the forest again came out to meet them as they left behind the idefatigable clamor of the Malleco.

The first firefly floated before them.

"The first firefly! It always settles on María Griselda's shoulder as if guiding her," Rodolfo explained to her in sudden rapture.

From time to time, a fox let loose its macabre and strident sound, and from the opposite ravine, another quickly answered it with the precision of an echo.

The lilies began silently to open their heavy, wax petals and the honeysuckle inclined, perspiring along the path. All of nature seemed to breathe and to surrender in exhaustion...

While they returned on a path that differed from the one from which they had come, still eagerly following María Griselda's tracks, she finally managed to overcome the shyness and fatigue that had paralyzed her before.

"Rodolfo, I have come to find out what is happening between you and Anita. Is it true that you no longer love her?"

She had asked with caution, preparing herself for a negative or an evasive response. But he shamelessly and vehemently accused himself immediately!

Yes, it was true that he no longer loved Anita. And what they were saying was true: that he was in love with María Griselda.

He was not ashamed of this, however, nor was Griselda, nor anyone. Only God, who had created a being so wonderfully beautiful, was to blame.

His innocence was such, that even Alberto knowing about his love, instead of condemning him, commiserated with him. He also permitted him to continue working at the estate because he understood; he knew that once one had met María Griselda, it was necessary to be able to see her every day in order to continue to live.

To see her, to see her! He, however, always avoided looking at her, suddenly afraid and fearful that his heart abruptly would stop beating. Like someone who prudently enters glacial water, he slowly faced the gaze of her green eyes, the spectacle of her luminous pallor.

No, he would never get tired of seeing her, his desire for her would never extinguish because the beauty of that woman never totally would become familiar to him, for María Griselda changed imperceptibly, according to the time, the light and the mood, and she rejuvenated like the leaves on the trees, like the face of the sky, like everything living and natural.

Anita was also pretty, and he truly loved her, but... She remembers that her daughter's name, intermingled suddenly with such a confession, ended up wounding her in an unexpected way.

"Let's not talk now about Anita," she violently interrupted and then said: "Let's pick up our pace; it's getting late."

Rodolfo respected her silence, and as he guided her in the obscurity of the woods, he helped her clear the enormous twisted roots that stood about a meter high.

The silence was broken only farther on when a commotion of doves ended up thrashing them in the face.

"They are María Griselda's doves," he could not refrain from explaining to her, still with devotion.

María Griselda! María Griselda! She remembers that her foot had stumbled upon something soft in the middle of the front steps; it was that frog who was also waiting eternally for María Griselda...

She also remembers how a wave of anger made her stoop down to catch it brutally between her twitching fingers and throw it far,

far away. Then she started to run toward her room with her fist clenched and with the horrible sensation of having squeezed in her hand a palpitating and cold entrail.

How long did she sleep stretched out on the bed?

She doesn't know. She only knows that...

Noise. Latches being unbolted by an insecure hand. And above all, a hoarse, unknown voice but, nevertheless, a voice similar to Alberto's tore apart her slumber.

Zoila had not lied; no, she hadn't. Neither had Fred alerted her in vain because that was her son, Alberto, who arrived drunk and talking alone. She remembers how, by straining her ears, she had sustained for an instant in her mind, the echo of some shattered footsteps along the hallway.

Afterward...yes, she must have slept again, until the explosion of the shot in the garden, which, together with an enormous agitation of frightened wings, forced her to jump out of bed and run out of the room.

The door of the hallway opened wide toward a throbbing night of lightning flashes and listless fireflies. And in the garden with revolver in hand, a man was pursuing the doves of María Griselda.

She had seen him shoot down one after another, and then fling himself over their soft bodies only managing to capture between his greedy palms, bodies to which a few blood-stained feathers clung.

"Alberto!" she cried out.

"There is always something fleeing from the whole!" that man moaned, falling into her arms.

"As with María Griselda!" he almost shouted suddenly, detaching himself. "What use is it for her to tell me: I am yours, I am yours! If she barely moves, I feel that she is far away! She barely dresses, and it seems that I have never possessed her!"

Alberto then began to explain to her the anguish that was consuming and destroying him, like that of all the inhabitants of that somber mansion.

Yes, it was in vain that so as to calm himself, he would remember and count the many intimate embraces through which she was attached to him. In vain! For barely separating from his body, the body of María Griselda seemed always and forever detached from his physical life. And it was in vain that he would then fling himself over her again, trying to impart to her his warmth and scent... From his desperate embrace, María Griselda would spring up again, distant as if untouched.

"Alberto, Alberto, my son..." She tried to silence him by reminding him that she was his mother.

He, however, continued speaking and drifting aimlessly through the hall...ignoring her laments as well as the presence of Fred, whom, having also run in alarm at the shots, he considered with sorrow.

Jealousy? Perhaps it was possible that it was. Strange jealousy! Jealousy of that "something" that pertained to María Griselda and that always escaped from him in each embrace. Ah, that incomprehensible anguish that tortured him! How could he capture, know and exhaust each and every moment of that woman? If he could have surrounded her with a tightly woven net of patience and memory, perhaps he would have managed to understand and to imprison the reason for her beauty and for his own grief!

But he couldn't!

For just when his loving furor began to soften in the contemplation of those round knees so ingenuously arranged, one behind the other, when her arms already began to stretch harmoniously, and he still had not acquainted himself with the thousands of waves that this gesture had imprinted on her slender waist, when... No! No!

Of what use was it to him to possess her, if...

He could not continue talking. Silvia was coming down the stairs, uncombed, pale and barefooted, getting tangled up on each step in her long sheer dressing gown.

"Silvia, what is wrong with you?" Fred had managed to babble when a horribly sharp voice had begun to erupt from that fragile body.

"Everyone, everyone is the same!" shouted the strange voice. "Everyone is in love with María Griselda!... Alberto, Rodolfo, and

even Fred... Yes, you too, Fred! You even write poems to her!...
Alberto, you have known about it for a while. Your beloved brother
writes love poems to your wife. He writes them behind my back.
He thinks that I don't know where he keeps them. Señora, I can
show them to you.

She didn't respond, fearful that an awkward remark could fling
that wild and restless being into madness.

"No, Silvia, I am not in love with María Griselda," she suddenly
heard Fred say with fearful gravity... "But it is true that something within me changed when I saw her... It was as if some kind
of indescribable presence suddenly had ignited in the deepest part
of my being because it was through María Griselda that I finally
found my true vocation, through her."

Fred than had begun to tell them about his meeting with María
Griselda...

As newlyweds, Silvia and he had taken the country estate by
surprise and María Griselda was not at home.

But anxious to meet her as soon as possible, they quickly went
out searching for her, guided by Alberto.

And this is how it had been when, suddenly, in the middle of
the forest, he stayed behind, quiet and motionless and almost sensing within his heart, the echo of some very light steps.

Then turning off the path and accidentally making a partial clearing through the foliage, he saw her pass by, slender, melancholy
and childishly dragging along the train of her Amazonian riding
skirt..."

María Griselda!

She carried a yellow flower prominently in her hand, as if it were
a golden sceptre, and her horse followed her at a short distance
without her having to guide it. Her narrow eyes were green like
the foliage! Her posture serene, her hand tiny and pale! María
Griselda! He saw her pass by, and through her, through her pure
beauty, he suddenly touched another infinite sweet world...algae,
water, tepid sands visited by the moon, roots that silently decay
growing under the mud, as far as his own anguished heart.

From the depths of his being, enraptured exclamations began

to break out, never before heard of melodies, verses and notes that until then, had been dormant within his blood and that now suddenly rose and fell triumphantly together with his breath, with the regularity of his breath.

And he discovered a happiness that was both serious and light, nameless and without origin, and a sadness both resigned and abundant in unruly sensations.

And he understood what the soul was, and he accepted it as shy, unsteady and anxious, and he also accepted life as it was: ephemeral, mysterious and useless with its magical death that perhaps leads to nothing.

And he breathed and finally discovered what it was to breathe. . .because he had to put his two hands on his chest, take a few steps and throw himself on the ground among the tall roots.

And while they called him and looked for him for a long time in the growing darkness, remember?, he composed his first verses with his head buried in the grass.

Fred was speaking in this manner while Silvia drew back slowly, silent and paler by the second.

And, oh my God, who could have forseen that gesture in the spoiled, beautiful and foolish girl?

Rapidly taking hold of the revolver that Alberto carelessly had thrown on top of the table moments before, she had positioned the barrel against her cheek and without even shutting her eyes, valiantly pulled the trigger like a man.

"Mother! Come! María Griselda has fainted, and I cannot revive her! Whatever could have injured his wife from that horrible drama was, from the start, all that grieved Alberto; it was the spring that made him hasten automatically, not toward Silvia suffering from the bullet wound, but toward the door of his own room, in order to prevent María Griselda all access to the mishap that she unwillingly had provoked.

"Come, mother I can't revive her! For God's sake, come!"

She came promptly, and once she was inside the room, she approached the border of the large conjugal bed with hatred and prudence, indifferent to the expressions of foolish restraint with which Alberto cloyed her.

María Griselda! She looked lifeless. However, lying on her back and on the surface of the pillows, her face emerged, serene.

Never, oh never, had she seen eyebrows so perfectly arched! It was as if a slender and melancholy swallow had opened its wings over the eyes of her daughter-in-law and remained motionless there in the middle of her white forehead. Her eyelashes! Her dark, thick and glittering eyelashes. In what pure and generous blood did they have to submerge their roots so as to grow with so much violence? And her nose! Her small haughty nose with delicately opened wings. And the constrained arch of her enchanting mouth! And her slender neck! And her shoulders as plump as ripe fruit! And...

Since she eventually had to help her out of her swoon, she grasped the bedspread and hurling it backwards, suddenly uncovered the half-undressed body. Ah, the firm and small breasts densely attached to her torso, with that fine celestial blue vein meandering in the middle! And the extraordinary and round hips! And the endless legs!

Alberto had taken hold of the candlelabrum, whose tapers were dripping, and suspended it foolishly over his wife's face.

"Open your eyes! Open your eyes!" he shouted at her, he ordered her, he implored her, and as if through enchantment, María Griselda had obeyed, half-conscious. Her eyes! From how many colors was the uniform color of her eyes composed? From how many shades of green, their dark green? There wasn't anything more detailed or more intricate than the pupil of María Griselda.

A golden ring, a light green one, another misty green, another very black and then the golden ring again, and a light green one, and...the result: María Griselda's eyes were green like the moss that adheres to the trunks of wet trees in the winter; deep within those eyes, the flame of the tapers twinkled and multiplied!

All of that radiant water contained there as if by a miracle! To pierce those pupils with the point of a needle would have been like rupturing a star...

She was sure that some kind of golden mercury immediately would have risen out oozing, in order to burn the fingers of the criminal who dared.

"María Griselda, this is my mother," Alberto explained to his wife, helping her to sit up among the pillows.

The green gaze had apprehended her and quivered, clearing up in seconds... And suddenly, she felt a weight over her heart. It was María Griselda who had flung her head against her chest.

Astonished, she remained motionless, motionless and stirred by a strange, extraordinary and bewildering emotion.

"Excuse me," said a serious voice hastily.

Because excuse me was the first thing María Griselda said.

A cry escaped immediately from the depths of her deep-felt tenderness.

"Pardon you for what? Are you perhaps to blame for being so beautiful?"

"Oh, Señora, if only you knew!"

She doesn't remember well, how exactly María Griselda then had begun to complain about her beauty as if it were a sickness, a vice.

It always, always had been like that, she said. Ever since she was a girl, she had to suffer because of her beauty. Her sisters didn't love her and her parents, as if trying to compensate them for all the beauty they had bestowed upon her, always devoted their affection and love to them. As for her, no one ever spoiled her, and no one could ever be happy by her side.

There was Alberto, loving her with that sad dispassionate love that seemed to look for and pursue something beyond her, leaving her desperately alone. Anita suffering because of her! And Rodolfo also! And Fred and Silvia! Ah, poor Silvia!

A child! If she could have a child! perhaps seeing her linked maternally through a child, Alberto's spirit would manage to rest assured... But, it still hadn't materialized, as if she had been chosen and predestined to a solitary beauty, and nature—no one knows why—even had prevented her from giving birth!

And in its cruelty, it seemed as if destiny had not wanted to grant her the insignificant privilege of a visible lineage... because neither her parents nor her grandparents resembled her in the least;

and in the old family portraits, it was never possible to find the common trait, the expression that could have made her recognize herself as a link in the human chain.

Ah, the solitude, boundless solitude!

This is how María Griselda spoke, and she remembers how her rancor began vanishing as she listened to her speak.

She remembers the love, the involuntary gratitude toward her daughter- in-law that began invading her through each of the gestures with which María Griselda caressed her, through each of the words that she addressed to her.

It was like a consolation, like a kind of candid satisfaction very similar to the spontaneous and irrational confidence that is awakened in us and that is offered us by a reticent animal or insecure child.

Yes, how could one resist the tranquil haughtiness, the tender look of those eyes so strangely linked together!

She remembers that she, musing, compared the beauty of presumptuous Silvia and that of her magnificent daughter Anita with the beauty of María Griselda. They were both pretty, but their beauty was like an almost conscious medium of expression that they could have perhaps substituted with another. On the other hand was the pure and veiled beauty of María Griselda, beauty that was nothing but a natural flow, something cogenital and intimately linked to her being. It was inconceivable that María Griselda could exist without those eyes and that presence; and it was inconceivable that her voice could have a tonality other than the one that was hers, low-pitched and assuming in its velvety muteness.

María Griselda! She still sees her live and move silently and modestly, carrying her beauty like a sweet hidden lamp that, from a secret charm, kindled her gaze, her gait and her most minimal gestures; the gesture of sinking her hand into a crystal box to extract from its contents the comb with which she would comb her long black hair. . . She still, yes, she still seems to be hearing the ticktock of the invisible clock that there, in that far away house in the south, indefatigably marked each passing second of that unforgetttable afternoon. That tick-tock implacably cutting through the sea of time, toward the future, always toward the future, and the waters of the past immediately closing behind, immutable, compact and solitary.

And you Anita. So arrogant! Here you are and there you have that man who didn't love you and whom you forced and conquered! That man who later on without thinking will admit in confidence to another woman: "I got married because of an engagement."

You hate him, you despise him, you adore him and each of his embraces leaves you more and more disenheartened and much more in love.

To be afraid of the past, of the present, of the future; of the suspicion, the gossip or the mere premonition that will come to threaten the tranquility that you must fabricate for yourself day by day. And feigning, smiling, to fight for the conquest of a piece of soul from day to day...that will be your life.

Rodolfo! Here he is at my side and at yours, helping you to attend to the candles and the flowers and squeezing your hand as you desire it.

Carrying out an infinite number of actions that are foreign to his desire, engaging in them with false enthusiasm, while a thirst that he knows is insatiable will devour him from within...that will be his life.

Ah, my poor Anita, perhaps that will be everyone's life. Fleeing from or losing our true life by concealing it behind an infinite number of trivialities that have the appearance of being important!

Translated by Celeste Kostopulos-Cooperman.

---

*Chunco: a species of owl that can be found in Chile.

# The Little Island

## Luisa Mercedes Levinson

In the middle of Montiel forest is a pasture where proportion
and harmony have prevailed. The trees are loosely separated one
from another and they look symmetrical and plump. They are the
same trees that are native to the zone, *algarrobos* and *nandubays*,
but having unrestricted oxygen and sunlight, they have spread out,
having grown fuller perhaps because a stream glides along the
pasture's edge, clear and steady. It is the Lucas; we are in Lucas
South.

This pasture of "La Luisita" was the place chosen for the yearly
country picnic, at noon on a certain day in March, the month
of our vacation at the ranch, where we had the custom of getting
together, once a season, with the neighbors from "La Nueva Alema-
nia," the other ranch four leagues away.

Colored tablecloths, crystal and inviting delicacies were spread
out over the pasture's grassy shoreline while the old foreman bar-
becued the ribs, and the guests arrived, gentlemen and beautiful,
blonde ladies in very low-necked dresses, very tall—the ladies were
just visible to the fledgling child that I once was. Enormous felt

hats adorned with pheasant and bird of paradise feathers protected their whiteness from the rays of the Entre Rios sun. The gentlemen were wearing hunting garb, a few of them with red jackets, and others more severely attired in black velvet. They were very large, imposing and handsome, always standing sideways and staring emptily.

In the distance, the sheep and their young, so intensely white, were grazing and even bleating defiantly.

The stream flowed on, murmuring persistently. That noon, the discovery took place, a surprise to everyone: a mother-of-pearl shell brought to rest in a bend in the shoreline by "adventures on distant seas centuries ago," father commented humorously, perhaps because the statuesque ladies laughed with voices as crystalline as the clink of the tall glasses scarcely darkened by the transparent wines. Had Papa said remote seas? Did he mean to say that everything was a transformed sea? At that moment, the ladies stood up in unison while the younger ones rambled about letting the gossamer stoles, which just minutes before had softened their gently rounded pearly necklines, slip away.

One of them blindfolded a gentleman, using a dark handkerchief. Another, the blondest one, imitated her and covered with a black shawl the entire stunning face of the man in the red jacket. The couples, with laughter that was perhaps a little raucous, played blind man's bluff. I observed this scene, which I felt I had already seen in the land portrayed on my grandmother's fan. I was standing on tiptoe at the very edge of the little island that seen from afar did not impair the harmony of the landscape with its rounded shady harmony, but from its tangible limit, it recovered its threatening power of a forbidden thing. Perhaps it represented America's mysterious appeal in a landscape that looked like it was painted by Corot, but this thought belongs to the present. Then, the little island was, for me, only self-absorption, mystery, the tantalizing beauty of fear, a tangle of vines and trees transforming things into ghosts, and inevitable misfortune. I stared toward the center of it and heard dark cries and even more sininster silences because the presences that they muffled were invisible. Then came the hissing of the snakes. Some terrified bird that had committed the folly of going into that dense woods gave its last cry. But the lusty fragrant flowers of climbing vines stood out along the edges of that stormy, dark mass, devoid of even a chink of forgiveness for light to enter: *pitas* with the color of a deceptive radiant sun, violet *mburucuyas* with the seven thorns of Christ's crown and the elongated white waxy incense candles of the *nino-urupa* flower. I never saw the others, the devouring carnivorous flowers. On the other hand, on one occasion I found among the ferns the dazzling skins that the elegant and terrible *yarara* snakes had shed as they glided along. Papa had explained this to me, and I recognized them.

He also said that in the middle of the little island the coral snakes and voracious wild boars made their nests, and he added that no one had ever penetrated the deepest part of the island. But I saw a woman go in there, the blondest and most beautiful of the tall ladies. The man with the covered face and the red jacket followed, groping after her, trying to push aside the branches with no success in keeping the thorns from digging into his flesh and the lianas from wrapping around his hands. The young blonde woman continued on ahead, enclosing herself in the darkness until she disappeared. The aroma from the flowers and the lichens was unbearable now, but I stayed there, feeling very tiny, while the shadows lengthened, now gigantic, enveloping me. And through it all, I saw the hungry flower—flashing as if giving off white flames—carnivorous, opening its petals, tentacles, blonde pistils, and the snake, struggling, lashing out with its fangs.

Afterwards, there was nothing, only darkness, and the heavy breathing of the little island.

I closed my eyes tightly, squeezing them together. The blackness engulfed the field, the water of the stream and the lambs. Perhaps the sky was left face down. Perhaps the world had been devoured and turned into a little island.

I do not know how long I stayed there in the dark. Suddenly Mama, Papa, the tall ladies and the great gentlemen began to shout. Where, where is she? Perhaps they searched for minutes, or for years. They passed alongside me, almost trampling me. I thought they were looking for me, that I had become invisible. But no, they were shouting some name that was hard to pronounce. The red jackets and the black velvet ones, the trembling necklines and the birds of paradise became wildly jumbled together. Only the foreman was stomping around the little island's perimeter. He went in. A long sinuous whine could be heard, and I saw the flash of lightning. A flash of lightning, yes, although it was daytime. A flash of lightning that persisted and was as intense as if it had been a moonless night. The foreman emerged from the little island, his face as expressionless as always.

I wanted to explain what I had seen, but my voice didn't come out or nobody heard me. Nevertheless, on passing next to me, everybody looked down. But they did not fix their gaze on the little girl, awkwardly bearing her five years, but on something the color of pearl that was lying in the grass.

"It's the stole," someone said.

"And that, that?" others chimed in.

"It's the skin of a rare species of *yarara*," added the foreman in a very low voice.

A gossamer stole, the color of a woman's neckline, interwoven with blonde hairs. But it sketched or wrote out secret things, and it seemed to extend itself, to drag itself along. Had she been transformed into. . .?

But I never said it. To anyone.

Translated by Elaine Dorough Johnson.

# The Boy Who Saw God's Tears

## Luisa Mercedes Levinson

The first time he saw it was after the seventh day of his newborn brother's life. The boy was climbing up the slope. Some buds were opening up, just when he was passing by, but not even that miracle could compete with the other one, with the bud that had burst forth there below, from his mother, and he smiled at him and stretched his little arms out toward him.

The boy needed to share his happiness, he needed to communicate, he did not know what. He went right by the dens of the little forest animals who were his friends, and he jumped without letting himself be caressed by the streams that ran down from the mountaintop. He did not stop next to the trees that were filled with fruit and squirrels who, with their little cries, begged him to stop. The slope was already becoming less green, for the tender new vegetation was being replaced by the cactus plants with their fleshy flowers, and the singing of the birds was becoming scarce. But the boy did not feel either the perspiration first, or the cold afterwards, and he kept climbing farther and farther, up to the first hint of the summit where the sun, nearby, was nevertheless pale and the waterfalls remained stiff like crossed stalactites. The boy was having a little trouble breathing, but he was happy. The clouds had wings, and they wanted to carry him away.

There above him was the great stone, smooth and grey. He contemplated it for a long time, squatting, until he could no longer see it, nor feel the cold, nor remember why he felt so contented, only mindful of something unattainable that was issuing forth from the stone and encompassing the summit and the sky and him . . . It was the Gaze, because the stone had a gaze that penetrated his innermost being with a soft glow, like a balm, with a smile that was serious yet sweet; it was the Balm of God.

The boy was there for a long time, deep in thought, perhaps that entire day, perhaps longer, without feeling hunger or thirst. One evening at dusk he began to descend, gently, surprised to see again there down below, the initial cause for wonderment: plump, small and sweet with another kind of sweetness. Everything was new and exciting—the fleshy fruits and their nectar, the taste of honey—yet he was a little sad too, because he was losing the other, the sublime, the Balm, within. But the tiny arms of the little one were there and the noble daily tasks: bringing water from the river, milking the goat. It was a loss and a recovery, but it was also coming to understand the tides, and it was good that things were this way, he thought.

The brother was growing. One morning he ran trotting after a colored bird. The bird perched on his head and then on his shoulder, and the little one began to laugh. The boy wanted to participate, but his movements were abrupt and the bird flew away. Why? He had reached the summit and felt the gaze of God upon his innermost self, and the little one could not, even by crawling, climb up to the base of the mountain. Another afternoon they were returning from a long walk and the little one felt tired; he threw his arms around his brother's legs so that he would pick him up, but the boy kept right on going, without looking at him, and the little one's feet began to bleed.

Already in the cave, the mother looked harshly at the older son, made a growling sound and then gathered the little one up into her arms and covered him with kisses. When the gruff looking man arrived, he examined the little one's feet. He stayed there for a while observing the two of them, and finally he turned the older one over and thrashed him. Something began to grow inside the boy, like a parasitical, harsh life, within his own life, something that would grow to resemble resentment. In vain, the brother reached out his little arms and handed him a pebble, inviting him to play.

Once when the little one was chasing a squirrel that was hopping over the lowest branches of a bush to let the little hands just barely touch it, the boy came up to touch it too, but the squirrel slipped away. The boy turned his back on them to leave, but he remained hidden behind some brush, and he saw that the little one was starting to laugh and the squirrel was starting to hop once again. The boy could feel that the parasitic life inside him was taking on a solid body, which left his tongue feeling bitter and his hands feverish. He picked up a stone from the ground and threw it at the squirrel.

The little one waited, astonished, then he went up to his playmate, that had fallen near his feet. He picked it up and held it against his chest; the squirrel was still. The little one raised his terror-filled eyes to the sky. He had discovered death.

The boy moved away and ran and ran. He came to the foot of the mountain and began to climb. He needed the Balm. He reached the summit panting, and he prostrated himself in front of the stone, waiting. It was already getting dark, but the gaze was not forthcoming. Suddenly, drops that were like a balm perhaps, but dark, started dripping from the cracks in the stone, something that cast a cloud over him made him one with the night. The frightenend boy, dragging himself along, descended the mountain slope. Some brambles ripped at his sides, but he did not notice. He was not sure if he had seen the liquid blackness; he felt it inside himself, like a blood that was different and terrible because it was so sad. Out of the stone had come tears, God's tears. The merciless, implacable night was inside him although the sun might devour the plain, and his brother, already without memory of his hurt, stretched his little arms out to him, smiling. But the mother rushed to raise the little one up in her arms, keeping him away from the older brother. Later the gruff man arrived, and taking the mother by the waist and putting the little boy upon his shoulders, the three of them stretched out under the almond tree, busying themselves with eating the heart of the fruits that they split open against a sharp rock. Then the man got up and began tossing the little one up into the blue air and catching him with fear and pleasure. The man did not seem gruff under the tree, next to the woman and the little one. A branch was coiled around his head through his shaggy mane. The boy had never seen him like that.

Suddenly the boy heard, very close by, his brother's laughter. He had discovered him. The little one opened his tiny arms, calling him. The boy forgot about everything that had happened before; he only felt beneath his skin that sweet laugh, and he remembered his warmth and his smell of honey and milk. The man and the woman were frolicking about beneath the almond tree turning somersaults over each other. Their laughter was husky now, and they were no longer paying attention to the little one. The boy turned his back on them and walked toward the sea. Nor did he turn around to look at the brother who, with his short little steps, was following him. The boy was hungry. He had not gone near the cave for days; his insides ached. With one hop, he was on top of a rocky little mound that was turning black with mollusks. In desperation, he started ripping them off and sucking on them, opening some with his teeth. They had a harsh taste, an iron-flavored edge that burned a little. He remembered that blackness that dripped from the stone at the summit. Salt, or tears, began to gush from his eyes. He felt that all was well at last.

Suddenly he heard the brother's little voice again. The little one was trying to climb up the rocks above the sea, but he was not succeeding. A wave wrapped around him from behind, coming up to his neck. He could only reach the boy's feet, so powerful looking up there above. The trusting eyes of the little one softened the older boy. The boy picked him up and held him in his arms. His feet were aching now. With the added weight of the brother, they were being impaled on the jagged edges of the partially-opened, stony shells. But that pain was also a deep contentment; it was like coming to understand the peace of the first world.

The black mollusks, against the afternoon sun, were gathering in purple reflections. The boy took two mollusks and opened them. He passed one to his brother, and he put the other one up to his mouth. The little shell contained the sea and something else; it had the taste of God's tears.

Far away were heard the voices of the mother and the man. They were walking hurriedly, like errant travelers, looking in every direction except towards the sea. Now they were running and calling Yahaiii, Yahii. . .; the boy looked at them with surprise, for he had dreamed something like that once: two figures leaving the forest and the world behind, advancing toward the sea. The boy was lost in his thoughts. Suddenly a big wave caught him squarely on his back. He lost his balance and the brother fell from his arms and onto the sharp-edged mollusks. The little one screamed and screamed. The mother and the man found them, the boy standing up, with his arms to his sides and the little one there among the rocks, frightened. He had scraped his forehead and his knees, and he was bleeding. A wave covered him up momentarily, and the mother arrived and picked him up in her arms, whimpering. The man threw himself onto the older one, ground him down into the sharp open mollusk shells on the rock, held him under the waves for a long time and began beating on him and battering him again.

The mother caressed the little one and immersed him in the milky flowering of her breasts.

The man was still pounding as the mother and the little one moved away. The boy did not know what was happening under the elemental fury of the strong arms. There were no longer any mollusks in his mouth, but he tasted a sharper, more bitter flavor. And already growing, was that ancient parasite-like entity inside him, now with a life of its own, made heavier by dark memories, something that perhaps could be called injustice.

The little one, contented, was already playing on the white sand, while the mother returned to the cave alone. But the man was still meting out his punishment, now with his fists, on the neck and the back of the boy who was bending down so far that he could touch the humid sand with his fingertips. And then something solid that was right there: a ragged stone, weighty, like a question, like the blows that were resounding in his head. He picked it up and took it firmly in his burning hand, and he threw it at the other bewildered head that was also his, his brother's... There was a single scream and then nothing, neither the man's fists nor the noise of the sea.

The boy picked himself up slowly. He was alone now. The wailing wind was rising in the distance. The boy ran; he fled up the mountain, upward, falling down among the brambles and cactus, climbing again, breathless, up to the summit.

He fell down in front of the Stone and he waited; there was only light and barrenness to acknowledge his presence, then night, and again, a blinding radiance. Suddenly came bursting forth a howling sound that shook the mountain and the earth; from the stone, the blackish liquid began to gush out, to explode, in a torrent, a stony oil now, inundating the summit, the slope, the sky, a vortex from the depths of nature, sweeping over everything, a mineral snake with lion heads, with flames for a body, with separate fin-shaped lungs, breathing in the heavens. An oily-black river over the sea and sun.

Rent asunder are the chains of men pursued by ferruginous wombs; stars beseiged by subterranean spiders that have come forth into the light; dismembered moons showing their other face, the one that was never to be seen by man or beast; terrible, frightful fungi falling from on high, covering birds, squirrels, women, fish, worms, children; tigers with their venomous membranes, making them indistinguishable one from another; terrified human mountains, fleeing from the decapitated suns, a tower of flesh putrefying under the triumphant greenish-black venomous liquid tower, with its mechanical laugh of death mixing blood with stony annihilating oil. Laughter...

Translated by Elaine Dorough Johnson.

# And The Wheel Still Spins

# An Eternal Fear

## Elvira Orpheé

Doña Elvira was always afraid of them. She didn't have many friends, but every time the opportunity arose, she told the ones she had that she would never travel by sea. She hated the idea of dying in the water, so much so that it reminded us of a lullaby: "I give my soul to God, my body to the salt water, and my heart to the Virgin Mary." Only in no way did Doña Elvira want to give her body to the salt water or even fresh water. What she feared most was suddenly bumping into a shark that would eat her. I never knew anyone who was so afraid of sharks and with so little reason. She lived at the foot of a mountain and didn't have the slightest chance of ever traveling by sea. She was as poor as the rest of us, and her husband was a clerk like any other. How was she going to take an ocean voyage? But she couldn't stop dying from fright just thinking about it. And if someone told her a boat had sunk, she would get goosebumps. Nevertheless, she herself would start conversations about the sea and sharks although no one would remember that.

Doña Elvira was very beautiful, but she didn't know it. And she became ugly when she wore a sour expression. Practically every time she wore that expression, it was because of her husband.

I was a girl, but I remember that sometimes when he wasn't around and two or three of her friends were visiting, the friends would ask her to put on the clothes she wore before she got married. Then she would make-up her eyes, style her hair, and put on a transparent blouse with a stem of yellow rosebuds. Years later I saw a picture in a magazine of a woman who was as beautiful as Doña Elvira, an empress from a place called Persia, with green eyes, a full lower lip, and a round face. They looked so much alike that they could have been related in a different life, and it must have been because of that memory hidden in her heart that Doña Elvira hated her name and would have liked to have been called Zobeida, Zoraida, or even Sulamita.

She read a lot, although she also worked because she didn't want her husband to be embarrassed about not having enough money to support her well. But it seemed to me that it didn't matter to him whether he supported her well or not. I am inclined to believe that he preferred not to support her well because her expression would turn bitter and hide her great beauty. Even though I was a girl while Doña Elvira was an old woman of 30, I realized how beautiful she was.

She loved her husband, as a single woman, as a married woman, and even in death, as you will see. Who knows if he loved her or not. Every weekend he said that he was going hunting. He would put on a canvas outfit with a cartridge belt that Doña Elvira had made. And he returned every Sunday night with partridges and sometimes even chinchillas. But his eyes were always sunken and very red, as if he hadn't slept for two nights. I always suspected he hadn't slept. I once heard him tell of the daughter of a gaucho in the country who put him and his buddies up on his ranch when they found themselves without a tent. She told him he had the jawline of a saint. I don't know what saints' jawlines are like, since they always cover them with beards, but I didn't like the idea of her calling a guy a saint as an excuse to touch his "jaw." Especially when, behind a door, he asked me if I wanted to touch his jaw as that country girl had done.

I never said, as did the stupid women in town, that Don Eduardo was a rascal. Stupid people refer to "a rascal like him" with sympathy and almost admiration, and they could be talking about anyone. I was one later on; only instead of calling me a rascal, they called me something else, but it didn't matter to me. For some, it was very costly that I was a rascal. And I'm not only talking about money, I'm talking about how they missed me for the rest of their lives.

But returning to Doña Elvira (so beautiful without knowing it), her great fear was of sharks. Her great fault was the love she had for her husband, who didn't deserve it. He repeated the same jokes. He always seemed to have a mirror in front of him so he could look at himself while he talked. He would keep people waiting an entire evening with their fingers raised, wanting to say "I think so-and-so," until they lowered them out of frustration when they understood that once he started to talk no one could stop him. And the things he said came from the last article he had read in one of those silly magazines that squeeze in many different topics but don't cover any of them in depth. Or he would insist on one point, either because it really concerned him or because it seemed very up-to-date; I don't know. You could say he had a "one-track mind," as they say about every boy and old man in town who has only one idea in his head. But I don't know why people didn't say it about him as well.

I think it was because he was partly blonde. And instead of getting sunburned, he tanned, giving him an aristocratic air.

Townswomen are so stupid, so stupid. To avoid being considered spinsters, they allowed themselves to be the lover-of-the-week of a guy as vile as Don Eduardo who, after messing with them, would tell Doña Elvira that they were no longer allowed in the house.

For a long, time Doña Elvira was ignorant of her husband's adventures, even though they brought fleas into the house, if not worse things. It was like this: one day a man from the country appeared at the door, the gaucho who gave Don Eduardo a place to sleep when he went hunting. Don Eduardo hadn't arrived home from the office yet. Doña Elvira was upset. The gaucho sat in the hall, still and silent, smoking and spitting large balls of phlegm from time to time. Doña Elvira saw this filth on her shining floors and almost fainted. She ran to my house to borrow a spittoon and returned to put it next to the gaucho. But he ignored it and continued to spit on the floor. Doña Elvira ran to another house to get another spittoon. I think she managed to find four in all. And the gaucho continued to let loose phlegm balls. Don Eduardo arrived just as she was asking the gaucho why, if he wanted to spit, he didn't do it in the round thing that she had brought for that purpose. Don Eduardo greeted his friend with a hug and then took Doña Elvira inside and told her off: that she had no respect, that his friends received him in their house without telling him how to behave, that she only thought of herself, and that she was incapable of helping him as other wives helped her husbands. Another spat occurred when she refused to eat dinner in the dining room with the gaucho because she was afraid she would get sick if she saw the phlegm. But I was there to defend her. My mother had sent me to see if everything was all right with poor Doña Elvira. Don Eduardo came to let the maid know that he and his friend were going into the dining room, and Dona Elvira told him that she had a headache and was going to skip dinner. So Don Eduardo turned to me and tried to get me to criticize her:

"Do you see what married women are good for? First they want someone to support them, then they aren't able to help you entertain."

I was only fifteen years old but very bold. I said to him:

"You don't really support her, Don Eduardo. She is a mathematics teacher. And any clean woman, even if she wasn't married, would get far away from a spitting gaucho, who isn't at all entertaining, just like his daughter who touched your jaw."

I didn't say it in a bad way, but he interpreted it as I intended it—as an insult. So, to show how manly he was he began to insult Doña Elvira. And, though it wasn't true, I told him that, since I had never heard a man insult a woman, I was leaving so I wouldn't learn bad manners.

I didn't find out what happened between them after I left, but I did know that Doña Elvira was panicked by the old gaucho's visits. Fortunately, there weren't many. Someone must have told him that he wasn't welcome in that house. Especially since he left some fleas there although they could have come from his dog.

Meanwhile, Doña Elvira continued to teach her classes, love her repetitive and boring husband, and dress up when he wasn't around. Better said, she dressed as a woman of her beauty should have dressed.

And one day when her friends asked her to dress up, she refused and was very sad. My mother coaxed the truth out of her. It seems that a woman had arrived at her door looking for Don Eduardo. Doña Elvira said that he wasn't home and asked the woman who she was. The woman answered with her toothless mouth that she was someone who had the right to know. Still not comprehending, Doña Elvira looked at the little boy whose hand the woman held and found a great resemblance to her own ten-year-old daughter. An alarm went off in her head. She asked:

"Your last name is Delgado?"

The woman said that it was. Doña Elvira remembered that Don Eduardo always spoke of a friend whom he helped and who was always asking for more help. He said that instead of being named Angel Delgado, he should have been named Devil Gordo* and right then and there Doña Elvira figured out why he gave money to Devil Gordo or to his sister and why the gaucho came to spit on her house as if he were an in-law.

She could have left, could have gotten a pass to go to the city. They would have given it to her because she was friends with women who had relatives in the government. But she stayed home. I would have kicked her to get her to go, but my mother and her other friends convinced her that Don Eduardo would attract more interest and attention from the local girls. Being a mathematics teacher and not a rascal, no one thought that Doña Elvira would have been able to go to the city and find a rich man who adored her. But what did it matter if she was married or not? No one in the city knew her. Well, she was stupid enough to stay with him. She was stupid enough to believe all the idiotic lies he told her. And one day she found herself pregnant again.

She was happy enough, I was furious, and Don Eduardo strutted around like the cock of the walk. However, in private he told her that he couldn't afford another child and that she would have to find a way to get rid of it. And she tried to find a way since he had demanded it. She went to see La Palma. Although La Palma was already very old, around forty, men and women still considered her attractive. She was blonde, tall, foreign, and had brought into the world many children from decent homes whose parents could pay her price. But it was said—and not in secret—that she was addicted to morphine, a terrible drug, according to my mother, one that makes people see the world as it isn't and become so used to it that they squirm like dogs if they are deprived of it.

I don't know what La Palma told her, probably that she should return to her house and La Palma would meet her there with everything she needed. But some rotten idea crossed through Doña Elvira's head. I think she remembered how beautful La Palma was, how Don Eduardo was always throwing her compliments, and she thought that while she was laid up, Don Eduardo would take advantage of the opportunity to do who-knows-what with La Palma. Poor Doña Elvira, how stupid! She should have known that La Palma wouldn't get involved with a clerk; the least she accepted were doctors. The fact is that she bypassed La Palma; she did I-don't-know-what by herself, and she came down with a fever that made her delirious. It goes without saying that Don Eduardo received visitors, smiling, making jokes. He had to know that she was dying, if even I knew it. And not because anyone told me. Not even the doctors, who ran around like chickens with their heads cut off (we had seen them in anatomy class). Even Doña Elvira knew she was dying although she didn't tell me this; with the fever, she didn't even know what she was saying. She turned violet from the fever. But she spoke of her dream, and alone with her, I listened to how it progressed. On an old ship, a pirate captain was punishing a young nobleman. He suspended him from a rope passed through a pulley and submerged him head first in the ocean numerous times. A shark circled, and when it approached, the sailors shouted to frighten the man. Then they submerged him in the water just a little, not so he would drown but so he would think the shark was going to eat him. And when the shark was so close that the man could see it, they would pull the rope through the pulley and leave him hanging halfway between the deck and the water, where the shark couldn't reach him even if it jumped. Sometimes, instead of tying him by both legs, they tied him by one. His desperation make the whole crew laugh.

And Doña Elvira's dream progressed as her beautiful olive skin turned red and raw. She spoke of her dream in spurts. I was the only one who knew of it because I didn't move from her side, even at night. My mother called me a saint, a martyr.

The moment arrived when the pirate captain decided to end the game. He had his crew cut the young nobleman's arm so the blood would make the shark crazy with desire, and then they submerged the man in the ocean. Suddenly, there was a commotion on deck: a woman was slashing herself. Before anyone could stop her, she threw herself in the water. The shark, who was trying to reach the man, went right for its new prey. And I *saw* how it ripped Doña Elvira's body to shreds. I heard her screams, and I saw her relive her previous death in this new agony, all because of that trash named Eduardo.

What I don't know is if the next time she lives, she will have a great fear of rejected children who are capable of killing, or if the memory of the shark will continue to be stronger. I also don't know if the pirate captain (and I suspect who this is because of his particular trait of punishing stupid love) will make her different: deaf to lies and capable of demanding an eye for an eye for the pain they cause her.

Translated by Janice Molloy.

---

*Angel Delgado: Skinny Angel; Devil Gordo: Fat Devil.

# I Will Return, Mommy

## Elvira Orpheé

The woman tells it in her language, and I will tell it that way because I am talking to her. We both came from the same place, far away. She says: Then, I wasn't so old, and I was with my husband in his parents' country. Here they call them Turks, but they aren't Turks. I already had my daughter Palisava, and everyone watched her because she was sweet, solid, and beautiful, with her dark red hair and her eyes so large that it seemed impossible that any sleep could close them completely, expect a long sleep, as high as flying.

One holiday, as my husband and I were walking unhurriedly, strolling through those streets, Palisava saw us from inside an unfamiliar house and came out to meet us, so sweet. Mommy, she said to me, I must appear before the court tomorrow to die.

It takes one a moment to understand that the time has come for weeping, so I asked her why, for what reason, as if reason still existed for me and for this world, since I was already alone in the grasp of desperation and since the world never had reasons when it was capable of killing Palisava, its jewel, in such a way. "Tomorrow," she said, "they summoned me to die tomorrow because I don't share their beliefs."

I begged her to let me appear in her place (at that moment, tears had squeezed my heart without squeezing my eyes). "We would both die," she said. "We are women; we shouldn't think or believe, only obey. We shouldn't think that the court is bad; the ones who are bad are the ones who order us not to think."

I was always a poor woman. I didn't understand why the court was like God who saw everything. I didn't understand how she was unable to escape if she was free to appear on her own, without being arrested. I looked at my husband with the hope that he would say: I will appear in her place, I am a man, I don't wear a veil over my face, I am authorized to defend myself. He didn't say anything, he just looked away vaguely and tenderly.

Palisava hugged me: "I will return, mommy. Don't throw out my things. I will return, and we will be so close that you won't know whether I am in front of you or inside you." I saw her poor, little violet T-shirt. I remembered all of her poor, little T-shirts, her poor, open shoes that she wore with tights to keep out the cold and the dirt. And for a long time, I didn't remember anything else because even my memories left, dragged away by the tears that I shed in my heart.

While I couldn't remember, my husband and I went somewhere else, to a country that had the ocean and pink houses. How did he manage to leave that closed country of his parents and grandparents? I don't know. Maybe he ingratiated himself with the court, maybe they noticed his tender, vague gaze, maybe they knew that he never got angry or cried and decided that it wasn't worthwhile to kill such a man.

I think that I remember a little about that country with an ocean because my husband, who before was already an adult, became a boy. And I almost became a girl. I say almost because even the youngest mothers always seem older than their husbands. It's because they worry more. And one day, when my husband was sitting on a low wall playing with something on the ground with his foot, two little green snakes appeared, thin, thin and short, very light green, almost transparent. He played with them without fear. I must have been remembering poorly in that moment because the time didn't correspond with the memory. I was remembering that Palisava was near me, a baby with curlers in her short hair (she died very young, with long hair), and until that moment I had been watching her and suddenly I didn't see her again. My memory is so bad that now I don't even know if we were in the country of pink houses before or after she died. I think it was after, because my husband played with the little snakes and called them Palisava. Would he have given them her name if she had been with us? And if she weren't there, it was awful of him to have given animals the name of a loved one. But, how strange, it didn't bother me so much. The little snakes didn't seem bad. They had no interest in me. How could they have been Palisava, whom I loved so much, who loved me so much? My husband talked with them. I don't know what he said to them. Was it good or bad that he talked to them and gave them his daughter's name? To them, all green, while my beautiful Palisava was dark with red hair. I am a poor woman who never learned too many things. Was it good? Was it bad?

That was like the sun shining in the middle of the darkness of a long sorrow. I immediately returned to forgetfulness, to obscurity, to a time without memories. Maybe I was dead, me too, and it was better. Now I have returned to life to suffer again, perhaps even more than before.

We came to this country and to this town, from which my husband left with his cart to sell knick-knacks. I must have done something as well because if not, how would we have eaten? Maybe the women here were good and helped me to make things. They felt for the soul of a woman whose daughter was dead although it had never happened to them.

One day the memories suddenly returned to me of when Palisava was alive (the later ones never returned), and it was awful. A furious, great, large, light green snake appeared on my house's earthen patio. Very bright and shrill. Furious with me. My husband and the snake understood one another, and it spoke to him. I know this, although I didn't understand it, because my husband repeated what it was saying, and in this way I learned that it wanted to come over to me, like an undulating and lashing fury. My husband repeated what it said and called it Palisava. The snake claimed her things, Palisava's little T-shirts. It said that I had thrown them out despite the fact that she told me she would return, and she had returned. It said this, but I didn't believe it. This awful terrifying creature was my sweet Pailsava?

The creature even guessed my thoughts. It knew what I had thought. Why did this dirty reptile need Palisava's poor little shoes, with the stockings that protected her feet from the street's dust? Guessing my thoughts, it answered through my husband that it wouldn't need them anymore. Why didn't I run, why didn't I escape, as Palisava didn't escape from her assassins? People don't escape because they never believe that such a terrifying thing could happen to them until it actually takes place.

All of a sudden, I remembered that I hadn't thrown out Palisava's things. Even with my memory loss, I wouldn't have been able to. Never, never would I have parted with anything that had touched her body because her sweet spirit inhabited it. Sweet and desperate when she left to die. Who, then, had thrown out her little T-shirts? The creature didn't hear that thought. It didn't matter anyway because it threw itself on me in a fury. Better said, it threw itself inside me. I don't know how it did it, but it got inside me, in my spine, from the bottom to my skull, contracted because it was twice my size and thick. Now it is always pressing against my bones, until it makes me scream. It is squeezing everything in my body: what I breathe, what I eat, what I dream. Because even during the little sleep that the pain allows me, Palisava's voice as she left to die says to me, "I will return and we will be so close that *you won't even know whether I am in front of you or inside you.*"

Translated by Janice Molloy.

# How the Little Crocodiles Cry!

## Elvira Orpheé

My two oldest daughters have strange marriages. Girls today aren't prejudiced.

But the worst thing is that I believe that I am responsible for their marriages because of my love for animals, principally cats.

One day, I heard a loud uproar in the street and went out to look. People were piling up and fleeing at the same time. They fled in groups. A woman calmly came walking down the middle of the street with a white crocodile tied to a string.

We weren't familiar with crocodiles, except through the movie theater on the other block, but we knew they were ferocious. We saw them eat men in shorts and lash their tails furiously. We wouldn't even have imagined that white crocodiles existed because in the movies they were always black and muddy.

The one coming down the middle of the street had a powerful tail, but it was so young that it almost seemed comical, with its bulging eyes that didn't know where to look.

Suddenly, the woman's calmness ended. The little crocodile pulled on the cord and, with a lizard's quickness, it slipped into a hedge.

The crowd cautiously started to approach, and the woman explained that he was like that, very curious, and that he was often overcome by curiosity. The people became bolder and asked her questions. She said that he was very good, as affectionate as a kitten.

I watched from the sidewalk in front, interested but fearful. I would have liked to have approached it and touched it, but was the woman trustworthy? Who knew her and where was she from? In a town, everyone knows everyone else.

Beneath the hedge appeared the white tail that, although strong, was really just a little white tail ending in a pointed tip. He began to move it, like a cat waiting for something exciting.

That gesture won me over, and I began to approach. The people crowded together more, and I couldn't see. They must have wanted to pat it, as I did. It was so small. But when I got close, I saw that someone was already patting it: my daughter Laura.

The crocodile had stuck his face out of the hedge, and while the woman held the cord, Laura passed the back of her hand along the animal's long face.

"Laura!" I believe I shouted.

I must have barely whispered it because no one looked at me, including her. The animal's gestures were exactly like those of a cat. He held his head so it could be caressed; he rubbed against the back of her hand and closed his eyes with the same ecstatic love which a cat devotes to a caress.

Well, the later oddities began there. Laura began to object: "But mama, didn't you tell us of a French writer who used to take a lobser for walks down the street with a loop around its back and held by a string?"

"He was crazy."

"But what you said was very sensible."

Oh, why did I have to tell my daughters about my readings in the library? In reality, yes, it was very sensible. Laura repeated it to me.

"His friends criticized him, as you are doing to me now, but he told them that if people walked dogs, so annoying, so noisy, and so dirty that they even eat excrement, why couldn't he walk lobsters, which are very clean, quiet, and know the mystery of love's secrets."

"What? Of love, no; only of the sea."

"Well, I was mistaken; that know the mysteries of the ocean's secrets."

My second daughter, Paula, is even more open-minded than Laura, and much prettier. I don't know how she met another little white crocodile, but one fine day my two daughters went off to marry them. "Marry" is a figure of speech. I don't believe there is an employee in the civil registry who would have agreed to marry them.

The facts are they left, I didn't see them again, they had children, and they separated from their husbands. I don't believe that the crocodiles fathered those children. What I do believe is that, under the pretext of marriage, my daughters managed to leave home and go to the city where they didn't have anyone to watch over them. I also suspect that their little crocodile husbands were the kind that don't grow, or else they would have eaten my daughters. Finally, I am convinced that all the crocodiles asked was that my daughters pat their heads and take them for walks on a leash down the street.

The fact is my daughters now live with their children, completely human creatures and, in my opinion, children of fathers who aren't the ones that my daughters claim.

And one fine day I discovered that I am to blame for everything, not only because of my love for a man whom I married a year before my daughters left. "I married" is a figure of speech.

That man swindled me. He cheated me out of seven years of my life. He rubbed his head against my hand, and every day he spoke to me of his deep love for me. He told me I had changed his chaotic life, and swore that I improved his work when I got involved in it. He made so many promises that I'm not going to exhaust myself repeating them.

Love numbs, as smoking opium seems to numb. And it was that way for me. Always so perceptive, I didn't notice the cruelty with which he tricked me. But one day I regained my senses and saw what isn't seen and what isn't known. A few words from him gave me a name, a slight clue brought me to the second woman, a detail in a letter produced the third. And in this way, I learned of all his affairs as if he had told me about them himself. He was obsessed with falling in love, making love, and believing himself polygamous and crafty. He wanted to convince himself of his power and brought these women to my house, making me serve them cocktails and meals. He was the child who presents his girlfriends to his mother (although he was eighteen years older than I), because the mother is the one who must seem like the ultimate idiot to make her son feel certain that his lies will be believed by the rest of the world.

He now knows that, even though he may have made me into his mother, not even mothers excuse the mockery of a man blinded by vanity.

And I believe that he will cry. Because I will no longer listen to his lies or because that type always cries.

When I learned of his hypocrisy and faults, I began to see the details of his physical appearance. What were they? A very long face, with some kind of scales on his eyelids, and although his eyes weren't globular, the eyes of the women he deceived were. Ana's eyes bulged; Lea's were like hard-boiled eggs; Edna's matched her jaw, the eyes of a poor spinster, as scaly as a crocodile. Maria Juana, who tried to destroy me from the beginning, had eyes that seemed to spring from their sockets as if attached by rubberbands. Because of my love for animals, I found a man more like a crocodile that cries!

This was the reason that my daughters married whom they married.

Translated by Janice Molloy.

# For Friends and Enemies

## Olga Orozco

A yellow glimmer, that's all. At one o'clock, all the lights are turned out. The glimmer, fish-shaped, sinks in my eyes, and when the house is dark, anything can happen; it can even begin to move. The house may already be moving around, slowly and majestically, with the nocturnal garden steeped in a brilliant greenness, as if it had emerged from the bottom of a lake. It puts on a bridal crown and walks away. Or it's a black stanhope that tumbles away, swept off by the whistle of the pack or whipped by an invisible coach-man. Sometimes there's a cetacean tremor, and a large crack appears along one flank; it's about to push me overboard. Other times I hear a powerful calcareous grinding, and I say to myself: it's pull-ing up its roots and moving away; and we go off, except I mean the grinding doesn't move from bottom to top, like bones being yanked up, but just opposite. It's more like a vault that is about to collapse on shaky columns, that's it. And is this catastrophe that I'm making up to distract the blackness any better than the inevitable appearance of the blackness itself? Wouldn't it be better for the shapeless thing crouching in the space between the wall and wardrobe to appear suddenly: Quick, a spell. I forgot to say the shapelessness is the worst. It can even be a chair with a hippopotamus head, a loose veil blindly looking for me, a mollusklike palpitation that slowly devours the room—furniture, Laura and all.

Laura is sleeping. Recently she has taken to whistling in her sleep. Perhaps she's afraid. I hope I won't imagine her transformed into marmite, marmot, dumb, dead, bean-pole. Just as well. It's a good thing. The door appears, just in time; it began to appear little by little in another glimmer because Grandmother scrapes matches as white as little bones, lights the candles and begins to pray:

"I pray for friends and enemies, for acquaintances and strangers, for the living and the dead. Enlighten them, dear God."

The glimmer is not enough. It only helps to see or not see what should not be there. The glimmer is the devil's palette and makes things worse.

"For my grandmother, Florencia, to whom we are all so endebted, you will set things right with her, Lord, although you may not want to, because of her great memory, her prudence and her orderliness."

The darkness is orderly and foresees what it left behind yesterday and before that. If I help it a little, we could take an inventory of all the possible and impossible monsters in the world. Each night is a review augmented by new combinations, by half lights that open like a trap to let something emerge. And something always emerges from the rarified light over the blackness, from the rarified blackness over the light.

"For my father, who sired so many children, the ones I know as well as the ones I don't know, all of whom he would prefer not to recognize when You call him to You, because he was forgetful, and unless You have cured him it will be very difficult for him to recognize those who don't recognize him."

The monsters recognize me. That's why they come back every night. They come close to me, and I never know exactly how many there are, because they are countless in their metamorphoses. Sometimes I give them names, to help recognize them. But they must lose them at dawn or else someone gives them another name. Sometimes the same ones come back, and I still don't know their real names.

"For my mother, who must look much younger than I. I could make her pray until her knees hurt, like mine, because I no longer felt like picking the threads out of six frayed trousseaus."

Now I am going to feel cold pricking my face, then the slight touch of a brush and a ribbon that circles my head. I wish I could go to sleep before they come, go to sleep on this side, which is my great-grandmother's side. With the last "amen" of the Ave María, if only I could tuck myself in those hems, in those cottony, soft clouds, and fall in the chest where my six great-aunts' sheets and tablecloths lie, smelling of apple, of lavender, of heliotrope, of jasmine, of rosemary, of forget-me-not, forever, forever after.

"I pray for my sister Gertrudis, who had as much patience as time for her worst deeds, but better means, such as lying, craft, and imagination; for my sister Cecilia, may You rest her soul, but keep her alone, so that she won't wake up anyone, so no one will have to help her darn, clean, and mend everything You have to clean, darn, and mend, and even the little that You may have left sound in this world; for my sister Eduvigis: improve her complexion and her character, so that she won't have to hide or feel embarrassed, and no one will have to hide from her; for my sister Valeria, forget that she never was around when she was needed, except when she died; for my sister Viviana, although she never learned to say thank you, in spite of the fact that she talked so much, and perhaps she was right; for my sister Patricia, may her beauty, her indifference and her stinginess be of some use to her."

No one is trying to cure me with this frozen ribbon around my head. These are not blood ties, and if they are, they may be treacherous. They are probably dragging me right now to the middle of a circle where my six great-aunts surround me spinning, the six of them with their hair loose and cold, all six the color of celestial statues or faded earthworms. They are tying me to a cage forever, and they go on spinning forever around me in this bare garden where the wind blows. I don't want anything to do with ties or ribbons, even if I have to protect my forehead all night long with my hands.

"I pray for my four brothers, all womanizers, all brave, so that at least they won't defy You when You plunge them in hell. But first don't neglect their good deeds, even if they're the deeds of war and others that I can't name because it wouldn't be proper and because they still have much to learn."

I'll never learn to tolerate the night. Night learns me, if it does not know me already, because it feels the length and breadth and depth of my skin. It covers me with its smooth touch, it wraps me up in blind bandages changing me into a larva, and it does not leave me even an inch of porous skin to breathe. It's better to try to not move, on the edge of the unnamed thing that is on its way. I don't know if it's possible. And besides, what would I move and where?

"I pray for my uncle Julián Ezcurra, the cross-eyed slavery supporter, and if You can't save him, Lord, don't worry, because his bones would make a good kindling for all those who will have to burn with him, like his son Faustino, so hard that no mortar could grind him down."

If only I could grind up this vague organism that approaches, breathes and hesitates in order to torture me all the more; if only I could send it away with one powerful word that I will never manage to formulate but that I feel is somewhere about; if only I could dissolve it in all the fears of the future, even if each one grew a little afterwards, although I know that they will also be unbearable when the time comes. All right, let it devour me once and for all.

"I pray for my son-in-law Francisco, may You keep a throne for him in this world, as is only fitting for the best man on earth; for everything that You must have to do to finish Your work. And don't tell me that the reward is greater beyond because I say that if You can't do it You should hand it over to some greater god, but let him get going, because I, for one, want to see, and I'm impatient and in a hurry to die."

Now I am going to start to fall in something that isn't even death. It's a kind of vertigo on the inside. It begins with that taste of viscera, with that indigestion in my body, so foreign and so obvious, that I can't get rid of it. It's an excess substance, and I don't know where it is sewed to me or where I am stuck to it. And suddenly an abyss opens. There is a distance between the two, as if what's outside were inside, and this is where I am falling, because it won't hold me anymore, in some way, because it has already make a pact with that other darkness that closes up and pushes me backwards. Where, where am I going?

"I pray for my daughter Sofía, so generous and proud, as immoderate in her goodness as in her anger. Spare her tears and bitterness, never make her bow her head in humiliation, sickness, or poverty. But lower her voice. And if You have time, teach her restraint, but not the timid restraint of others because then it would be better if she stayed the way she is."

And that's my mother, who weeping or smiling snatches me from the depths of an abyss, from this very abyss that I was about to reach because she is my only reference in this world, my door of wisdom or my wall of ignorance. That's my mother, who destroys the cyclone and prevents the ant from exceeding its normal size. That's my mother, like a festive tower on holiday, a bristling fortress, as grand as a cathedral and as tender as the light of a candle or the touch of warm feathers on heavy eyelids at sleep's threshold.

"I pray for my daughter Lidia, who died very young. I won't make any charges, or call You to account. I will be as sparing with You as You were in bargaining for her future. I commend her to the Virgin because She will know how to care for her better than You: Let the Virgin remind her to starch her blouses, keep her paintbrushes neat and change the water in the flower vases. And dress warmly, because she was always very cold, and she went out in her slip and she never once wore her shawls, gloves and cape."

Heavy eyelids. No. I thought that it was inside, but it's outside where it begins to form, that thing that begins as a misty condensation that spreads and takes shape and ends up as a lady. She's an old woman composed of tulle and transparent fumes. She always shows up when Lidia is named, with time, with night, with fear and with patience. She dilates my eyes to get in, with her rocking chair, so that she's there and she isn't.

"For my daughter Adelaida. Lord, I earnestly pray for You to improve her in any way possible, even if it means she will always be a spinster. Erase her so that no one realizes it and draw her again as I remember her; copy her from any portrait when she was seventeen, make her face as oval as a medallion once again, with nothing left over, her waist so slim that two hands can encircle it, the rest of her formed in the most perfect of molds so that she can wear white organza or red velvet once again. And if that's not possible, go back twenty years, even if those of us who are here now may not be all those who were there then."

That's it. Now she has taken shape completely. She sways, as slight or as diffuse as if she had come to rest on a branch of cotton or were imprisoned in a stormy winter window. Tomorrow they will tell me not to be frightened, that it's great-grandmother Florencia, dead for fifty years. But I can't look at her as if she were a picture. Besides, no picture comes alone. And what if she suddenly approached? Laura must also be looking at her. It's best not to lose sight of those who have disappeared when they do appear because you never know how they come and go. Without taking my eyes off her, I stretch out an arm toward Laura's side of the bed and I immediately find her hand that has come to meet mine. It always happens that way.

"For my grandson Alejandro, dead at twenty. You must know why You did what You did. It's useless to try to excuse Yourself by telling me that God takes the best first, because You will make me pray for the perversity of those who are left behind. He was handsome; he was intelligent, noble and saintly. So You weren't satisfied with all the angels and archangels of Your court? So You needed one more angel? I'll tell You face to face, without humility or resignation: You'll share your position at the right hand of God the Almighty Father with him, and even so, who knows if You can count on my forgiveness."

Laura's hand is warm, moist and trembling. And what if it's not Laura's hand? I look, although Great-grandmother Florencia might take advantage of this moment to come forward, rarified, irrevocably riding her rocking chair. The vague form that is Laura looks like any night condensation: an immense, folded insect that will jump suddenly, a drowned girl who floats in her bed of tangled vegetation, a boat's figurehead ready to plunge me into the depths. I try to let go of her hand, but she grasps me with the strength of desperate cohesion.

"I pray for my granddaughter María de las Nieves, who has so much suffering in store for her and so few masquerade balls and lighted gardens, which is what she likes most. She'll be married young to a man with a tiger's gaze and a sentimental heart, with the stripes of a beast and a dove. Don't let him corrupt her skin or take away her happiness. May she have many children because she is the last of our line. Let her preserve our family in other names and other memories that will recognize us and exalt the nobility and truth above all else."

Perhaps it's my own hand that invents the other hand, my own blood that projects itself to defend me or to protect me. No, and yes, perhaps, because I hear Laura's very soft voice, like the voice she uses to announce dates, illness, or eclipses, that is almost like an official document: "Lía, do you see her? Do you see her now?"

"Who," I ask afraid that she's not talking about the same thing.

"Her, who else?"

"Yes, I see her. What do you think she'll do?"

"Anything."

"And what is anything?"

"Everything, except rock in her chair."

"But that's what she's doing."

"And do you think she came to do that?"

"I don't know. She probably forgot something."

"And what if we gave her Lidia's clothes and paintbox and the skeleton that's in Alejandro's room?"

"Wouldn't it be better to ask her what she wants?"

"No, can't you see that she's already leaving?"

"For my granddaughter Laura. Now she's charming and wild, especially when she whinnies or makes faces. That has its charm. But I want her to be like the little First Communion pictures, inside and out. See to it, Lord, and develop her openness until it becomes concern for others; develop her neutrality so that it may become warmth; develop her outspokenness so that no one may feel alone when her name is spoken."

"Grandmother Florencia, go away," I whisper, and I blow silently. My great-grandmother goes off riding her disperse cloud; she penetrates the shutters invisibly and becomes part of the misty assemblage that is corporealizing on the other side because now I hear muffled confabulations, deadened footsteps, a soft rebounding against the walls. They're falling in flocks from the sky. Don't you hear something spinning like a pinwheel with big feathers tapping against the peephole?

"For my granddaughter Lía, who's timid and melancholy and likes to keep to herself. May she be able to hold something in her hands that are the hands of the dispossessed. Make strength out of her weakness. Remember she nearly died when she was a year old and perhaps she has left much of life somewhere else, not in this world. Repay her at least in intelligence in faith and charity, because I am very much afraid that she will have nothing to do with hope. I don't ask you to give her beauty because it wouldn't do her any good."

I only hope that this growing rustle against the shutters will finally stop. It spins with a tapping that is ever more powerful, ever more urgent. "Laura," I whisper at the moment when I feel that the house is going to move, lifted up above by this wheel of wings. But Laura is already asleep, grasping a kind of handle that it is always so difficult to detach her from, unless she lets go herself. "Laura," I insist anyway, about to move, almost walking.

"I pray for myself, who am nothing, but should be the last to die so that no one will mourn me."

There is someone. It should be better to know that there is someone. I get out of bed and walk forward trying to support myself forcefully on this floor that sways as it ascends, that is going to hurl me in any direction. Breathlessly, I reach the shutters, the fragile wall against the unknown. Where will I find the strength to open the peephole? First I look, without moving, toward the glimmer, toward the open door, by the bed where grandmother is engraved, almost phosphorescent against the pillows, a little more corporeal, a little more tenacious than her grandmother Florencia.

"What's the matter, child? Where are you going? Why aren't you asleep?" she asks with a voice that is a gust of air.

"I hear noises, Grandmother. Don't you hear them?" I say, trying to counter with a gust that will unite us and push back what is outside.

"Yes, I hear them. Go back to bed and don't worry. Go to sleep. They are the ghosts, that's all, just the ghosts."

Translated by Alison Weber.

# And the Wheel Still Spins

## Olga Orozco

Our progress is irrevocable, as if we were inside a wheel, but we ride on horseback. At a gallop, on a white horse, from Telén to Toay. To me it is just like riding on the croup of the stormy wind, and although the horse may not leave the wheel's circle, I cling desperately to Grandfather Damián's poncho.

We left at dusk, when sadness falls like an enormous bird from blue to grey, shaking handfuls of ash, and with failing strength covers the plain, blocking the day's retreat, the day that perhaps is disappearing at my back beneath these wings that have not yet closed.

I don't know. I vowed not to turn my head so that nothing could make us return. I can't look sideways either or the house will come back, and I will sink again in those rooms that smell of never leaving. Those rooms where the dark furniture peeps hungrily through the keyholes, where the fleshy plants swell imperceptibly in the shadows and the lamps lower a yellow eyelid to conceal what is not seen.

Perhaps Aunt Valeria is still there behind the grille, I told myself, perhaps she is futilely waving a handkerchief she can't even cry into. Perhaps she is still there, absent-minded, idly growing pale, and perhaps it's already night, I tell myself.

"Good-bye, Aunt Valeria. You will be locked up forever in smoked glass, like an eclipse. It doesn't matter. They will see you just the same. All the drawers in your house are spying on you and want to eat you up, and the plants cut you up while you sleep, and in every corner there are hooded things with shining eyes that make signs like Bengal tigers. Good-bye, Aunt Valeria. You have cold hands like widows who pet flocks of black birds. It doesn't matter. I love you just the same, even though your voice is far away, so distant that it floats in the air like the gauze of someone else's mourning. I love you because your name is Valeria even on the moon, because in three days you didn't spy on me to try to see me cry and because I know that you know that I know. Good-bye, Aunt Valeria. We will never see each other again." Years later I will see your last photograph, and you will be even more pale among the plants that are even more fleshy, looking like you know that I know that Alejandro is dead.

I know. When everyone else believes that you don't know, they look at each other with such complicity that it's enough to give it away, or perhaps that's precisely why they do it, giving in to sheer temptation; when they suspect that you suspect, they sniff apprehensively, as if there were a dead dog around somewhere, while they speak hypocritically about the exquisite perfumes of the season; when they know that you already know—like Valeria—they conspire with each other so that they can be simply stubborn and indifferent witnesses to "what happened," which no one can undo, because it already happened, and therefore it will keep on happening, even if it is forgotten. I know. It's useless for Grandfather Damián to have brought me here, "before," three days ago, and for him to bring me back punctually, exactly when he promised, with a storm and night coming on, as if he were only trying to escape the wind, as if, in the meantime, the wind had passed over my house, slamming a door closed that we will find closed forever when we return. I know that it was much more than the wind, much more than a door. It was a precipice that they have not allowed me to cross with the others, for the first time. They dug it deeper for me during the three days of the two absences, without knowing that I have been infected by that death, whatever the distance, and that I will never be free of it.

How and when did I find out? I found out just as I learned many other things, trying to see until I couldn't see, or the other way around. I don't really understand the game because I later caught it, and now I can't begin again without knowing. I held the likeness of death ten days ago. I looked at it just to see what it was like, and I kept on looking at it until I got dizzy, or until my gaze sunk under water or turned to the edge of a flame, and then, in that figure that was the likeness of a tremor or a shiver, only motionless, the face of my brother Alejandro appeared. I closed my eyes and with my eyes closed, I saw him with his eyes closed. His cheeks were more sunken, his lips were pale, and his complexion was very sad, a color that would never be another color, but would instead gradually disappear more and more within that same color. Then I forgot, until Grandfather Damián came for me and brought me to Telen three days ago, and I didn't ask anymore because I knew that was the face that brought us, the face that was spinning in the wheels of the car with its color that meant it would not return. If I knew nothing else, I knew that that was being dead. Only I have been infected by it ever since because since then I feel beneath my eyelids other closed eyelids that no effort, no astonishment can open again; my blood flows sweeping along with it motionless blood, heavy as a stone that persists until my blood is also stone; my heart beats above a heart permanently paralyzed by frost. This very moment it is freezing my tears.

We have stopped. Grandfather Damián dismounts and ties the horse to a post. I rub my eyes with my fists so that he will think that I am only sleepy. When I look again—now I can look to the sides because I know that nothing can stop the wheel that carries us back without the car—he is already inside the store, inside the gasping blue cold illuminated by two alcohol lamps. He is as alien and as near as a tree. It all depends on whether you find protection or abandonment in silence. He is made, like trees, out of an arrogant, impassive, calm, pensive and sleepless substance. He is "Grandfather Damián" and not "Grandfather" plain and simple because he is not my mother's father but her uncle. For others, he is "Grandfather" plain and simple, but that doesn't make him less tree-like, especially at night when he and the trees isolate themselves in their patriarchal dominion, in that slightly hazy mystery that looks like sleep on the outside, and that must be the instrument that fashions them—the trees and him—and keeps them from sleeping. Just like now, as he approaches—although it always seems as if you were the one who was approaching him—and holds out a package that does not look like a gift but like something that was left for someone on the branch of a tree, and he unties and mounts the horse.

We spin once more in a spoke of the wheel; at the axis is Alejandro's face. Again, we gallop. But I am no longer afraid of the beasts that the night harbors at my back or the unimaginable hand that stretches out to snatch me because Grandfather Damián has placed me in front of him in the saddle and protects my back with his body and my sides with the barrier formed by his arm and the two reins. Who told him I was afraid?

From now on, we both see the road take shape at the same moment. I am always less afraid of what I can confront with my eyes than what may surprise me unseen. That's why I sleep with my back pressed to the wall and I can only sit facing an open door. Although I may hear nothing, there are balls of yarn that mean something else, that fall and bounce and slip away in astute silence; even though I may not see anything, they are weaving something to catch me. Of course now everything is so dark that it is almost as if it were happening behind us, as if what's behind were the entire night that is plotting to envelope us. I feel the night working, close by, crouching in the agitated brush that opens and thickens at the edge of fields, open but impenetrable against the darkened sky; I feel the night preparing its materials, in the distance dissolving those pallid glimmers that suddenly hint at salvation, incorporating them into its own substance into the skein of horror; I feel the night at my sides stretching taut threads to bind us. I don't want to look down to see the trap that the road has become, and still it hurls us forward, but at any moment it will close in below and behind and catch in the sack, any moment now. . . If I look I'll slip, I'll fall inward and downward, I'll fall like a cold stone through the stomach's mouth, who knows how deep if I can't grasp onto something while I'm still outside. Leaning forward, I cling to the horse's mane with both hands. I want to press against it; I'd like to get inside its skin, if it would let me. I really should walk on four or more feet. They have put me on two feet to measure me against a world I don't belong to, that takes a different path, that slides away carrying off the deepest part of my organism, and that's why it is gradually unwinding me from this wheel of nothingness that revolves at a diabolical speed in the core of my being. I spoke of weavings! They are unweaving me, they are unraveling my mysterious skein, they are detaching me from a scheme I thought I was woven into until the end of time. And the hollow of the wheel widens inside dizzyingly; it devours my substance with something that tastes like pulverized grey, like swelling wind, like vomit on an empty stomach. I don't understand the substance that abandons me nor can I assimilate this gyrating nausea that replaces it. If I throw myself right now from the horse, the substance that leaves me will snap back to my insides like a rubber band, filling my nausea to overflowing, and I will explode in a thousand pieces; if I stay on the horse, it will keep on moving backwards, and the wheel of nausea, after touching bottom, will hurl my empty shell against some wall of the universe. Why are they turning me backwards? And for how long?

The horse shakes its head, neighs, and slackens its pace. Grandfather Damián's arm presses against my waist and his hand throws my head backwards while supporting it firmly against his stomach. We come to a halt. He dismounts and lifts me down from the horse. I am trembling from head to toe. It's a rising vibration, knocks against my height and leaves me as limp as a rag. I don't feel it subside, but it rises again and will keep on rising for the rest of my life, knocking against all the ciphers of my years.

I sink to the parched earth and cry. The measure of my weeping is the measure of my recovering strength, my consciousness of abandonment, my reincorporation into the wall that opposes. That opposes what? Something that seeks me and that I halfheartedly reject, something that I cannot resolve to explore, but that doesn't let me in, unless I completely let go of my insides and abandon myself to its strength without resorting to any of my powers.

Grandfather Damián, squatting at my side, strokes my head and whispers, "Poor thing!" If he says something else, it is something that is indistinguishable from my voice and my thoughts. "Poor thing! Poor thing!" That's all. It's like being alone with God, with God who breaks into pieces to act with my acts and feel with my feelings, who moves away from his unity with my desecrations and advances toward it with my love. An impartial witness throughout the inevitable journey between nightmares to the end of time. We could stay here until then, until we are covered by this sand that begins to rise and swirl, thicker and thicker, faster and faster.

We are on horseback once again. We advance slowly against the wind, almost broadside against the thirsty whirlwinds. It's going to rain. These thousand mouths that hurl their desolate breath in every direction are clamoring for rain. Suddenly they become silent, surprised by the unexpected warning of a lightning bolt. It disappears and lights up: irascible, threatening. Even though I go on believing otherwise, it is not the brilliance of a door that opens, closes and bangs open offering a glimpse of an unknown, surprising interior, whose very splendor blinds us and will not let us see. It is not a fleeting concession of the miracle. It is rather a warning signal from the watchman in high towers, or a gathering of arms prepared for the day of annihilation. It rolls down the steps. In that light I am entranced staring at the candies that Grandfather Damián gave me, as if he had left them on a branch the first time we stopped, the candies I have clutched all this time without realizing that the paper has come off and that they are candies and that my hand is sticky. They are perfect little opaque pebbles—pink, blue, and grey, with the irregularities, the hollows, the bumps of any pebble that you save to keep you company or to look at in the light and remember. Perhaps these will let me forget. They must be sweet but sad, like any memory that is savored before it is forgotten. They are a bribe to compensate for my grief and fear. I contemplate them in their humility in another light, with infinite compassion, with a pity of crystalized honey that hurts my throat. I see them as something as helpless as I. Because I have never found in this world an object to exchange for my grief or for my fear. Each coin received in exchange only increases them because it changes immediately in value; it acquires the price of my compassion at the expense of my helplessness, even when that coin is stamped with the image of the adverse. Swindles, revenge, resentment, they didn't buy in me more than a patch of compassion where the thickets of another grief and another fear grow like wild, sheltered by my own abandonment. I establish this dominion with these insoluble opaque pebbles—pink, blue, and grey. Upon them I build the dwelling place of my fortitude and my need, while the sand ceaselessly stings my cheeks.

The horse whinnies, rears up and shakes its head nervously, refusing to go on. Something is approaching. Something is rolling down the road without a wheel. Between two blinks of lightning I make out a nebulous mass. It is an immense grayish, spiny organism, composed of atmosphere and aggression. It advances swaying lightly without skin or heart and, therefore, apparently without mystery. But it belongs to the world of unfathomable repetition that grows from without; to the world of involuntary, blind threats, perhaps the most dangerous world, because a powerful negation of will acts everywhere but does not show itself. Who knows from what distance it orders this emissary of fate to emit an extension of the unformed to envelop us and incorporate us like water, shadow or stain! Well, let it come, let it invade us, and change us into another adhesion identical to the rest of its bristling nothingness. The horse, old man, and little girl will keep on riding within another wheel of uncontrolled and irreversible fate, whose center will continue spinning simply with the hands of the clock until the absurd termination of the absurd universe. But no; it brushes past us and goes on. And it will keep growing in its aridity, adding to its gigantic bulk more identical bulk, without roots or final destiny. I have known similar atrocious moments.

"It was a tumbleweed," Grandfather Damián states simply.

And the horse, old man and child continue their irrevocable journey, in silence, penury, and obstinacy. And what if we were traveling within another similar wheel? It can't be similar, because wherever we go, at the end of all weakening, all perseverance, lies the house. It is within my eyes and shines in the stormy shadows of the distance like a jewel, like an ember, like a phosphorescent diamond. I know that within one of the faces of that crystal an opaque bolt of lightning has suddenly flashed; I know that one of the walls of that house has now opened in a fissure from which it will begin to crumble. I try not to see that face clouded by the death of the face that draws us. I try to imagine myself with my back to the wound in that wall that is bleeding us. I want to see only the luminous heads around the lamps without counting how many there are, feel the brush of the warm sheets without thinking about the ones that will grow cold on a bed that no one will rumple again, smell the woody perfume inside and the scent of sugared lemon that seeps in without looking beneath the hint of lavender that will slowly vanish, absorbed by the damp handkerchiefs, the scent that perhaps has already disappeared. And nevertheless I cannot erase it because that perfume is Alejandro and it is Alejandro who draws me, who submerges me in immobility, who imprisons me like a butterfly beneath the frost of his heart.

It is impossible to breathe in the motionless cold. I cannot absorb this frozen mask affixed to my face. Everything has stopped. I am an inhabitant of the mummy world. They have embalmed the air and the landscape that I cannot see. Perhaps they have also embalmed Grandfather Damián and the horse in this swaying to and fro and up and down like an infinite carousel. If only something would move, although it might only be a rope crossing the road. . . I prefer the sandy gusts of wind to this paralysis that stops my nose and ears. It is an unbearable suspense, an empty basin that one does not know how to fill. But they are already filling it. Enormous rain drops have begun to fall against my maskless face, against the avid earth. I cannot see the ground, but I suppose that it absorbs the rain drops, that it keeps them intact, that it hides them avariciously. And now that the rain drops are beginning to fall more rapidly, more incessantly, the earth must hide them quickly, in its deepest corners, beneath a fold. In a thousand years, people may excavate and find this buried rain, and I will explain to them how it happened. Perhaps my fears, the vertigo, Grandfather Damián, the tumbleweed, the horse and the insoluble stones will still be alive, all of them witnesses to this journey that never ends. Each one may claim a portion of the distributed consolation. I breathe in deeply the air mixed with rain.

Grandfather Damián covers my head and wraps me almost two times round in his poncho. *"Thus did the grandfather, in days of yore, return from Vercelli bearing the dead woman's body."** It is a signal. Immediately the lightning answers him, the thunder and the veins traced by the bolt that will soon fall, that is already falling. The poncho is white, so is the horse; we only need a mirror to see the lightning. We will attract it. We are shouting to it with our whiteness that pretends to repel but only brings on the worst. White forebodes catastrophes; black reports that they have already passed. We will cross from one to the other, from this opaque ice to coal. We will remain intact, transformed into our mourning (How the crepe-like rustle of your voice will change, Aunt Valeria!), into the statues of our own grief. I know because I have heard the stories: the man who killed his brother and stole the treasure in a white sheet, the bride who fled through the countryside wrapped in veils, and the little thorn that snagged the saint's tunic were the black testimony of their own punishment. But why are we punished? Because of the future, surely, because of our weakness, our abdications, our excessive patience, and its counterpart in obstinacy and pride, always present throughout future years. They made this journey possible when I was only five years old. The punishment heaps on me dozens of years anticipated by the wheel and makes me part of a monument to the somber pilgrimmage, until these dozens of years have truly passed and I am transformed

into a little pile of dull ash, and anyone can blow away each parti-
cle of obstinacy and pride. And even so, after infinite turns of the
wheel in limitless time, the ashes will draw together again animated
by the same weakness, abdications, and excessive patience, so that
the journey may continue because I must reach the house anyway.

But the bolt doesn't fall. It has gone back through those doors
that the lightning opens and closes. And doors and walls are bumping together up there and keeping it from getting out. The battle
is deafening and dazzling, behind a blinding thickness of water.

"No. Not here," I cry, because I have just seen.

"There's nothing we can do. There's no other road," says the
voice of God, the voice of Grandfather Damián. The gallop
quickens, and the embrace that holds me tightens.

I have just seen. By that vein of light that stretches to the roofs
of the earth, I have just seen, engraved in mists by the rain, the
cupolas adorned with absorbed crosses that arise from the top of
the wall, and above the entrance, the irremediable angel who calls
us. God, Grandfather Damián, I ask, "Was this cruelty necessary?"

"There's nothing we can do. There's no other road that will reach
Alejandro, reach his eyes like new green silk beneath the yellow
fires, reach the empty hands of a young and bashful champion.
But Alejandro's eyes are now an acid bath in which all the portraits of the world are submerged and erased, and his hands hold
only the threatening banner of an immobile victory over time. No.
There is no other road. Outside is this funnel of panic through
which they suck me from the cold of my hair, dragging me to the
assembly of nameless bones, presided over by that lady to whom
all faces can easily be proved. Within is this endless incline down
which I fall tumbling beneath the boiling of my blood that is still
alive among the dead.

"Alejandro: this is not just your game. If it were, I wouldn't mind
following you because I know that we are the same color, and no
strange color can make us different. Being alone with you, wherever it may be, is proof of previous ramification, whatever test we
are subjected to. The mystery has the same beginning and perhaps the same end that you may already know. But this is a game

for both of us. You're making a pact against me. You're joining the enemy. You?"

"It's not true. He's not there," I tell myself, and I close my eyes so that what I tell myself will be true.

I order the panic without Alejandro. I corporealize it in those small closed niches on All Soul's Day, where all objects are useless, and nevertheless they seem recently touched by someone who has just hidden, has just dissolved in that impregnated, taut, almost organic air because it's only the rarified deposit, the amorphous body where the molecules of the invisible remain suspended. At any moment these particles may look for each other; they must be seeking each other now, trying to recover their cohesion in an easy effort of memory. They do not even seek each other; they attract each other. The dead, *they* remake themselves. Because just as here, there is in every substance a part that struggles to fall; because it is condemned to death, there must be here, also in every substance, a part that struggles to rise up because it is condemned to life. This mixture of forces in a single substance nauseates me, and nevertheless it is in me, in my own seed, in the beginning of the cadaver that I will become. I have been locked up with my own enemy ever since I was born, but I have not known him. Don't let him make a pact with *them*, the ones like him, that's all I ask, now, as they approach. They are dense transparencies, armies fashioned from rarified smoke clouds, gusts of vibrations given to random metamorphoses. And at their head the lady, with her hat trimmed in flowers and her jaws strong from chewing butterflies. I cannot bear to think of the moistness of those flowers or the crunch of those butterflies. Or of the blurred faces that are approaching. It is a cold and misty tide, with circles that advance like moire. It's now here. It rises, it freezes us, and the circles tighten and imprison us as they rise. They adhere in blue streaks from our feet to our necks; we are imprisoned in marble. This light is the last streak, the luminous blindfold that binds our eyes forever. I scream just as the bolt deafens us. I hear myself howl in the din of the sky that collapses and splits the flagstones and sweeps us along with the falling columns that supported the vault of its immense cathedral. They pull us up by the roots from the world of the living and bury us indiscriminately with the dead. I am an interminable moan that turns inward, taking me down to the subsoil. It will suddenly become mute against the stone door that will put out this light on my face. My last appearance is this well opened by my own lament, and they are going to close it on me.

"Blessed Saint Jerome, Virgin Saint Barbara!" Grandfather Damián says softly, stopping the expectation of the fall, turning the well upward, making my ears emerge again. "It struck next to the church."

I return from the depths with the moist puff of air that puts out the fire in my face. We are incredibly in the present. Then I turn to see, as if through a glass on which all the tears in the world have condensed, the ragged night, still standing upon the earth, clothed in wintry steam, with its old garland of yellow lights in shreds. It advances toward us across the plaza; it jumps over the fences dripping water. I would also like to hold its hand and run, dishevelled and barefoot, over the immortal land.

But I am still tied to the wheel that bears us, and perhaps I no longer even know how to walk. Because wrapped in the poncho that smells of savage storms, crossing confused underground sheets of cold and of heat, I am no longer anything more than a pitiful larva, clinging not to memory, not even to the promise of sunshine, but simply to the effort of breathing, of contracting and expanding the miserable portion of air that sustains me. I can scarcely breathe, shaken who knows how long by the echo of the broken sob that was buried deep inside me. I am expelling it in little pieces, in a kind of muffled hiccough, all through the Larrain ranch.

And in front of us is the darkened house, encased in grief.

When Grandfather Damián deposits me on the ground, I feel that I really am something without beginning or end, without hands or feet, an undifferentiated continuity of cold and heat, still displaced by the impetus of the wheel that wobbles now in the emptiness of my heart. It's possible that it will eventually stop and that I will collapse on nothingness, like a rag. But no. I am still the shell of the sob that I have not completely released. Perhaps it has dug down in me to the last day of life, because it is still there when I see my sister María de las Nieves sitting in the galley, so pale and dressed in black, and I hear her say from so far away as if she were speaking forever:

"Alejandro went away. Elijah came for him in a fiery chariot and they went up to heaven three days ago. Just now when the lightning struck, it looked like a chariot's wheel and I thought that they were coming back. I lifted my feet, and it rolled by beneath my legs and fell in the cistern."

Then the wheel of the journey, the wheel of fire, passes over me, over Alejandro's face, over the repetition of the sob. Still.

Translated by Alison Weber.

---

*La Berline arrétée dans la nuit, by O. V. de L. Milosz.

# The Wild Mirrors

# The Mirror of Melancholy

## Alejandra Pizarnik

*Everything is a mirror!*
—Octavio Paz

...she lived in front of a great gloomy mirror, the famous mirror for which she herself had drawn the model... So designed for comfort that it projected arm-rests to allow her to remain leaning there without getting tired throughout the long hours. We can suppose that having thought to design a mirror, Erzsebet had also drawn the plans for her dwelling place. And we can understand why only the most captivatingly sad music of her gypsy orchestra, dangerous hunts, the violent perfume of magic herbs in the sorceress's cabin or—above all—cellars awash with human blood would kindle anything resembling a living flame in the eyes of that perfect face. For no one thirsts more for cold mirrors. Speaking of mirrors, no one was ever able to confirm the truth of the rumors about the countess's homosexuality. We will never know whether she ignored the tendency or, on the contrary, admitted it as a right she accorded herself along with all the other rights. Essentially, she lived submerged in an exclusively feminine universe. Only women populated her nights of crime. Certain details are obviously revealing. For example, in the torture chamber, at the moments of greatest tension, she herself would thrust a burning candle into the victim's vagina. Witnesses told of less solitary lecheries; a servant swore during the trial that a mysterious aristocratic lady disguised as a boy would visit the countess. On one occasion, she found them together, torturing a girl. But she couldn't say whether they shared other, less sadistic, pleasures.

Back to the theme of the mirror. This sinister figure cannot really be explained, but I must point out that she suffered the sickness of the sixteenth century, melancholia. The melancholy are governed by one unchanging color; their interior is a space the color of mourning. A space where nothing and no one enters. It is a stage without scenery, where the inert ego is attended by the ego that suffers from this inertia. The latter wishes to free the prisoner, but all attempts fail, just as Theseus would have failed had he been— besides himself—the Minotaur. Killing him would have also meant killing himself. But there are fleeting remedies. Sexual pleasures, for example, can briefly blot out the silent gallery of echoes and mirrors that constitute the melancholy soul. They can even illuminate such a mournful confine by turning it into a kind of music box whose bright, gay figures dance and sing delightfully. But then, when the spring runs down, everything again returns to stillness and silence. The music box is not a gratuitous analogy. Melancholy is, in fact, a musical problem, a dissonance, a disturbed rhythm. While outside things whirl vertiginously, within throbs water's exasperating, slow dripping, drop by drop. This outside seen from within the melancholic becomes absurd and unreal, the "farce we must all perform." For a moment, though—whether through savage music, or some frug or the most violent sexual act— melancholy's painfully slow rhythm not only keeps pace with that of the world but surpasses it with unspeakably delicious excess. The ego vibrates, animated with delirious energies.

Time reveals itself to the melancholic as the suspension of its passing—time really does pass, but its slowness evokes the growing of nails on a corpse—which precedes and continues the fatally ephemeral violence. Between two silences or two deaths, a prodigious whirling speed disguised in forms varying from innocent debauchery to sexual perversions and even to crime. Thus I think of Erzsebet Bathory and the rhythm of her nights measured by the cries of young girls. The book I am glossing in these notes carries a portrait of the countess; the beautiful and somber lady resembles the allegory of melancholy shown in the old engravings. Let us remember, too, that in her era a melancholic meant one possessed by the devil.

Translated by Suzanne Jill Levine.

# Blood Baths

## Alejandra Pizarnik

> *Si te vas a ba*ñar, Juanilla,
> dima a cuales banos vas.
> —Song of Upsala

The rumor ran about that from the moment of Darvulia's arrival, Countess Erzsebet, to keep her beauty, bathed in blood. And it was true that Darvulia, like any good sorceress, believed in the restorative properties of "human fluids." She extolled the qualities of young girls' blood—virgins' if possible—as the means to defeat the devil of decrepitude, and the countess accepted this prescription as if it were merely a matter of taking sitz baths. Dorko would thus pitilessly cut open veins and arteries in the torture chamber. The blood was collected in vats and when the donors were finally exsanguinated, Dorko would spill the warm, red liquid over the pale body of the countess who sat erect, so silent, so patiently waiting.

Despite her timeless beauty, time did inflict cruel signs of its passage on Erzsebet. Around 1610, Darvulia mysteriously disappeared and Erzsebet, now close to fifty, complained to her new sorceress about the inefficacy of the blood baths. If the truth be told, more than complain, she threatened to kill her if those detested signs

of advancing age were not arrested. The sorceress reached the conclusion that the problem lay in the use of peasant blood. She
pronounced—or predicted—that a change of tone, from red to blue,
would soon chase away shameful old age. Thus they went searching for daughters of the lesser aristocracy. To attract them to the
desolate castle, Erzsebet's henchmen would announce that the
countess suffered for the lack of good company. How to dispel her
loneliness? By filling the halls with girls of noble birth who, in
return, for their lively companionship, would be fully instructed
in etiquette and all the social graces. In a fortnight, only two of
the twenty-five pupils who had rushed to learn the ways of the
nobility were still alive; one died shortly after, exsanguinated, and
the other managed to commit suicide.

Translated by Suzanne Jill Levine.

# Severe Measures

## Alejandra Pizarnik

> . . . la loi, froide par elle-meme, ne
> saurait etre accessible aux passions
> qui peuvent legitimer la cruelle
> action due meutre.
>
> —Sade

For six years the countess murdered with impunity. During that period the sad rumors ran about like wildfire, but the illustrious name of Bathory, under the protection of the Hapsburgs, kept the denouncers at bay.

By 1610 the king had gathered the most sinister information—and evidence—about the countess. After considerable hesitation he had no choice but to take severe measures. He charged the powerful Palatine Thurzó with the task of investigating the lurid deeds of Csejthe and punishing the guilty parties.

Accompanied by his armed men, Thurzó arrived unannounced at the castle. In the cellars, strewn with the remains of the bloody ceremony of the night before, he found a beautiful mutilated corpse and two dying girls. But that wasn't all: he breathed in the stench of corpses, saw bloodied walls, the Iron Virgin, the cage, instruments of torture, vats of dried blood, the cells—in one he saw a group of girls waiting their turn to die. They told him how, after several days of fasting, they had been served grilled flesh that had once been the beautiful bodies of their dead companions.

The countess, without denying Thurzó's accusations, proclaimed that all this she had every right to indulge in as a member of the highest nobility. To which the Palatine responded: I condemn you to perpetual imprisonment in your own castle.

In his heart, Thurzó knew that the countess should be beheaded, but such an exemplary punishment would have excited the reprobation not only of the Bathorys but of all the nobility. Meanwhile, in the countess's room, they found a small notebook where she had inscribed the names and descriptions of her victims, which by then numbered about 610... As for Erzsebet's accomplices, they were tried. After confessing to unbelievable deeds they died at the stake.

The prison rose up round about her. They walled up the doors and windows of her room. In one thick wall they left only a slit to permit passage of food and water. And when everything else was finished, four scaffolds were erected at the four corners of the castle to show that inside lived someone condemned to death.

She lived in this way for more than three years, half-dead of cold and hunger, but never revealing the slightest remorse. She never understood why she had been condemned. On August 21, 1614, a contemporary chronicler wrote: She died towards nightfall, abandoned by all.

She felt no fear nor did she ever tremble. Thus we can feel no pity, no emotion or admiration for her. Just a suspended gasp over the excess of horror, a fascination with that white dress turned red, with the very idea of an absolute wantonness, with the evocation of a silence starred by screams where everything was the image of unacceptable beauty.

Like Sade in his writings and Gilles de Rais in his crimes, the

Countess Bathory reached, beyond all limits, the final abyss of abandon. She is yet another proof that the absolute freedom of the human creature is horrible.

Translated by Suzanne Jill Levine.

# Excerpts from The Wild Papers

## Marosa Di Giorgio

Some mushrooms are born stealthily; some are born in silence; others, with a bit of a shriek, a touch of thunder. Some are white, others pink, that one's gray and looks like a pigeon, the statue of a pigeon; others can be golden or purple. Each one carries— and this is the awful part—the initial of the dead person it comes from. I don't dare devour them; that delicate flesh is a relative.

But in the afternoon the mushroom buyer comes along and starts harvesting. My mother gives her permission. He chooses like an eagle. That one, white as sugar, another pink, still another gray.

Mother doesn't realize she's betraying her race.

\*     \*     \*

Last night it returned again, the Shadow; though a good hundred years had passed, we recognized her all right. She bypassed the violet garden, the bedroom, the kitchen; she went around the candy dish, the dinner plates white as bone, the candy dishes that smelled of roses. She went back to the bedroom, interrupted love-making, caresses; those who were awake froze with their eyes staring ahead; those who were dreaming saw her just the same. The mirror in which she looked at herself, or didn't look, fell and shattered. It seemed that she wanted to kill someone. But she went out to the garden. She hovered, digging in the same place, as if there were someone buried beneath. The poor cow, grazing near the violets, went mad, moaning like a woman or a wolf. But the Shadow flew away, heading south. She'll be back in a century.

*   *   *

When I paid a visit to the altar, I wore a sky-blue organdy dress longer than I was tall, where, at times, a golden foot, so exquisitely embossed peeked out from the very breast of my mother. My hair, too, was sky-blue organza, longer than the dress, but it could turn pink and even pale topaz.

As soon as I arrived, the inhabitants began to pray and thus the novel, the novena began. Hummingbirds and colibris laced the prayers, going in and out of them; their ephemeral presence produced, first a stir, then lent skill and intensity to the sacred murmuring.

Some beings were there on a visit, outside, and for a moment; the sad-faced Cow came; the Hare, the Snow, and a fly.

While I was there, the inhabitants prayed fervently, not taking their eyes off my veil, my hair, that in a few seconds turned from blue to pink and even light ruby, in a completely natural way.

*   *   *

The wolf attended her baptism and her communion; to the baptism he wore a skirt; to the communion, a pink dress. The wolf wasn't noticed; only his pointy ears stuck out a little.

He pursued her to school, darting from rosebush to cabbage patch; he spied on her during exam period, when she trembled a little...

He spotted the first suitor, the second and the third, who only visited her at the garden gate. She in her filmy organdy that sheltered girls wore back then. And pearls in her hair, on her neckline, on her hem, heavy and splendid pearls (they were the only things holding up the dress.) When she moved, one or two pearls got lost. But the suitors disappeared, and no one knew why.

Her friends got married, one after another; she attended their big parties; she was there when each of her friends gave birth.

And the years passed, flying by, and she was lost in bewilderment. One day she turned to someone and said: It's the wolf.

Though, to tell the truth she had never seen a wolf. Until one extraordinary night, amid the camellias and the stars.

Behind the gate, the wolf appeared; he came as a suitor, as a man who spoke in a soft, wheedling voice. He said: Come. She obeyed; one of her pearls fell off. She went out. He said: Here?

But they walked passed camellias and rosebushes, blackened by the darkness, to a hole that had been specially dug. She knelt down; he knelt down. He stuck out his long tongue and licked her. He asked her: How would you like it?

She didn't answer. She was a queen. She only smiled slightly, as she had seen her friends do at their weddings.

He pulled off one of her hands, then the other hand; one foot, the other foot; he contemplated her briefly like that. Then he took off her head; took out her eyes, he set them down on either side; he took out her ribs and all.

But particularly, he devoured her blood, with dispatch, mastery, and real virility.

Translated by Lorraine Elena Roses.

# *Excerpts from* Dream Time

## Ana María Shua

I'm wide awake. I'm lying along the edge of a deep dream. I can't see the bottom. The water is sticky and murky. Sometimes, monsters surface. But I'm not scared. I'm keeping watch; I'm dry and safe. A good strong blow and crash: monster to the water again. It's a shame. With so much commotion, I'll never get to sleep.

In the jungle of insomnia, it's not necessary to go deeper in. It grows up all around me. Crickets are the most ferocious of the beasts. In a clearing, I think I can make out a dream. I approach slowly, so the noise of my footsteps won't wake it. But when I gather my net, I find it empty.

Smoking, I fall asleep. In one way, I'm happy: It's a good dream-sleep. The cigarette falls on the rug and starts a fire. The rug starts a fire on the curtain. The curtain starts a fire on the mattress. The mattress burns the sheets. There's nothing left of the house but a pile of ashes. In one way, I'm still happy; now nothing can force me to wake up.

"What are dreams made of?" I don't know about yours, sir. Mine are made of Gruyere cheese, very delicious and a little spicy. One thing you can be sure of: you have to watch out for the holes.

Crouching, terrified, each cell in my body imprisoned in the throbbing of my blood, heart, pulse. Unable to remember the reason for the fear, the nightmare. Awake? Asleep? Awake?

In the darkness, I mistake the clothes piled up on a chair for a shapeless beast that hurries over to gobble me up. When I turn on a light, I calm down, but I'm wide awake. Unfortunately, I can't even read. My blue shirt sinking its teeth into my neck makes it impossible for me to concentrate.

If the heat makes the walls of the room soft like butter (and they even start to melt a little), don't turn on the air conditioner. For you, anyway, it's too late. And the cost of the electricity wouldn't be worth it.

The first shriek makes my skin break out in a green trembling. The second shriek lands deep in my eyes, and it's a burning ember. On the third shriek, I recognize my own voice and wake up. "What did you see?" they ask me. "I wish I knew," I tell them. But that's a lie.

From the hollow of a tree a man calls to me. "Save me, señorita," he begs. "I've been bewitched for several centuries waiting for a virgin to save." "I'm not a señorita, you boor, I'm a señora," I answer him insulted. (An old man, several hundred years old, is far too old for me).

Translated by Regina Harrison.

# Other/Other

## Ana María Shua

Yesterday I got even. But I don't want to think right now about my revenge, about that concrete act—accomplished—of my revenge. What I want to do is to think very calmly, taking my time about it—since yesterday I have all the time in the world—about all the steps that led up to that act. I wouldn't be disorderly about listing each and every step, each and every reason. Disorder bothers me; I am a meticulous and methodical person. I think that the important thing in life is to set up a strict system and then stick to it no matter what. The German nation is a clear example. Ignorant people talk about the German miracle; there's no such miracle. A disciplined and methodical nation can meet any challenge, that's all. Of course I don't share all the Nazi ideas, like racism—all I ask of blacks is that they bathe. But it seems to me that if the Germans had won the war, today's world, and this I can guarantee, would be much more orderly.

In this case, being methodical should allow me to set out the facts in their chronological order and run them past my conscience—in my new state, I still have a conscience—in order to fully understand the succession of causes and effects that carried me to such an extremity of hatred. Were I not to do this, I might get confused. I might even start thinking that Alicia was the main cause. And that confusion would be serious, because in that case my revenge would seem really out of proportion. When your conscience is the only active part of you, you have to be extra careful with your thoughts. Organize them; control them.

Even for me, it's not easy to think that way, methodically, with pauses, with parentheses, with separate paragraphs. Even as meticulous a person as I could commit digressions every once in a while. I'm going to try to avoid this pitfall because, in order to understand the process, it's crucial to respect the exact order in which things happened. I'm aware that what happened with Alicia is a key point. If it's considered out of its context, it gets blown way out of proportion. Because anybody would think that I made the decision—or began to make it—when I saw my brother in bed—in my bed—with Alicia. They were both naked and they didn't see me. I went away trying not to make any noise and trying to scrub that nasty scene out of my eyes. It was clear that for Alicia the contact of her body with my brother's was producing uncontrollable pleasure.

It made me feel sick to my stomach.

Except for that moment of nausea, the event didn't bother me too much. I think this was the only occasion in my entire life when I felt grateful to my brother for something. Thanks to him, I discovered that Alicia wasn't the serene and responsible person I had thought I would be marrying. It's not that I don't think that sex is an obvious necessity. In fact, I myself have had sexual relations periodically—although I've never had the poor taste to do it with my own fiancee—and I have always found this activity beneficial, since it makes it possible for me to get back to my daily pursuits feeling more relaxed, with complete control over my body again. But the gestures and, above all, the abandon, the out-and-out disorder demonstrated by Alicia in bed with my brother, seemed to me incomprehensible and disgusting.

Just as soon as I had a chance to speak with her alone, I explained that our engagement would have to be broken. I should say in my favor that I sought this chance despite the repugnance I felt in her presence. I've never been one to prolong situations of this sort. She tried to persuade me first with rational arguments, which provided the best possible demonstration of the superiority of a methodical mind like mine over a totally chaotic, confused and primitive system of thought like hers. Her arguments were more or less the following: that we'd already been given a washing machine, that we had a joint savings account, that we were making the mortgage payments on the apartment, that—how were we ever going to tell our families?

I quickly sketched an outline of a plan that took into account and tidily solved all the economic and social relations problems. On the other hand, I found myself in an extremely uncomfortable state when she came over and brushed her body right against mine and tried, by means I'd rather forget, to arouse my irrational instincts. I am deeply proud of being a human in the fullest sense of the word, that is, of always putting my reason ahead of my animal urges. Her demonstration disgusted me. It's true that it also proved to me what I'd already suspected: my brother, always quick to exploit our identical appearance, had let her think it was me. The words Alicia used to remind me of promises I'd never made and things I'd never done, confirmed her confusion. Of course, that didn't at all affect the feeling of repugnance that Alicia's physical presence aroused in me, but at the least it was pleasing to my self-esteem; I was sure that she had not decieved me intentionally. After this conversation, which was lengthy and tense, a shower felt very good to me.

I've tried to restage mentally this episode for myself, attempting to remember every detail and every image in order to demonstrate to myself yet again that the memories don't cause me pain or sadness or hatred. It really was not important at all. If it had any effect on my revenge it was to make me doubt its justice for just a second, only a second. I assume that if my brother had understood he was doing me a favor—he was too insensitive to even notice—it's very probable that he wouldn't have gone to bed with Alicia.

In any case, it is this supposition that tipped the balance against him, when at that final instant a single blink of mine could have stopped it all. (But could I, can I still blink?)

If I think hard about it, there are many details of our life together that were a thousand times more exasperating to me than the business with Alicia, although they didn't have anything to do with our similarity but rather, a lot to do with our differences. Our shoes, for instance. When I go to bed, I always leave my shoes lined up precisely at the edge of the bed. The left one on the left, the right one on the right, fairly close together and exactly parallel to each other. This way I could jump right into them if it were necessary. In case of a sudden fire in the middle of the night, for example, I could leap out of bed and have my shoes on straight away. My brother, on the other hand, left his shoes thrown around helter skelter, generally tossed right into the bedroom doorway, giving off a foul odor—I always spray my shoes with deodorant right when I take them off. Of course, when he got up at night to go to the bathroom he put on the shoes that were closest to hand, that is, mine. And he used them like slippers. The worst of it isn't just that he ruined the heels. The worst of it is that while I lived in the same house with my brother I constantly ran the risk of finding myself barefoot in the middle of the street while my house was burning down. But that is just a detail, although a fairly important one, and what I need to do now is concentrate my effort, and I repeat this, on an orderly chronological listing of events. (I am no longer so sure that I can do this.)

I don't think that anyone can have the slightest idea of what it means to have to share everything with a person like my brother. And when I say *everything*, I mean every single thing right from that moment when the egg and sperm met, everything since we were just a pair of cells in the uterus. It was there, I am certain, in a dark corner of our mother's uterus, as I was trying to protect myself from the menacing shadow of my brother who was growing and growing, that the embryo of hatred began to form. I myself was a peaceful embryo—and later a tranquil fetus—with very moderate habits, who limited himself to the methodical absorption of vital fluids, who divided and multiplied his cells in a rythmic continuous manner. But even so, I wasn't happy. Any wretch, any tramp has known at least a moment's hapiness in his life, that moment when he's lulled by a warm and velvety darkness that protects him from the chaos and disorder of the world outside. I didn't even have that brief moment of peace; my brother was there occupying, as always, more than his fair share of space. As soon as his limbs developed, he started flailing them in all directions, setting off uncomfortable currents in the amniotic fluid. I tried to avoid all contact with him by keeping very still and curling up in order to occupy the least amount of space.

From the moment of gestation on, my brother managed to generate that confusion between our persons that would mark my life. Because of my economical outlay of energy, achieved thanks to a rigorously disciplined growth that triumphed over adverse conditions, I weighed a few more grams at birth. And logically, since I was bigger, Mom always blamed me for the digestive upsets she suffered during pregnancy, as if it had been I and not my brother who had constantly kicked her in the liver.

The confusion had already begun, and it wouldn't end until its culmination and my revenge. More than once after our birth, my brother received a double share of milk while I, who wailed desparately in hunger, just received calming pats that were supposed to make me burp, as though I had already eaten. But it didn't take Mom long to be able to tell us apart, thanks to certain characteristics of my personality which soon manifested themselves fully. In effect, I was a very organized, methodical, meticulous baby who excreted his digestive wastes according to plan, four times a day, at specific times. My brother, as could be expected, defecated in a disorderly fashion at the most unexpected or inconvenient moments—when Aunt Rosalba was holding him, for example, or just when Mom had finished changing his diaper. But when one of his helter skelter deposits coincided by chance with one of mine, Mom would still get us mixed up and I, resigned, would get an unjust scolding for dirtying my diaper.

From the time of our birth until the age of rebellion, we were always dressed identically, as if adults were amused by setting the stage for that monstrous confusion. Later, as adolescents and young adults, each of us developed his own style and no one could have possibly confused me with that slovenly man who wore pullovers in strident colors. That is, no one could have confused me with that slovenly man if he hadn't actually caused confusion by wearing, when he felt like it, the same gray or brown or dark blue shades of my discrete elegance.

In primary school, my white smock was my shield, my armour, an almost inviolable protection. On Monday mornings, it's true, we both showed up looking identical, with our hair neatly slicked back and our smocks spotlessly white and well-ironed. By Tuesday, it was easy to recognize me. And by Friday, no confusion was possible. Not only did I stand out in contrast to my brother in his filthy smock, stained with ink, rumpled, but my tidiness distinguished me from all the other children at the school.

The possibilities of imposture being thus reduced to Monday mornings, the rest of the week my brother had to fall back on other methods.

We were in the same grade, and in order to torment us even more efficiently, the teacher sat us on the same bench. There are images which have remained vivid in my mind, which endlessly recur in my nightmares. I see my brother's right hand, with its dirty nails and splotches of tempera paint left over from art class, reaching out cruelly for my notebook, meticulously covered in crisp blue paper. I am paralyzed in desperation: I can't yell, I can't move. Very slowly, the hand flattens itself against the notebook page. The fingers press down on the white page and leave five sticky fingerprints horribly identical to my own. The cry that is stuck in my throat manages to squeeze itself out as a grunt that wakes me. Yes, my brother tortured me in every possible way—and a boy can think of an infinite number of ways. He switched my colored pencils around when I had them all lined up in order of the spectrum. He stuffed my inkwell full of blotting paper. He jiggled the bench while I was drawing maps with a quill pen and india ink. He stuck chewing gum on my seat. He sat down as though by accident on my cardboard polyhedrons. Shaking his fountain pen, he made blotches in my notebook, then he tore holes in the pages with the ink eraser, trying to rub out the spots. He drew in moustaches on the few clean-shaven leaders of the Wars of Independence pictured in my reading books. He organized and urged on the choruses of kids who called me a creep as I left school. He broke my pencil leads. He snitched my pencil sharpener. He drew obscenities on my desktop. He stepped on my plastic ruler. He jabbed me with the compass. Every day at morning recess they gave us a bread roll; on Mondays and Thursdays, it was a sweet bun. On the only day of the week when he could get away with it, my brother took advantage of our likeness to get my sweet bun.

I think it was one of those sunny Monday mornings, eating the dust of humiliation in the courtyard—"you're really asking for trouble, you little bastard," the teacher had said to me—when I first began to plan my revenge. At that point I wasn't even thinking yet about the things that eventually happened. I was much too young; I was very fond of the slice of life that had been dished out to me, and I still imagined that it would be enough to put physical space between us in order to create distance between my brother and myself. But even so my first schemes were based on the same idea: to get even for once for all his perverse imposturing so that finally and forever our inconceivable similarity should be turned against him and should devour him.

In truth this similarity between us was so great—when he chose that it should seem so—that I can't blame the witnesses to the holdup. Not even Dad could tell us apart after our baths—Mom, on the other hand, could always cleverly recognize me by looking behind my ears. Dad was a carpenter, he had a little shop of his own, and things were going well. But his real vocation was law, or perhaps, more exactly, justice. Afterwards, as years went by, I discovered in the weekly magazines that doctors want to be actors, actors want to be doctors, almost no one wants to be a door-to-door salesman and everyone wants to be president for a day. But that was afterwards. At the time Dad's constant passion for equality pleased me insofar as it coincided with my need for order, but there were times when for all of us it was asphyxiating. For Dad, not being able to determine which of the two of us had been the guilty party in any given transgression, even when he had seen it committed with his own eyes, was a very serious worry. One night I listened to him pacing up and down for hours in the sleeping house, pulling the milk out of the refrigerator every once in a while to calm his ulcer. The day before, my brother had used my chemistry set to set off an explosion that was followed by the beginnings of a fire. The next morning, Dad had circles under his eyes, but he had made up his mind: from that time on, every time one of us was naughty, both of us would receive an equal spanking, applied in the same zone and with the same severity. In order that fatigue would not influence the degree of relative intensity, Dad would wait a suitable amount of time between the first spanking and the second. What he didn't know, what he never would believe, was that sometimes I got both of them. With this system, Dad thought, not only would the guilty party receive his punishment, the collective sanction would also stimulate our sense of joint

responsibility. Dad thought he was creating loyal citizens; by associating us in punishment, he was associating us in the fulfillment of duty. From that time on, our reciprocal hatred was augmented by a mutual vigilance that turned into espionage on rainy days.

Going back to the question of the witnesses (Should I just give up this attempt at chronology altogether, since it is impossible for me to follow it? Or can it be that logical and chronological thought never did coincide in this story?) I never held anything against them. They didn't have any way to tell us apart any more easily than our own father could. My brother had put on a suit of mine, which was later found in my closet, and during the holdup he had let the handkerchief which covered his face fall, as if by accident. I had been sick for two days, and I was astonished that after- noon when I saw the police entering my apartment. I almost went crazy seeing how they messed up my drawers, how they tossed my newly-washed underwear on the floor, how they put handkerchiefs back on the sock shelf. I yelled, and that was held against me.

In reality, there wasn't anything in the entire trial that was in my favor. My defense lawyer wasn't able to produce much evidence on my behalf. He affirmed in his written summary, as a basic assumption, that no person of normal intelligence would commit the folly of holding up the bank where he was an employee. To prove that I was a person of normal intelligence, he included the results of a test given by a famous psychologist. I wanted to present a more important line of reasoning, but my lawyer either didn't choose or didn't understand how to use it: the brown suit that was used the day of the holdup had a big tomato sauce stain on the lapel, conclusive proof that my brother had been wearing it, not me. The lawyer, a man lacking in imagination, responded that the stain didn't have a signature attached. This answer, which demonstrated a total lack of intuitive perception, of intelligence, of observational powers, left me speechless. From then on I preferred to remain silent and not bother to try to help him obtain the rightful verdict, which, after all, was his problem; it would have been very important for his career. Unfortunately, that young man did not have an organized and methodical mind like mine; therefore, it is logical that we were unable to understand one another.

I should acknowledge that these characteristics, typical of my superior personality, qualities of which I am very proud, brought me some small problems during the trial. I am, and I must reiterate this, a person who is meticulous, methodical, orderly. I find the unforseen profoundly disagreeable. One of my theories is that unforseen occurrences are an invention of fools. Therefore, although I've never lost anything, I always keep two of everything at home just in case: two military registration cards, two voter's registration cards, two passports. Unfortunately the police were not able to understand that the fact that I was in possession of duplicate copies of all my documents was actually proof of my excellent organization. Before the judge, it finally turned out to be a strike against me.

If you discount my poor relations with my cellmates, as squalid and disorderly a lot as I've ever seen, the years I spent in prison were not the worst in my life. Some aspects gave me great pleasure, like the existence of fixed schedules for all the activities. What

I lamented, and what I have not been able to forgive my brother, was the loss of my job at the bank.

I was happy at the bank. The main advantage was, of course, the lack of my brother's presence (since yesterday, I have to think about his absence). The purity of the numbers, the orderliness of the columns of deposits and withdrawals, filled me with joy. At the beginning, when they put me at the teller's window, I suffered a little; the new bills, which had just come from the printer's, were a great pleasure, but it turned out to be unbearable for me to have to be in constant contact with the used bills, tattered and crumpled, that people handed to me. Who could tell how many people had handled them before they arrived in my hands. Who knows what microbes they were harboring. I never could understand those tellers who, ignorant of the most elementary rules of hygiene, wet a fingertip with their tongues to count out the bills and, in mid-count, would again lick that finger, which was now covered with pathogenic germs. In any case, I very quickly resolved the problem of dirty bills by working in lightweight rubber gloves like surgeons wear. The others gave me a hard time at first but then they got used to it.

Even that job at the bank, which I liked so much, was a substitute for my true dream: to be a Certified Public Accountant. A truly fascinating career, interesting, full of excitement. Nothing satisfied me so much as finding a discrepancy in a total: a completely engrossing enterprise of detection. But once again my brother interfered, a dark shadow between me and my dream.

He was studying Political Science at the same university, and I, to win his good favor—it had been years since I had been afraid of him—had agreed to take his exams for him. One day I had the bad luck to flunk an exam in his name, and I didn't have to wait long for punishment. He put a stink bomb in the dean's office with everyone watching, and they expelled me from the university.

Now as I go over the list of injuries and sufferings item by item, I feel a gentle tickle of irresistible laughter creeping up my back. The great revenge takes it all into account, remembers and responds to each and every grievance.

I think of all the payments I made in his name, of all the blows I received in his name, of all the persecutions I received in his name, of all the love I lost in his name... I think about Aunt Rosalba, who won't speak to me anymore since he poisoned her little dog. I think of the restaurants I can't enter because he left without paying.

I think in an orderly fashion, meticulous, organized and method-ical, about each one of the times, about each one of the spaces I had to share with that monster who only differed from me in his disorder, his messiness, his disorganization and his lack of method. I think, and a great guffaw almost shakes my inert body.

Yesterday, my revenge was culminated. Yesterday I finally achieved the ultimate confusion. Yesterday I killed myself. And they buried him.

Translated by Mary G. Berg.

# Fishing Days

## Ana María Shua

When I was little, I went fishing with my Dad every summer. The tackle box was made of wood, and it was painted green. In it were different size hooks; the tiniest were for minnows, and the biggest ones were for sharks. There were lead sinkers too. Most of the sinkers were shaped like pyramids. They were really heavy. They were shaped like that so they wouldn't snag on the rocks. We used to go fishing off the pier or at Burriquetas Cove, and we always got our sinkers snagged because there were so many rocks. I say "we," but the only one who fished was my Dad. That's to say, he was the only one who held the fishing rod, since there weren't too many fish biting in Miramar. I had a little rod, but I hardly ever took it along; I didn't like to use it. What I did like was standing alongside my Dad. On the pier, they knew us, and we knew the ones who were usually there. Skinny, for instance, who had blonde hair and eyebrows that were completely black, and an older man (older than my Dad) named Ibarra. I felt really proud of all the things I was learning, and I tried to show them off every chance I got. I knew, for example, that grouper, even though they were small, pull hard, and at times, because of the way they bend your rod, you can mistake them for a much bigger fish. When one of the fisherman was straining to pull in his line and the rod bent and trembled, I went over to him and said, "That's just a grouper you've got there." I knew how to recognize the bonefish, too, that are sort of like little sharks; the ones with dark spots on them were called dappled bones. They pulled the hooks out of bonefish and just threw them back in the water. Once in a while we landed a tarpon. Dad used to say that with tarpon you had to let them take line from the reel because they thrash around, so if you don't give them line, they'll break it. Then they lie on the bottom, and you have to pull them up. Once Dad went fishing alone, and when he came back, he told about how he'd had an incredible bite. He was holding his reel loosely and suddenly something (he never found out what) swallowed the hook and began to thrash around so hard that the nylon line burned his thumb as it spun out. I have a very clear memory of the white line of that burn on Dad's thumb. And even so, my Dad died. Isn't that incredible?

He felt the first yank in his spine, at about the height of his waist, the night after the fall. He never again felt such a sharp pain. That morning there were sheets on the floor, and I didn't know why. "He had to sleep on the floor all night long," Mom told me. "He couldn't even turn over in the bed." That night he came back tired but in less pain. "Getting up from the floor was really a struggle," he told me. He had gone to the doctor that afternoon. "A herniated disk," they diagnosed. "Try taking a sedative."

In the green tackle box, we also had some mackerel that we used as bait. Sometimes Dad let me cut up the mackerel, but he always baited the hook himself because he was afraid I'd get stuck. (Dad was always afraid of my hurting myself. Around that time, he invented a wire guard that he fastened onto the knife blade so that I could learn how to peel oranges without cutting myself). Mackerel has a strong smell, and Mom would get angry when she saw the tackle box inside the house. We kept it in the trunk of the car. On very special occasions, Dad would buy little squids and put them in the freezer: luxury bait. On the pier, it was always pretty windy. I would put on a thick mustard-yellow pullover that Mom knitted for me and play at being a basket. The game was to squat on my heels and pull down the sweater, which was big on me, until it covered up my legs completely, then stuff the edges in the sides of my shoes to anchor it. Another way of protecting myself from the wind was to lean up against the walls of the hut out at the end of the pier. I switched walls according to the direction that the wind was blowing. I entertained myself by trying to guess how many shrimp the drag nets would have in them each time they were raised. Generally, they didn't have any. I had learned how to grab shrimp, which tickled as they moved in my hand, and put them in the fishing can. I liked the smell of the mixture, the chum, that the net casters threw into the water every once in a while in order to attract shrimp. On the pier, the only thing we could catch were bonefish. At Burriquetas Cove, we had better luck. You had to go down a kind of natural stairway down the side of the cliff. To me it seemed very dangerous and a lot of fun. The cove was a little beach that was narrow and quite long. Dad used it to practice casting with his rod and measuring how far he could get the sinker. He did the measuring with his strides; each stride was a meter long. I always wished his casts would go really far, but they were never farther than seventy meters. I remember clearly the distance between Dad's footprints in the sand, stretching seventy meters more or less down the length of the beach. And even so, my Dad died. Isn't that incredible?

He started to feel the yanks next in his right leg. First in the foot. Then in the calf. His back-bone didn't hurt him anymore. Just then there were financial problems at the factory, and he had to walk around a lot in the center of town, from bank to bank. "Stop complaining and go see a doctor like anyone else would," Mom said to him, and she wasn't usually big on doctors. "That guy at the health plan clinic doesn't know anything." The truth is that Dad was limping quite a lot, and during the Three Kings Day weekend, he couldn't find any position that was comfortable. Mom was in Mar del Plata with Grandma and Grandad, and I felt responsible for seeing that Dad was as comfortable as possible.

He felt tugging now in his thigh; he ate half lying down in the armchair in the living room.

Where we did our serious fishing was at what Dad called Stinky Cove. We didn't go often because it was a long way away. It's the place where the sewer from Mar del Plata hits the sea and where fish processing plants throw their leftover garbage. To go to Stinky Cove, we had to get up early. The day before, Mom would fix sandwiches and drinks. You could fish from up on the cliff. The ground was covered with little fish bones and all sorts of junk. Flies that were bright green or blue and sticky buzzed loudly and flew slowly. Stupid flies, Dad said, because they were so heavy. We fished for catfish there, big fat catfish, with whiskers and a bad smell. Right away Dad cut off their whiskers, where they had a sharp pricker. Later, that night, complaining a lot, Mom would cook the catfish in a fish mayonnaise. While we were fishing, we hardly talked at all. We had to be really quiet in order not to frighten the fish. Dad held his rod tightly in both hands, and he held the nylon line between the thumb and the index finger of his upper hand so that he would feel the slightest nibble. When he let me hold the rod for a little while, it always seemed to me that there was a nibble, and I pulled it up right away. We had two problems: the snags and the snarls. When there was a snag, Dad left the rod on the ground and pulled at the nylon line. He pulled it as tight as he could and then let it go suddenly. If it just wouldn't unsnag, he cut the line, but either way, it was a lot of work. The snarls were the worst. And sometimes they happened at the the same time as the snags. The line on the reel snarled in such a way that we had to give up and go back home to untangle it carefully. A fierce snarl could hold up our fishing for a whole week.

The part I liked the best was operating on the fish. Dad slit them open with the knife he kept in the green box, the one he also used to cut the whiskers off the catfish and the tails off the tarpon. He pulled their guts out. We opened up their intestines to see what they'd been eating. While we were doing this, I kept imagining that we were going to find all sorts of marvelous things, like magic rings or fragments of glass. But I never felt disappointed because Dad, peering closely at the mess, gave me a long explanation about what the fish had been eating. And sometimes we found snails or little crabs. Once we caught a black corvina with her guts all swollen full of eggs. Since it was really a big fish, Dad took a photo with the corvina still dangling from the hook. I still have the photo. And even so, my Dad died. Isn't it incredible?

Mom had to come back from Mar del Plata so she could decide about the operation. First an orthopedic surgeon saw him, then a neurologist. They said, "Without surgery, he'll lose the foot." Mom and Dad didn't like that idea. "His sciatic nerve is being pinched. You don't want to drag around a numb foot, do you?" they told him, because they knew he wasn't happy about it. "There isn't any alternative. You have to have surgery," they told him, because they wanted to see what was inside.

Twice we had bites at Miramar. One was the day the schools of fish went by. It was a rainy day, and we were using it to fix up our lines. I liked the little nylon knots on the hooks. Suddenly the bell rang and Skinny was there. "There's a school out there right off the pier," he said, and ran off. The pier was full of people bristling with fishing poles. There were high waves. Dad was afraid I'd get hit in the head with a lead sinker, and he made me stay right by his side. We didn't have our pole. The usual people were there and lots of others. It was a school of whiting followed by a school of anchovies. Ibarra had caught fifty one and a half whitings—the other half had been eaten by an anchovy as he was pulling it in. The anchovies had sharp teeth and seemed fierce. The whiting were more peaceful. The schools had almost gone by, and it didn't seem worth going to get our rod.

The other time there was good fishing we didn't get anything either. That was at the shark-fishing contest at Universal Cove. Universal Cove is a huge beach at the entrance to Miramar. Dad hadn't taken the fishing rod, but he did have his movie camera, and he took pictures of what people were catching. In this film I'm not so small. I'm wearing a blue pullover which is big on me but not so big that it hides how my body is changing. I have bangs that are really ugly. You can see lots of sharks, mostly females, pregnant. In one shot, a tough-looking guy is stepping on the belly of a shark and six or seven little sharks are popping out, still moving around. Dad doesn't appear in any of the shots, but you know all the time he's right there, on the other side of the camera. And even so, my Dad died. Isn't that incredible?

The day before, in the hospital, he asked if we would film him. Three days had gone by since the operation. Dad liked to have all the important events registered on film: the car upside down that time when it got flipped over; the strikers' attack on the factory; me with chicken pox. I didn't really feel like filming him. He was lying on his back, and he couldn't move. He had a needle stuck in his arm. The needle was connected to a little plastic tube that came out of a Liquid-filled bag held up by a tall stand. But Dad was feeling better, and he asked me to bring him some marzipan.

The hook didn't always stick right in the fish's mouth. Sometimes they swallowed it and getting it out was a real mess because you had to operate on them alive. Other times it was caught on a fin or stuck into their bodies. When that happened, Dad would say the fish was gaffed. When we were going to Stinky Cove, we always took the gaff along; it's a great big giant fishhook with four pointed barbs (or like four giant fishhooks stuck together). The gaff is used for lifting the heaviest fish without cutting the line. When it looked as though a big fish was hooked, Dad would tell me, as he was reeling, to start getting the gaff ready. As they were being pulled out of the water, croakers made a strange continuous sound, like a snore or a croak. That's why they're called croakers. The ones that could last the longest out in the air were the sharks. Tarpon lasted a really long time, too, and when Dad cut off their tails with the fishing knife, lots of blood came out. I never thought of asking Dad why fish died when they were taken out of the water. Since they didn't have noses, it seemed natural that they couldn't breathe. Dad really liked to explain things to me, and while we were fishing, I tried to think up hard questions so that he could answer them. And even so, my Dad died. Isn't that incredible?

He said "I'm drowning," Mom told me, crying. When she looked at him, she saw frantic desperation in his eyes. They couldn't do anything with oxygen, or with chest massages. Coramine didn't work either. He didn't start breathing again. "They did all they could," Mom told me, crying. "It was an embolism. His lungs."

When I was little, every summer I went fishing with my Dad. And even so, my Dad died. Isn't that incredible? You see, he was hooked and couldn't get loose.

Translated by Mary G. Berg.

# The Man in the Araucaria

## Sara Gallardo

A man spent twenty years making himself a pair of wings. In 1924, he tried them out, at dawn. They worked with a slow swinging motion. They didn't take him any higher than thirty-six feet, as high as an araucaria in the Plaza of San Martín.

The man abandoned his wife and children to spend more hours in the top of the tree. He worked for an insurance company. He moved into a boarding house. Each night at midnight, he put sewing machine oil on his wings and walked off to the plaza. He carried them in a violincello case.

He had a nest at the top of the tree, comfortable enough. It even had pillows.

At night, life in the plaza is extraordinarily complex, but he never bothered to get into it. The foliage, the dark houses, and especially the stars, were enough for him. The nights when the moon was out were the best.

Our problem is not accepting limits. He got it in his head to spend a whole day in his nest. It was a company holiday.

The sun came up. There's nothing like dawn in the treetops.

Very high up, a flock of birds passed, leaving the city at their feet. He contemplated them with a kind of dizziness, with tears.

That was what he had dreamed about during the twenty years he had dedicated to constructing his wings. Not about an araucaria.

He blessed the birds. He lost his heart to them.

A maid opened the shutters in the house of an aged, sleepless woman. She saw the man in his nest. The old lady called the police and the fire department.

With loudspeakers, with ladders, they surrounded him.

It took him some time to see what was happening. He put on his wings. He stood up.

The cars put on their brakes. People gathered. Windows opened. He saw his children, with their school smocks. His wife with her shopping bag. The maids and the old ladies holding on to each other.

The wings worked, slowly. He touched branches.

But he lost altitude. He went down as far as the monument. He leapt. He got entangled in the horse's haunches. He grabbed San Martin by the waist. He was smiling.

He got as far as the English tower; the wind helped him along toward the south.

He lives between the smoke pipes of a factory. He is old and eats chocolate.

Translated by Elizabeth Rhodes.

# The Blue Stone Emperor's Thirty-three Wives

## Sara Gallardo

### 1

Behind the great king hangs a painted leather hide. It can waver; it is the wind. Or not waver; the queen is listening. I count within myself those dead at his command. Those dead at his hands are within me. Foolish women, those who bewail their lost youth; they do not know the secrets of fermentation. May they see drunkenness beneath the stars; if water is for daytime then alcohol is for power.

Alcohol is old age. I lost my teeth; my nourishment is to influence. I braid my grey hair; what gets braided without me?

I have a whim, nonetheless. I'd like to have that girl killed. And her child in her arms.

### 2

For me, stretching leather. Eating. Going for water. Sewing the skins, preparing the threads, weaving. Looking at the smoke, whether it will rain tomorrow. Relieving myself calmly among the rushes. Seasoning the venison through the wound in the flesh. Preparing maté and drinking it. Dying ostrich feathers.

To each day its own. A good life. Sleeping.

### 3

I make people travel. Careful, horseman. Not a word of what we said can be repeated. The most terrible of the kings moans like a calf. I never needed beauty.

I am the one who travels. Door of journeys.

It is true that I take risks; I see death at every step. How can you fasten my body of a thousand lives to only one man?

No one is as young nor as old as I.

### 4

I tortured them, the women. I still thirst. I saw them die, naming unknown people in other languages. I did not satiate myself. If each grazing were the subject of humiliation and each star an eye to blind, my anxieties would go on.

### 5

Wool, wool, morning has come. Shake off the dew, scare off the cold. If you take in what is red, you warm your eye. Tie the strands of life together.* Grid what is black, cross what is white. The form of the woof; the woof is my shape. Here the line of silence, the border, madness, the little tracks of the skunk, the tips of the night, footsteps, footprints, tracks. Life is between these steps: the yes, the no, the now, the never.

This is the poncho I wove for the king.

### 6

Friend, give your mouth to me. Spread your legs for me. I used to pick fleas from your hair. Fat ones to you, medium ones to me, skinny to die between my fingernails. Something happened. To be the king's wife matters little to me. To be the king's wife matters little to you. Is it possible to hide it? There are so many eyes.

## 7

I won't speak of another time, of another language, of another man, other children.

Here the wind, the horror.

To rock to sleep, I am the oven and the bread. Nine bakings. Nine loaves of bread.

I see six with the riding master. One, the bola balls. One, the lance. One, the dagger. One, the hobbled gallop. One, the race on foot. One, the stretching out.

They will talk among themselves. I will be a single ear: horses, horses. Only horses. Can any other words matter to me? Can they?

There are two more; then run close to my steps. What steps do I hear if not those?

One remains, asleep. Happy lap. I had a garden. There are no petals besides those eyes.

Nine loaves of bread. I ran in this same wind to kill other children.

## 8

To go along, without footprints. Ant. Air. Nothing.

## 9

I glory in his glory.

I repeat that the wind might carry:

Two thousand five hundred leagues of confederation.

Two thousand lancers.

Four horses per lancer.

Thus is counted the greatness of my king.

I walk weighed down with splendors.

Why did he mount me but once?

## 10

The Marquis whispered: the carriage is tied. Madame, all we have to do is flee. She lifted her mask. Her heavenly pupils were farewell. A ring with a seal on it slipped through her hands.

I can't remember what came next...

## 11

I will always see him as ridiculous. Every night guarding his females. He found me with my friend. He buried my face in a blow. He went off to bed. In the morning, he called my companion. He asked him for twenty sheep.

I was blind after that.

Twenty sheep.

In the land of shadow, I still see him. Ridiculous.

## 12

My grandmother—it was so long ago on the other side of the great mountain—had an ear for the dead. Strolling through the countryside she used to say:

"Here, some buried people. Dig, you'll see."

We dug. The bones appeared.

With the years, that same ear opened itself to me.

Others know where the enemy is by the smell of the wind. I deal with the dead.

Looking for an herb to dye the wool, I walk a lot. At some point, someone dead calls.

They call, like a warrior in the alc.ohol of dreams, like the creatures in the night. Their yellow bones are not dust any more. I tell them to sleep.

"We walk by day. Soon the night will come."

## 13

Everything was glorious there. With my cousin, I used to run horse races. We broke them in. Mine used to halt without reins, didn't drink, knew how to wait. We had a specimen, the most beautiful: Nahuel, horse of my father. We were almost children.

One night I heard the witch sing like the water in the cauldron. She was talking with the devil. The smoke of her fire responded:

"What scared you, lord?"

"I shall tell you, I shall tell you."

"What drove you away?"

"I shall tell you."

"Return to me, I am an orphan, I can no longer fly."

"The small one that eats from the hand of the leader scares me. Its neigh startles me, its odor scares me, its mane drowns me. Its feet break my powers. Each time it swallows fodder, I am asphyxiated."

"Fear not, my lord, you shall return. He shall die."

"I dragged myself over and awoke my cousin. I told him what I'd heard. Nahuel, horse of my father, heard. He turned around in his stall. My cousin spoke into my ear: "Go to sleep." I didn't sleep. Almost a child, he cut the witch's throat. She woke up facing the fire burnt down to the bone.

There was a scream in the morning. We were playing with our horses.

What a meeting, what talk, what arms raised, the boys hid, the women filed their nails. My father put on his blanket, the woolen crown.

"She is dead," he said. "Dead she will remain."

There was a lot of low talking, not in front of him. Who killed her, why weren't people punished? He didn't know why himself. But a great prosperity followed.

What for?

The king of kings—but a king among kings—asked for my hand. I said to my cousin:

"We show our horses, don't we?"

And we escaped. My father mounted Nahuel. Nahuel caught up with us.

My father carried his lance. He raised it and shouted.

"It is true that I love you like a son. It is true that you were going to be leader."

He killed my cousin. He shut himself up in his tent. He drank for three days. On the third I said to him:

"Your prosperity is due to the one you killed. Nahuel as witness. Your prosperity attracted the king of kings. Now you will see what he leaves you."

They carried me covered with silver to the old man of the blue stone.

Nahuel has died, my father is a beggar, his dispersed tribe gnaws at remains.

### 14

He was born. I always feared it: blue eyes. The king, my cousin and uncle, came to see him. The wives hid their delight. I awaited death. He smiled:

"Good blood," he said. "He will be a king."

### 15

I wish he would die, defeated. I wish, foot on the ground, he would find himself chained up by soldiers without leaders. I wish that his children would betray him and that he would find out, that he would lose his manhood.

I wish he would die. And his race would be erased from the earth. I with it.

Cursing him.

### 16

My father found me trying to fly. I never understood men's taste. Women's less. Lives of shadows.

Now I know. I search for buried snake's eggs. Toads. Sleeping bats. May the enchantress receive my adulation.

I shall learn.

## 17

A traveller saw me: hopeless, dying, very beautiful.
It was a mistake. I never existed.
Outside I hear the birds' song.

## 18

I am two. I have two names, and I am two. One morning I lost
my first tooth. My mother—who used to cry all the time—said:
"Maria of the Angels, bury it, and a miracle will sprout."

I buried it next to the tent. The next day I went to get the miracle. I didn't see anything. I sat down and waited. When I returned,
my mother—she was counting her bones—had died. Beaten to
death. It seemed she was smiling.

No one else called me Maria of the Angels. Only I used to say
it. No one used to say miracle.

When I buried my eighth tooth, I screamed in the middle of
the field.

"Miracles! I won't wait any more! I will forget how to say Mary
of the Angels! I will only be White Cloud."

That night, asleep, I heard a song. It spoke that which I never
heard:

"Seaworthy boat, light oar.
Castle by the river, keep me from cold.
Mountain snow, goes where I go.
Angels, saints, sing their songs."

I asked a man, an interpreter, with a red beard: "What does boat
mean, and seaworthy, and oar, and castle, and snow, and mountain." He said it. He repeated it to me gathering wood, carrying
water.

One day an old man came:

"The king of kings who lives on the other side of the desert makes
known what he was found out from the red-bearded man. A white,
fat, blonde, girl child lives here. He demands that she be brought.
He will send this much livestock, this many vessels, this much silver."

"What girl child is that?" I asked.

I was warmly received. We were poor. That king didn't know our people, or our leader.

Now I am a wife far from there. I have two names, and I am two. When I find my mother, she will tell me why.

### 19

The pleasure I have left is to contemplate the new.

The dew in the brush. The coming out of the new queen, the favorite, with her child in her arms. She laughs. The king wants her close.

In the spider's web, dew drops.

In the afternoon, I lock myself in, light the fire.

In the afternoon, there is no dew in the brush. The web is loaded with insects. The dust clouds fly on the horizon.

### 20

Sometimes we run into the king. If he feels like it, he greets me and continues on his way. I don't know where youth went.

We have been accomplices.

It's not that he needs them. In the triumph, the punishment, the killing, the glory, the lust.

But only I saw his tears.

### 21

I gave myself to the mystery.
What was it?
A path of darkness
toward a land which perhaps does not exist.
I am faithful. I persevere.

### 22

This happened when we crossed the great mountain. Playing, my brother and I went up to where the ice is very quiet.

In a cave, a small girl was sleeping.

Gold in her crowns, on her chest. Her sandals were made of green beads. Little face mask of pearls. She was sleeping.

When we went down, he died from the cold. I lived.

We never told anything.

They call me wife of the king. I use a silver necklace.

Whoever did not see the princess who sleeps in the mountain will never know about kings.

### 23

I waited ten years. And he saw me.

He was coming back from the war. Black blood flowed from his chest. I saw his children, his grandchildren. The feathers of his lances, also black, crazy with victory. Women, the aged, dogs, children were one single howl. And the captive females the color of death.

I held his glance. His horse brushed by close to my feet. I did not move. My grandmother hit me.

They celebrated for many days. The warriors slept, vomited. I waited. The king walked among the tents. I saw the leather skin at my house open.

I never said his name. He never said mine. I was the king, he the girl. I learned to rule, he to laugh.

They usually talk. They know little of love.

### 24

The moon has a halo; kings are travelling.

My brother arrived.

The rain erases all the signals. I cry.

My brothers left.

### 25

The story, which still gives people something to talk about, really went like this.

My cousin had a favorite dog,used to biting people's heels. I saw that that young man had his heel wounded.

I got some poison seeds and held them in my hand.

While dying wool with the old queen, I cried. She promised me a pearl necklace if I would tell her why. A bead necklace.

I said: "My cousin and her sisters are preparing a poison. That young man brought them the seed. They want to kill the king."

I opened my hand and showed them to her.

My cousin, her sisters, that young man, were burned alive.

They have been dust and ash for seven years. I use the bead necklace.

That fire keeps me awake.

I asked him for his love; he laughed at me. And he visited my cousin at night?

## 26 and 27

We are sisters and we are different. The day of that double banquet—that hecatomb—we were working together. Unannouced the little leader and his two hundred men arrived for a visit. They were given lunch. They were eating and his brother arrived, four hundred lances in the dust. Another banquet.

And they satiated themselves both times.

The king inspected the rows of eaters and drinkers in person. He talked and laughed.

I guarantee it was a proud day. To be the wife of a king, to feed six hundred men, and laugh.

But my sister said: "I know what the salt of a king's kitchen is like. Tears and sweat. Grief and fatigue."

## 28

While filling the king's pipe, I've heard how he dictates his letters. The men who serve him make lines and dots, like the white men do.

In the afternoons, I sit down. I am old. Words do not interest me.

I see the birds. Lines, dots. Every afternoon in the sky, the same letter.

Always the same, that I cannot say.

Defeat, end.

### 29

My brother, lord of the apple tree country, wanted an alliance with the great one. His wife promised me. When I arrived, he was out hunting ostriches. He returned at night, left for the war. Later he wanted to see me.

He didn't like me.

He performed the ceremony for an alliance with the lord of the apple trees.

He never touched me.

I didn't have any women friends.

The witch asked a favor of me. I listen to all the conversations for her; I spy on every tent.

They call me names. The young boys set traps at my feet. I get hit. Still, my mother told me stories; she promised me happiness.

### 30

I dreamed: I lost a tooth.

What will I do without it, what will it do without me?

Wind has come come up over the river.

What will he do without me, what will I do without him?

### 31

It was raining. And it rained my lament. It is sad to be a wife of the old king. It was night, under the blanket. In autumn, things are like that.

My husband's son entered the darkness. He had been drinking. Perhaps he made a mistake.

What happened was a coming out into brilliance on a battle horse. It was running. It was conquering.

### 32

On the day of the first battle, his father told him:

"Let no woman matter more to you than war."
On the day of the first banquet, his father told him:
"No woman takes you further than alcohol."
On the day of the first sacrifice, his father told him:
"He who ties himself to a woman separates himself from the mystery."

He knew battle, alcohol, mystery. He tells me: "There are three shadows next to your red skirt."

33

I have seen a vision that is not a lie in the water of the well. I saw the king's funeral. It will not be long now. His horse dressed in silver will go with him. His wives in a line, their skulls broken. His favorite one, dressed in red, will carry her child in her arms. They will wrench it away from her at the same time they kill her. Thus I saw the funeral, with thirty-two wives. I am escaping tonight.

Translated by Elizabeth Rhodes.

---

*Translator's note*: The first four sentences of this paragraph are rhyming proverbs from the oral tradition. Since their elements figure in later sections of the story, they are translated literally. The first one might otherwise be rendered, "Out of bed, sleepyhead."

*Invisible Embroidery*

# The Condemned Dress In White

## Marcela Solá

It is a custom that rises from many years at home to keep vigil over everything that ends. A vigil is kept with an expert and guarded eye for all the signs of death.

It has been four years since my twin sister, Bellatrix, and I watched from our window the change in the color of the star.

It appeared red in the sky one summer night when Bellatrix had come out to see the light of the moon on the sidewalk, to walk her collection of worms. While I waited, laying down on the floor tiles, the worms undulated away in a wavy procession, and then I noticed the apparition.

"Bellatrix, there is a new light in the sky!" I shouted. "I know all of the stars by heart, and that one was not here last night."

"It is incredibly red!" Bellatrix told me in ecstacy. "Even my worms have changed color." And we ran home to communicate the news to our father, who left immediately to look at the light. He loved the sky, and that is why my sister had the name of a star. But he sighed when he saw it and said with a certain fatigue: "It is a changing star, a nova. It can disappear at any moment. We must keep a vigil over it."

Our hearts sank. We had spent an enormous period of time without sleep keeping watch over a relative who was nearing the end and before that it was the cat I had picked up and before that my grandmother and before that... I don't remember. At home, from the time we twins were born, the agonies were so prolonged that the habit of sleeping was lost.

For the ones who had previously known sleep, life became tough and that's why our father suffered from depression from time-to-time and our mother hid and cried. For those of us who had never known sleep, the problem was not that serious, although at times we asked ourselves how it would be to lose this thing called consciousness for such a long time. Often we were surprised to find ourselves thinking: "If one day I get to sleep...," and we imagined dreams. We wanted to understand what they were, but no one could explain.

"No one can be conscious of the act of sleeping," our mother said to us one day, "obviously, because you're sleeping."

Bellatrix became impatient with the lack of explanation. I still remember how she tortured her worms that night. She took them out of the can where she kept them and made them crawl in the darkness incessantly. She pushed the tails of the slow ones with a stick, and when the sun rose and the worms were canned again, the sidewalk was littered with their segments. Bellatrix cried desperately over them. Then the idea popped up to us, simultaneously.

"One of us has to sleep, so that the other one might know how it is," we said at the same time.

We did not need to speak to know what was going on inside of one another. That's why it was enough for only one of us to sleep. The other one would know immediately. That, they told us, is because you're not only twins, but identical twins.

From then on, delicious terror filled us.

But then the star appeared, and we had to wait. The vigilance was too extreme. This star, our father said, must be mourned with all the respect due its shine and great magnitude. He decided that we would all stand and keep a vigil in front of the largest window in the house, without ceasing to look at the star for an instant. Bellatrix and I told each other stories to keep from getting bored. I told the most dreadful, hair-raising stories, but in my sister's stories there was always someone who slept.

The only ones that benefitted from this situation were the worms, that now were crawling in sunlight and visibly growing, although Bellatrix did not like to parade them during the day.

"In the moonlight, they shine brighter because they're white," she said. And her hatred slowly began to incubate. From then on, she always dressed in white and I too, to give her company. Our mother liked to see us shine in the night in the framed window in our white clothing, like two more stars.

Finally, one night when the moon hung heavy over our dresses, like a shining blanket, Bellatrix revealed her rebellion to our father.

"This is the last time I will mourn," she said. "As soon as the star dies I will go to sleep."

A horror grew in the room when Bellatrix finished her phrase—an impalpable horror because our parents did not appear to have heard the words of my sister. To this day, they maintain that she would never have done anything that daring.

After a while, the star became white and shiny. The brighter it became, the closer it came to the point of extinction. We watched it from the window, the star was about to die. We consulted with Bellatrix. "Will it be tonight? Tomorrow?"

"I hope it's as soon as possible," Bellatrix said. "I'm tired of walking my worms in the sun and always wearing white. Besides, I want to taste sleep." She scowled, as she always did when she was filled with impatience.

Meanwhile, the worms continued to get larger in the eyes of all who looked at them, but a curious thing happened—they decreased in numbers. We discovered with Bellatrix that some had profited from the stroll in the sun by changing into butterflies and disappearing.

"They do not like the sun either. They are too white to go unnoticed, so they have to masquerade in colors," their owner said bitterly. They never would have escaped when she walked them at night.

That night the star gave off a blue light that overshadowed the brilliant light of the group. Bellatrix and I had the sensation of an immense void in the sky. The worst thing about mourning was always surviving what you mourned.

As soon as she was able to leave, unnoticed, Bellatrix moved away from the window and entered our room. I followed her because we had an unspoken agreement between us about what to do.

Bellatrix scanned the can of worms with her eyes. "Take care of them while I sleep." And she laid down on the floor. All dressed in white in the evening light, she looked like a huge worm. I did not want to look at her too much because I did not want to give the impression I was mourning her, but I could feel her moving from time to time. At times she put her hand over her forehead, or she sighed deeply. Other times she changed positions.

After a long period of time, it became obvious that the possibility of sleep eluded Bellatrix. At last she got up with a jump.

"It's useless, Betelgeuse," she huffed, "sleep is not for me, but if you sleep, I will learn how it is through you."

Then it was agreed that I would sleep. But we left it for the next day so as not to waste the moon. Bellatrix took the worms for a stroll and sang to them all night while she made them go round and round the block. "Healthy-worms-sleep-and-if-you-don't-know-how-I-will-know," she sang with the most crazy music.

This went on until dawn and the worms were canned again. We looked at ourselves and left once again for our room. I threw a large pillow on the floor to support my head and laid down. In the beginning, spider webs trembled in the inner vision of my eye; soon they calmed down, and inside of me everything started unraveling, leaving, disappearing. My eyes did not tremble any more.

The shouts of our parents woke me up. It was night again. Bellatrix was at my side, motionless, with closed eyes and her white dress covered with worms that crawled in every direction. On her face I saw three worms shining more white than ever beneath the splendor of the night.

I can't explain how they managed to escape from the can. Or

perhaps it was Bellatrix who let them loose. I will never know.

Now in the house we have returned to the vigil. This time it is the dog of our neighbor that agonizes with resignation. For a few minutes, our gazes meet over the body of the tired animal, and their eyes do not stop silently accusing me of having killed Beatrice in my sleep. The one thing they do not forgive me for, I suppose, is not having had the opportunity to mourn her. I, her identical twin, have not mourned her. But they do not understand that at times, when I look at the can of worms that is now, I think: who has died? Bellatrix or I?

Translated by Shaun T. Griffin and Emma Sepulveda-Pulvirenti.

# *Happiness*

## Marcela Solá

I have lost the capacity to be happy. The siren of a departing ship leaves me indifferent; it is no longer a sign of unknown lands. Where to go? With each visit, the places look more alike. There is no single place left in the world where one can be happy.

I did not lose my capacity to be happy in the remote places where the sirens of the ship took me, but rather here, in my city, where I live. It is subject to our judgment because of that. Before, judgment was the pri- vate domain of God; now it is not so. We do not belong to that kingdom, and maybe that is good because things do have an end. It is necessary that this story come to an end because the dead stand out in the city, and I have lost the capacity to be happy.

I would like to sketch an inventory of all those things that belong to life and perhaps will never return, but I only have one long street in mind where one hundred worlds fit into each block. The human current flowed and flowed, and in one of those blocks was a man selling a deck of Spanish cards. I remember the great crowd that surrounded him on the sidewalk, with thousands of staring eyes.

The juggler must have felt how their thin hopes were knotted with his gestures as he hid and exposed a card and the same one came out changed into a horse in the suit of goblets, the king of gold coins, the ace of clubs; how, after thousands of mutations, of cards hidden and transformed, a cathedral of faith was built in the night wind that left people in their places, motionless, anxiously waiting for the horse of swords to appear, not the seven of gold coins but the same face card of salvation. The juggler, I remember, perhaps sensing danger, pleaded with disillusioned believers—"This, ladies and gentlemen, is only a common, seedy trick." But the people preferred to believe, as in the miracle of the Eucharist, in the transformation of the seven of gold coins into the king of goblets, and demanded: "More, more."

In the city, the waters were accumulating in the various holes, pits, ditches and unseen spaces.

From a house where books and records were for sale flew Viennese waltzes;the lights were shaking. Passing by the railing, one heard the tinkling of the glasses, and all of this formed a strange world, unlike the one we could touch and see, that possessed the bodies, faces and voices that were walking or had stopped to see the continuing miracle. I told myself, "This city is happy." But the memory could be a trap for me. The past is very deep, an immaculately blue sea that never returns those who have drowned.

There is another class of those who have drowned, here, now, that the river incessantly returns to the coasts. It is difficult to live in the city; nature has fled the mother and abandoned the world of God. Dignity and piety are part of the same hand. And I like to point out those reasons that are foreign to this order. "The capacity to be happy exists in the world of God," they have told us, as is the balance of nature, I think.

Now it rains for endless periods, causing continual flooding, and they always find the corpses of the people who have drowned. Recently, people drown more and more. To observe our neighborhood and its people, one could get the wrong impression about the story I am telling. Down at his fruit stand, Don José keeps selling the "sweetest peaches in the world," almost effortlessly. In the kiosk, they almost always offer a complete variety of choco-lates and candies and even those day-old candies filled with fruit paste. Doña Rosa, the owner of the dry goods store, is very happy because she has just inherited her husband's estate. "There are no better people than those who secure the economic futures of those they love," she says and takes pity on all of us who have to work without a loved one's fortune. Ramón, the butcher, sharpens his knife against the stone as he greets us. As for us, his clients, we return to the house with the bloody cuts of meat and eat them with no problems.

No. Those who have drowned do not take part in our daily lives, and they were never part of the kingdom of God. To what reality do they belong then? Strangers to the questions and the way of life on the surface, the drowned travel through the channels and rivers that cross us, surround us and wrap us in their mystery.

I always thought that love would be happiness. It came. It proved to be so contagious that I began to love those who surrounded me without hesitation and so arrived among the drowned. I feel wretched knowing they are dead and think of those who cry for them. Loving, I have lost my capacity to be happy.

And it's true that it was beautiful to be under the sun, in spring, and feel a desire for everything growing in us, in those days when the river became blue and one could think that to navigate it would bring intelligence to the unknown.

To sit now, in front of the river means it is possible to see a drowned person emerge, between the waves, slowly getting closer, half-hidden and pallidly blue, with pupils dilated to the maximum and an air of petrified terror. The manuals teach us that man, despite living his first nine months submerged in water, spends the rest of his time afraid of dying under water, one form of asphyxia-tion. At that level, one discovers the Kingdom of God does not exist.

I do not speak about this world just to speak but because they have discussed it to the point of being absurd. I imagined it as they told it to me, a place where the light pierces us with its life, in the middle of an ex- tended feeling of serenity. There, one feels immune to death by submersion. But in this city, death is another one of the privileges that have been taken from the world of God. When I think about this, I wish it could exist. There, even death, if it exists, shows a more compassionate air.

Nevertheless, one day we will have to choose what kind of death we prefer and perhaps will finally realize that everything that exists in the world of God has been utilized as a trick, a deceit, for the mechanisms of the city. And asphyxiation has been transformed into something compulsory, that to drown is the only thing left before us.

I do not know what will come after this, if something comes, and I do not know if I would like to see it, if I will have the patience. I only hurt because of the fate of the people living now, those who live in the city, those like me who have lost their capacity to be happy because they perceive the horror that has displaced the natural order—those who listen to the violent gusts of wind and observe how the level of the water rises and know their only chance is a miracle.

Translated by Shaun T. Griffin and Emma Sepulveda-Pulvirenti.

# Invisible Embroidery

## Marcela Solá

I bring the dead back to life with my tears. It is intolerable to see them pallid, distant, resting, apparently tranquil, and unattached. I feel then a storm building behind my eyes, ready to flood from the sky to the heart of death. My tears begin, life flows through the torrent with the same impulse and energy that is needed to make a flower bud. The dead people come to life. They slowly begin to open their eyes, a little astonished by the miracle. Wide-eyed, they cannot take it all in. They timidly lift themselves, direct a smile to me and leave. They abandon their families and all who said they loved them but nevertheless left them to die. My tears become fright, hope, certainty, andhappiness.

But day, upon reviving a dead man whose wife was keeping a vigil over him, I took his place in hell. Upon hearing my screams penetrating the darkness my mother desperately searched the world for me. She did not find me. "Mother, why were you distracted?"

"My dear child, I had to play."

I played with the dead and remembered life. Who will bring me back to her, I thought, now that there are no more tears? How to return? How to revive myself? I shouted "I want to live!", but no one could lend me one moist eye. "The world is made of eyes but no one sees," I tell myself in desperation, ignoring the fact that there are certain frontiers many eyes do not trespass, do not want to cross. My resurrected ones were consumed with living and could not even remember how they had been rescued. I told them, "I cried for all of you," and they silently looked at their watches and stated, "There is no time," without knowing what question they were answering, whatvoice formulated it. Perhaps if I change my appearance I will find my way out through experiences I did not even suspect. The moment has arrived to take on other shapes.

A black bat flaps his wings near me, his tiny face ends in a curved beak that disappears between immense wings, unfurled, that fan the night. Is that how I will return to life? I fly in the night with my silk wings. Flap, creak, plain, delicate, they hiss when they move. I caress the forehead of the ones I love (will they listen to me?), but I do not drink their blood, only fly over their dreams. My appearance is frightening but my bat heart suffers infinitely every time it shatters against the windshield of a car and dies squashed between the wheels. The dust hardens the wings, smashes against the earth; the bat becomes stiff as cardboard, transparent as tissue paper. I abandon the body. Where will I go? There are no remains which can contain me. Abracadabra. I enter a white stone, I am the white stone, I am smooth, round, bright, heavy, tranquil. I do not break, I wear myself down. I expand in the sun, I live, the cold arrives, I contract, I get tired of being a stone. Abracadabra—foot of the goat. I am happier as a giraffe, I see into the distance from on high, I have much space, I will drink water from the lake when the sun goes down. I do not like the noises that I do not know, everything frightens me, nobody can look at me, anyone can be a lion. I flee, stretch my legs, I leave skipping, dancing. I love the solitude and the wilderness. I am far away. Bat-stone-giraffe. I am not human. Is this how one is to be saved? I am nocturnal, hard, long, tall, heavy, dis- agreeable, frightened and lonely, but I have the grace of immoderation and long eyelashes that listen to the wind. I fly awkwardly, I fall to the earth and remain, nevertheless, indestructible. I make many people stumble and many come to rest over me. I keep the heat of the sun although it may not remain. I indicate the location of the road. No one can reach me when I escape except a worthy enemy. A lion kills me, my skin decorates the hearth of the murderer, I live in his imagination, inside his eyes. I survive my murder. Beside me, no one can be a criminal, I am a metaphysical animal, beautiful in the eyes of the others. Multiple heart,I leave the battered earth behind me. Finally, no one is my master. Not living or dead, I enter the fist of a man.

I am tired of the conspiracies and the metamorphoses. Still, I remain in the darkness. Now I know that I must leave—return to my mother. I do not know how to do it. I already shouted once and still the earth devoured me and crying is beyond my reach. "The one thing I haven't tried is laughter." " I am astonished, "Why not?" I begin to laugh, harder each time. That's how it is; I begin to laugh in tremendous bursts, the waves provoke a great movement in the leaves of the trees. As the leaves scrape each other, they produce a deafening rumble like a great battle of birds. Now if my mother does not hear me it is because I do not have one! I thought. "Mother, in some part of your body, I am recorded as a form, as a beginning; return it to me, it belongs to me!" I shout one time, then another until it's deafening the sky. I laugh so much that she isforced to find me. "If I give you form, I will tear inside," my mother says, and the fight begins.

My God, what a battle it is! A whole day of fighting without a break. I trying to recover myself, she to remain intact. The howls of my mother deafen my ears: "I'll bite you," she flings herself over my arteries, in the cells, the neurons of your memory," trying to get closer to my head.

"Not that," I tell her. "It is the only thing that you will never be able to do because I will invent it again."

"I will break your bones, tear your muscles,". . . threat.

The science of mutation taught me to make a body out of everything, except myself, but I know about seduction. I adopt a dance position; I have a strong pulse in the wrists and ankles. I dance holding the head of a man on a silver tray. I give it to her. She begins to devour one ear. And then I begin to laugh, because I know something about the voracious- ness of my mother that she has overlooked. I know there is no place inside her for more bodies. Because of that law of physics and without her realizing it, her womb opens and my head appears. I am reborn.

We said a friendly goodbye at a crossroads. "Take care little one; let the dead die and don't call me again; patience has its limits," my mother said. I offered her a red flower that I brought from the depths, my last offering. "I will do that," I promised. And I have fulfilled my promise.

Translated by Shaun T. Griffin and Emma Sepulveda-Pulvirenti.

# The Storm

## Alina Diaconú

She had tried her hand at virtually every literary genre, immersing herself this time in an essay about Time, whose first seed had grown—like a revelation or a premonition—into a very brief story that critics would probably describe as "fantastic," and that she had roughed out some time ago without too much conviction.

The night to which we are alluding, she was very tired after spending all afternoon researching through bibliographic material, the only tangible result of which was an infinite number of notes on an equally countless number of manuscript pages.

When her husband planted a kiss on her left cheek, wishing her a good night's sleep, she knew she wouldn't be able to sleep well that night. She was now experiencing a total absence of sleep, which often happens when one's energy has been spent on exhaustive endeavors.

And so it was.

With her bedside lamp on, she stayed up awhile with a book by Donne in her hands, unable to concentrate on the text, allowing herself to be distracted by her sleeping husband's heavy, deliberate breathing, wary of a kind of frightful fit—his body was close to hers—he was heaving, as though someone were attacking him in some nightmarish battle.

Once again she envied the ease with which he fell softly—and at the same time abruptly—into that inexplicable dream state in which middle age leaves us.

She closed the book on page 49, turned off the bedside lamp on her night table and remained calm, her eyes open in the dark.

Little by little her husband's breathing became almost deafening, and to this was added the sound of footsteps on the floor above, right over her head. Then there was the growing sound of a persistent wind that had risen, at every moment increasing, pounding with no let-up against the windowpanes.

A storm.

She began to grow restless. She tossed in bed, one minute covering herself, the next throwing the covers off; one minute perspiring and the next shivering—all of which doubtless aggravated her chronic breathing problem.

Another asthma attack?

She thought that the best thing would be to remove, insofar as was possible, her usual haunts, to distract herself in some way and thus drive off the ghosts that came out at night to raise havoc with her breathing.

She tried to plan what she would write about the following day, but since nothing of real interest occurred to her, not a single idea stuck in her mind. Once again, as when she first began working on the essay, she pondered over the two meanings of the word "temporal," perhaps provoked by the howling wind and the violence raging outside.

And, to be sure, the hurricane-like gusts were lashing harder and harder against the windowpanes.

Curiously, her breathing quieted, and perhaps this is why she abandoned her fruitless digressions regarding the storm, and the transitory nature of time and, instead, resorted to repeating an old childhood prescription: pressing her eyes shut and imagining bucolic landscapes in meadowlands that never were, with streams that also never were, envisioned through a filmy, gossamer light as in a fairy tale.

But none of this worked, and she ended up slipping out of bed, feeling her way through the drawer of her night table where she kept her addictive sedatives. She broke the pill in half with her teeth and swallowed it. All this was done with the utmost stealth so as not to disturb the rhythmical movement of her husband's body that night after night for more than ten years had behaved in the same way: a condition of inertia that, especially in times of insomnia, had a calming effect on her.

In the distance, she heard two bells.

She envisioned the whole scenario. In five hours the alarm clock would jolt her from her finally-achieved state of unconsciousness or semi-unconsciousness. She would feel the usual palpitations in her breast and would give a start, as was also her habit. Her husband would leap out of bed pressed for time. Like a soldier, he would guide himself towards the bathroom, and from there she would hear the sound of the toilet flushing, the din of the shower, and, afterwards, the whirring of the hair dryer.

And when the alarm clock did go off, as usual she couldn't keep her heart from throbbing, and she woke up with her usual start. She was calming down a bit, counting the seconds when her husband would jump out of bed like every day. But, no, not this morning.

But, no, not this morning.

She waited a couple more minutes. Frightened, she touched the sheet draped over his warm back with the fingers of her right hand. Her husband seemed to respond with something like a grunt, in order to keep sleeping.

She had never, not in more than ten years, been in a situation like this, which disturbed her tremendously. Yet, she told herself that of course it was permissable and—why not—natural. "Whatever is unknown to us, vexes us." She had written this some time ago.

And she smiled, satisfied, not because of the meaning of the words, but for having at last managed to remember something of significance that she had written and that wasn't erased from her memory immediately after having typed it.

She turned on her night lamp and looked at the time. It was 7:04. Then she turned it off so as not to suddenly jar her husband awake.

She waited, motionless, five minutes more. But at 7:09, her husband was still asleep.

Making a major decision, she decided to move her body around in bed, but again grunts were the response that came from his side.

Exasperated, but still trying to retain her state of mind, she whispered a reproof.

"Come on, Thomas, you'll make yourself late..."

He didn't answer. He was sunk in the heaviest of sleeps.

Angry now, she again turned on the light, while with her other hand, she wanted to pound on her husband's back.

What a shock it must have been when her fingers sank into the inflated folds of the sheet, and there was nothing but air!

She leapt out of bed and standing before the abandoned, empty bed, she started to cry out:

Thomas!... Thomas!... Tho-mas... Tho-mas...

But no one was there, only her, only her, shouting.

Alone, she slowly calmed down, realizing that her confused mind had no doubt overlooked the obvious: Thomas had left the house very early and was probably at the office by now.

But his pajamas weren't anywhere around, and in the office no one answered the phone at 7:15 in the morning.

Short of breath, she went back to the bedroom.

Her head was exploding with anger mixed with an equally unexpected nostalgia for what had been her life with Thomas.

Feeling betrayed, defeated, she collapsed on the unmade bed, among the rumpled sheets, and then all of a sudden she again heard Thomas' calm, deliberate breathing, which became more and more resonant until it turned into the unmistakable sound of him snoring—only now with the difference that, for her, it was terrifying, unbearable.

Translated by Richard Schaaf

Translator's Note: The title of this story in the original Spanish, "Temporal," has two meanings. Used as an adjective, it means temporary or having to do with the temporal, material and mundane world. Used as a noun, it means a storm or a period of stormy weather. Since the story inextricably enmeshes both meanings, I have translated temporal as storm.

# Welcome to Albany

## Alina Diaconú

*to Ricardo Cordero*

He crossed 42nd Street and entered the PanAm Building.

In Grand Central Station, he bought a round-trip ticket to Albany.

"Be sure you sit on the left side of the train so you can get a good view of the landscape bordering the Hudson River," his friends at the Sterling Company advised him.

He looked at his old Girard-Pérregaux watch, and while checking the departure time (twenty minutes left), he thought one of the things he still ought to do on this work and pleasure trip (which is what these journeys are usually called to remove any cause for envy or remorse) was to buy himself a new watch, maybe a self-winding one, with a calendar.

A work and pleasure trip... He smiled to himself. Come on, man, when you're on vacation, work doesn't exist, even though today you have to take the train to Albany and from there go to the Rensselaer plant, where the company is conducting experiments with drugs on animals. What work? This really can be enjoyable too: to be in a new city, perhaps have a totally new, unique experience. . .

He got on the train. Heeding his counselors, he sat down on the left side, next to the window. The train was to leave at 1 o'clock. It was 12:50.

Some people, a few passengers. Better.

He took off his heavy coat, his scarf, and combed his hair. He exchanged his dark tinted glasses for his clear ones, then pulled out a folder from his briefcase. . . "Albany. Capital of the State of New York. Located on the Hudson River, 140 miles north of New York City. Population 180,000. A commercial and manufacturing city, etc., etc. . ."

Slowly, the train started to move.

He loved trains, their measured, rhythmic sound of a rocking chair, their brusqueness, the metallic whistles of the locomotives. It brought him back to his childhood, to books, films and fantasies, the Orient Express.

He had been in New York for a week now, and he still had three weeks ahead of him. The adventure was truly just beginning, and for perhaps the first time in his life, he became conscious of the importance that his very presence had acquired: Buenos Aires far away, and now, he, alone, traveling on an uncharted course with all his thoughts alert, his entire sensibility prepared to be surprised, amazed.

Through an overcast wintry sky, the sun only managed to accent the cold, platinum arrogance of the Hudson River, the mathematical filigree work of its magnificent bridges, suspended over the dense cover of a foggy horizon.

Some passengers at the other end of the car. . .their conversation resembling an almost indecipherable whisper, recognizeable only by an idiomatic musicality, yet as strange as the foggy landscape being con- tinuously framed in the train window.

Three hours later, he arrived at the Albany train station and took a taxi to the hotel where he already had reserved a room. The hotel was a modern, circular building, an archetypal North American hotel with plush wall-to-wall carpeting, excessive furniture, a roomy, comfortable bathroom and a great view.

Now he could rest, but the idea of walking through the city before it got dark was too tempting to pass up. The next morning he would go—as prearranged—to the Rensselear plant. For now, his time was his own.

In the hotel lobby, he asked for a map of the city and went out to confront his surroundings. It was very cold. The tallest buildings were in the city's center, as with geometrically planned cities, but compared to the skyscrapers of Manhattan, the Albany Public Library with its thirty-two stories made little or no impression on him. Much to his pleasure, however, he discovered the Capitol Building built with granite from Maine, and the Schuyler Mansion, a magnificent 18th century residence converted into a museum. Also, the massive structure of City Hall managed to provoke a certain emotion in him.

In this way, the city introduced itself to him, and he walked through it brimming with interest, recording some of his favorite images with his camera. It was still light. He walked down the solitary pathways of a public park, strolling among curiously lush trees and a strangely vital grass. He came across a plaque commemorating Edison: "Birthplace of Modern Electricity."

It was fifteen minutes before five when he emerged from his walk through the leaves. There was no longer enough light to take photographs. Implacably approaching were the shadows of dusk, but despite this, there still remained a certain interval of hazy twilight.

He walked down the street bordering the park, turned left and started down one of the wide avenues—perhaps the main avenue: huge department stores, neon signs, people bustling about this way and that, driven by the cold, cars braking and accelerating through traffic lights, lights multiplying on the asphalt, in the store windows, casting themselves into the distance.

He stopped at an intersection when a white truck the size of an elephant passed by. With the pedestrian crosswalk now clear, opposite him a small group of bundled-up people started to cross the street. It was at that moment he saw her walking towards him, frail and serene, wearing her maroon coat. It was she, his mother, who died three years ago on a terrible autumn night.

He just stood there, motionless. An inner voice wanted to call out "Mama!" but he contained himself and imagined that she, his mother, would pass by without looking at him, while he, imitating her cautious prudence, would go silently on his way as if he hadn't noticed her.

To be sure, the city of Albany had given him a welcome unlike any other he had ever had.

Translated by Richard Schaaf.

# The Widower

## Alina Diaconú

I don't like talking about myself, but since it is necessary that you learn about me somehow—who better than myself to do it?

I will be brief.

I am an architect. I turned twenty-eight last week, under the sign of Scorpio. I work in a studio that of course isn't mine, but is owned by another architect who is much more audacious and much less capable than I (if the truth be told), and, happily, I am still single.

In deference to the truth that is keeping me awake nights, I must also confess that I am a perfect neurotic, possessing some qualities that possibly may distinguish me from the rest of the neurotics; that is, from the majority of people. Namely: my sincerity, for example, as well as my honesty and a genuine concern for people and their problems, which has enabled me to make a few invaluable friends.

The fact is, people tacitly awaken in me a mixture of curiosity and compassion, and I can't think of any greater pleasure than sitting at a table in a bar and engaging in a kind of mental "voyeurism," imagining a unique human history behind each person's face.

It is important to underscore this aspect of my self-styled personality because this same mechanism was at work the day they introduced him to me.

He arrived at the architectural studio in a black suit and a black shirt, unbuttoned at the neck. His skin, on the other hand, was sickly white, or maybe it only seemed whiter by contrast. His hair was long and curly, and spilled wildly around his face like a charged, irascible halo.

I felt the same curiosity for him that I'd have felt had I met that individual on the street, or in a cafeteria, or anywhere. But this time my interest was heightened, knowing that the man in question would be from that moment on "our new co-worker," the fourth architect bent over a drafting table, tracing lines and copying designs.

It was winter and damned cold.

I shook his hand and made a remark that was so obvious it sounded almost ridiculous: "My hands are freezing," I said.

He didn't answer me except to force a strange, good-natured smile where one was able to decipher something like innocence, like naiveté, or possibly even cynicism.

A short while later, I learned that he was the same age as I (twenty-eight) and that he, like myself, had graduated (from a different university) a year and a half ago.

Nothing unusual happened the day we were introduced. But without a word he sat down at his drafting table and immediately knuckled down to the job they had entrusted to him—copying a floor plan—not raising his eyes from his drawing board for anything.

That noontime, the rest of us architects in the studio were remarking and cracking some malicious jokes about the man's demeanor, his dress, his attitude. I don't know whose idea it was or how it came up, but the point is we nicknamed him The Widower. Why The Widower? Because he was always in black down to his shoes and socks.

I couldn't help smiling, just as I also smiled the following morning, when on entering the studio (I am always the first one to arrive) there he was, at 8:50 in the morning, sitting at his drawing table, totally in black: hair, suit, shirt. Black and motionless, with that face of his that resembled a white-washed mask.

"I was waiting," he said to me. I smiled again, I just had to do it. The truth is, his words had totally baffled me. Later I realized that this phrase of his did in fact make total sense: inasmuch as I, and only I, was in a position to explain to him some detail of the job they had given him and without my instructions it was impossible for him to continue his work.

"Relax, don't be in such a rush," I advised him. "First have a cup of coffee, and then we'll talk."

He didn't answer me, but only smiled with that innocent (or dumb) smile of his that I already described.

This strange man had been working with us for a week and we still didn't know who he was, nor what he did after work, nor whom he went out with. No one called him on the telephone and he didn't call anyone. At times the situation became truly annoying since the rest of us no longer felt at liberty to talk and joke around among ourselves. The Widower and his recent arrival on the scene—which was, above all, an intrusion—had spoiled everything.

He was as industrious as a bee and when I'd say something to him, he'd respond in monosyllables. Or, he'd just smile.

One day, one of us shouted at him: "Hey you!. . . Are you deaf and dumb?"

But it was useless. The Widower just kept on smiling with the same stereotyped smile of his. So, ever since then, no one has said a word to him.

In spite of everything, though, I felt a certain friendly inclination toward him, a feeling that particularly surfaced when one time I found him reading a book that had excited me in my adolescence, entitled *Sharkskin*. When I saw him with that novel in his hands, it was impossible for me not to ask him what he thought of it.

"It's a book I read all the time," he spat out, and his yellowish-stained teeth described once again his now classic smile.

I do believe that that was probably the most penetrating idea that had issued from his lips until then.

"Oh, terrific," I said, to say something.

That same evening, at 6:30, when I took the elevator down to the street to begin my daily trip home, I ran into him in the lobby.

"I was waiting," he mumbled.

"Yes?"

"Where are you going?"

"To Retiro," I answered him. "I don't like to drive my car downtown. I take the train. And you?"

"Me too," The Widower jabbered. "I take the train also."

This was how I found out that he took the train to Retiro and that he, like myself, lived in Vicente López. And it quickly became crystal clear that we were going to travel home together that evening.

In the train car crammed full of people, he was observing me and smiling; he was smiling at me and observing. And as I can't tolerate long silences, I started talking. In fifteen minutes I told him my whole life story.

The Widower listened attentively. When we got off the train, before our paths separated, he whispered to me "See you tomorrow." And I, I also whispered back: "See you tomorrow."

The next morning when I arrived at the train station, guess who I saw on the platform? That's right, The Widower!

His face lit up when I went up to him, his complexion was even paler, ashen, and once again I heard that phrase of his: "I was waiting."

He was dressed exactly the same, black from head to toe (the same suit? or a different one just like it? I wasn't sure), and he was carrying that same old, worn copy of *Sharkskin* under his arm.

Again we rode the train together, squashed up against one another, but he didn't show any signs of discomfort nor did I hear any complaints from his lips.

To fill the silence I went on with my personal stories: I told him that I had had a fight with Estela, a girl to whom I was quite attracted; I told him that my mother had cataracts and had to have an operation...things like that.

"And you?" I asked him at the end of my confession. "What about you? Don't you have anything to talk about?"

"Me?" (he became pensive). "No. I have nothing to tell."

"You're strange. . ."

"Strange? No. . . I'm not strange."

He had the habit of repeating the question and then answering it affirmatively or negatively, as in an English language (or for that matter any language) class. At any rate, I have always remembered those absurd sentences they taught me: "Are you the teacher?. . . No, I am not the teacher; I am the pupil."

The Widower had this style of talking. Moreover, he would address me as "Mr." despite the fact that we were the same age and that I insisted he address me as a friend.

As the days passed one after the other, as is natural and inexorable, our relationship was becoming more and more of a nuisance, at least for me.

In the evenings when I was leaving work, he would hound me with his obsessive, "I was waiting," so that we'd take the train home together. And in the mornings without fail I'd find him on the train platform where, when he saw me, he'd again repeat the same performance, "I was waiting," and so I always felt forced to accept his company to the studio.

His presence had turned into a real nightmare.

I began to look for any pretext to get rid of him. I invented meetings downtown, movie engagements, anything. But that wasn't so easy.

One night—now reconciled with Estela—we went to have coffee in one of the bars along Libertador Avenue. When we went in, guess who I saw sitting at one of the tables? You guessed it, The Widower, as always reading that same book, *Sharkskin.* I was about to guide Estela toward the exit and get out of there as quickly as possible, when he raised his eyes from the book and sent one of his dumb, and now unbearable, smiles at me. He called out to us with his hand raised in the air, and thus it was im- possible to avoid him and not go over and join him at his table.

The whole night, ruined.
And many more nights as well.

Little by little, The Widower was waiting for me everywhere. He knew all my male friends, all my girlfriends. He went to see the same films as me, in the same movie theaters, seated—just by chance—only two or three seats away.

He took the same walks, ate in the same places, drank in the same bars. By means of some mysterious, magical intuition, always he was waiting for me.

The situation was now really out of hand.

I was walking through the city like someone being followed. I'd constantly turn around to see if he was walking behind me, if he was spying on me. Neither of us was sure who was keeping an eye on whom.

So I began living my life solely to avoid him, in a state of permanent flight from him and from myself, from everything that up until that time had constituted my existence, my precarious freedom.

From my initial curiosity about him, I ended up experiencing rage, intolerance, and finally fear. The fear then turned into panic.

I started looking for another job, in another architecture studio; I began asking my friends if they maybe knew of another opening for me.

My life was now sheer hell.

I met The Widower six months ago and for six months now I've been trying to escape him.

Today, shut inside these four walls, the walls of my room, I resist going out.

I'm not the slightest bit interested in my career, in women, in my family, not in anything related to the outside world.

I'm lying on my bed, thinking, muddling over things.

The worst of it is that in the course of trying to constantly escape him, now I am the one who is waiting.

No, he isn't going to come.

I am alone and safe, in here. Protected.

I look at the time: it's 10 o'clock in the morning. I amuse myself by imagining his astonishment when he doesn't find me this morning on the station platform.

Fortunately, though, the hour of our fated morning meeting has passed. I am free. I am fine.

I'm not going to leave my house, I'll make the most of my day, my time. It'll be all mine.

I get out of bed. I go into the bathroom and catch a glimpse of myself in the mirror. My complexion is pasty white, like a whitewashed mask.

My hair has curled up during the night, and it has grown out strangely. It is spilling wildly about my face, like a charged, irascible halo.

I turn away, spin completely around.

I run to my room.

Draped over the chair there is a black suit and a black shirt, both recently ironed. And a leather belt, also black.

Tranlated by Richard Schaaf.

# Country Carnival

## Luisa Valenzuela

When Eulalia saw him leaving the barn, heading toward the dance hall, she couldn't contain her disgust and shouted after him, "Surrealist!" She wasn't exactly sure what the word meant, but she suspected that it was just right for something all different colors, without rhyme or reason, like the cockatoo at the general store. Ermenegildo knew he'd dressed up in motley attire, but now he knew even more because of Eulalia, and when his friend asked him what he was dressed as, he answered without the slightest hesitation, "A surrealist."

There were more than a few remarks made along the way before they got to the dance hall. Once they were there, Ermenegildo and his friend stopped at the entrance so everyone could have a look at them and so they could scout things out a bit. It wasn't that the girls were skittish that sultry night, so full of bugs: gnats that sting and the other kind, the human ones that buzz around girls without letting them catch their breaths, to the point that the girls tilt their heads a little, as if those two-legged insects were at their beck and call, ready to shake their bones with anyone at hand.

Only a few were in costume. Every carnival, it was the same, and Erme should have known better, but, well, the temptation to make a splash had been too great, and almost without thinking he had thrown on every colorful rag he could find in the shack and ended up dressed like a surrealist. Pretty surprising.

On the dance floor, they were beginning to kick up some dust, and the two men went on scouting, disinclined to pay the admission fee if they were only going to end up wallflowers. The girls were getting pickier by the minute, and you had to ask yourself why they came to the dance in the first place because whenever some poor sap nodded to them they acted like they didn't understand and the fellow wound up embarrassed in the back of the shed, droopy-eared as a hound just pulled out of a well. Except, of course, the sap stayed down in the well, that deep hole that shapes itself around somebody who's all alone. A sad state of affairs, my friend, but Erme, dressed in all the colors of the rainbow, simply couldn't be sad or droopy-eared. He had to bust into the dance, his head held high with his cap on top and the pride of being one of the few people in costume in the whole place. So he came laughing onto the floor, something the girls seemed to like, just as they liked seeing him colorful as a cockatoo, shimmering among those pathetic clodhoppers in their black hats with kerchiefs around their necks.

The girls laughed; Ermenegildo laughed louder. If only Eulalia could have seen him, she would die of spite. The girls laughed with him, not at him like somebody else we could mention, and Erme took advantage of this by nodding at the snootiest of all the girls, so snooty she looked prudish. She accepted his invitation by barely tilting her head and raising her eyebrows, but she didn't move from her seat. In a jiffy, he was next to her and, as the polka started, not knowing what to talk to her about, he asked her her name.

"I'll tell you if you'll tell me first, what are you dressed up as?"

"A surrealist."

"That sounds impressive. What is it?"

"A surrealist? A surrealist... is a soldier from another time, when being a soldier was something merry."

"And brave."

"Of course."

"And beautiful."

"Ah-huh."

"And tender."

"If you say so. . ."

They danced the polka; they danced the chamamé till they almost dropped, and Erme was not the type that dropped easily. And she wasn't either. They sweated a lot during the dance like you're supposed to, and she, in the meantime, forgot to tell him her name. But during one of the intervals that evening, she said to him:

"Surrealist. Forward march. Let's go home."

"To your house?"

"Of course. Where else? I wouldn't be going to yours. I'm a decent girl."

Something any good surrealist ought to understand, Erme told himself, and so they set out on the road beneath the moon and through the countryside until they got to the army barracks.

"Halt! Who goes there?" a stern voice demanded.

"It's your daughter," Miss Prude replied, and Erme nearly had a heart attack. Even more so when that stern voice opened the gate and pulled them inside.

"And what's this?"

"He's a surrealist, Father."

"Looks like a cockatoo to me."

"No, Father, you're mistaken. He's a surrealist, a soldier from the time when being a soldier was something merry and brave and tender."

"Not these days."

"Not these days, no, Father. You know that very well."

"Well, you, my girl, should know that your father is always up to a good thrashing."

"This man is merry, Father."

"And I'll merrily let him have it."

"This man is brave."

"Brave? This I want to see."

"And tender."

"That I won't give him a chance to show us."

And, steaming, he went after Erme with a strap, and the poor fellow ended up like a ill-hatched parrot, half-plucked, just a rag. Though a colorful one.

The two men finally stood face-to-face. The barracks commander had lost his breath, but poor Ermenegildo had lost his spirit. The spirit of the carnival at least, and all for a girl who, when it came down to it, really wasn't that pretty, just prudish, and sly to boot. The silliness of the situation finally got to him, and he let out a guffaw there in the midst of all the hullabaloo.

"A surrealist doesn't laugh, he defends himself," Little Miss Prude spat.

"Laughter's the best defense."

To go to a dance and come out lashed; to go for wool and come out shorn. Only come out wasn't the right word because he had to stay for a year there at the barracks wearing fatigues. One more raw recruit.

Little Miss Prude walked among the troops, passing out words of encouragement as if they were orders, although with the surrealist, everything was so topsy-turvy that even orders turned to honey in her mouth, and drew flies. So it was that Ermengildo tolerated his recruitment without rebelling, in spite of the orders and the flies, for the honey that covered everything and gave it a golden shimmer. He remained and ended up doing the most unexpected tasks: chopping wood for the entire regiment or spending whole days on maneuvers. The training was constant: leapfrog, drop-drill, target practice, wrestling. Every so often, in the midst of his most extreme exertion—like the time they were clearing the thicket—the smile of Little Miss Prude would appear, and Erme would find new strength. It was true, of course, that there were long periods when he missed the barn and the cow Aurora more than any other one, and he even thought fondly of Eulalia, without considering it might be her fault that he was in this mess.

There are things a Christian doesn't rail against. And so he just went on—hup, two, three—there in the service, until war broke

out and he was sent to the front in recognition of his courage.
Courage? Indeed. It all began with a little set-to among the troops.
It seems that a real moron was making eyes—really making eyes—
at Little Miss Prude, and our poor Ermenegildo simply blew up.
His long military training had made him strong and tough, and
he was able to beat the fool single-handedly. This unexpected triumph established his prestige among the troops and earned him
a commission when the war broke out.

The fighting lasted several months, and it wasn't easy as it was
believed at first; the enemy knew how to vanish into the jungle
so well that the jungle itself became the enemy, which is the reason our hero Ermenegildo didn't have time to pine for anything.
Only during the moments he was setting up a bivouac or digging
a trench could he sigh for those old times when to be a soldier
was something merry, or at least safe, brave and tender, as Miss
Prude had added that night long ago when his misfortune began.
Miss Prude: she stayed behind at the barracks patching a colorful
costume, washing it and ironing it so he might someday recapture
that first day, when Eulalia yelled after him. What was it Eulalia
had shouted? Surrealist, she had yelled at him so long ago, and
he had believed her, and a surrealist he would be until the day
he died.

But phooey on death. He only had to last out the war—fighting—
and then return to the barracks covered in glory. His bravery in
every moment on the front finally brought him a night of love
with Little Miss Prude—the best reward—and a medal awarded by
her father in front of the entire regiment.

There was a long speech by the commander in which he spoke
of Ermenegildo's military valor. He lauded his strategy; he mentioned that day when he saw him arrive dressed in many colors
and chicken-hearted. He expounded upon the merits of military
life, which, in barely a year, turned cream puffs into warriors. He
sang the praises of physical training and the discipline of barracks
life. He did not speak of love, but, at the end of his long harangue,
he declared: "Private Ermenegildo, in recognition of your meritorious
service in time of war, you may ask of me what you will," and he

looked at him like a father-in-law.

Erme either misunderstood or pretended to, and he asked only that his suit of colors be returned to him and that he be released from any further service. There was no alternative but to do the hero's will, and everyone bade him farewell with tears in their eyes, Little Miss Prude especially.

And off he went at a comfortable pace. The road to the farm was a long one, and he had to walk all night by the light of the moon and arrived long after the first rays of dawn.

When she saw him, still far off, Eulalia yelled, "You bum!" And as he got closer, she added, "So you think this is a decent hour to get back, still dressed like a circus clown since Saturday night? Why haven't you changed? And what do you mean leaving me here all day Sunday without showing your face? And to make things worse, you've got that medal slung around your neck. You jackass."

Translated by Christopher Leland.

# Legend of the Self-Sufficient Child

## Luisa Valenzuela

"The way he shuffles the deck isn't manly. He's worse than a faggot. He's like a woman. Disgusting," remark the peasants as they play cards at night in the tavern.

"She looks at us like a man would. She must be a man dressed up like a woman to get near us. We shouldn't put up with something so wicked," the women remark in the morning in the general store.

The place is the same. Is it the same person?

A man who is a woman, a woman who's a man, or both at one time, interchangeable.

Poor little town. So much doubt, such metaphysical anguish even if it can't be expressed exactly... Town? Ha! Twenty or so houses, spread out and low slung so as not to offend the pampas, an abandoned church. A very few said to themselves: "Oh, if the padre were still alive, he'd help us figure out this mystery, he'd protect us." Most people decided to follow their own instincts and watch this strange being closely, yes, though not *too* closely, to avoid falling into the black pit of contagion.

In the town, one can see there are no natives, most have Italian blood; there are a couple of Englishmen who don't take sides (the gaucho has long left, but the devil remains). A gaucho would have known how to interpret the secrets in the whinnies of his own horse when this undefinable creature drew close to the hitching post. (The townspeople understand very little about horses. They tie them to posts and then don't give the poor animals a second thought as if, on the pampas, you shouldn't always carry your horse close to your heart, even at a distance or indoors.) As for this creature, it has neither horse nor dog—of course not: animals can smell the devil no matter how deep the devil hides himself.

At the first light of dawn, does this person scrape off his manhood to cast off the devil? And put it back on at nightfall for fear of having the devil bottled up in a jar?

Or does this endemoned creature really belong to the female sex? Does the devil get in when she's a woman, having sprouted breasts and bearing milk? Or is the Evil One always there, running up and down from breasts to balls for the sheer pleasure of traveling? Traveling on a schedule just like the bus that grinds down the dusty highway every Tuesday afternoon? But the Evil One is never delayed: with the evening star he becomes a man and wanders around all night like the town crier. Sometimes, people have seen him hunker down in the tall grass and sleep till the dew falls, then, as dawn approaches, return to his wagon and—in the blink of an eye— emerge, changed into a woman.

As night falls, these matters are discussed at the bar while the stranger leans on the counter a prudent distance away. Under that friendly roof, with the heat of gin upon them, the townspeople feel a certain brotherhood, free to talk about that person who, beneath the open sky, does things that make them tremble at the sacrilege. The barkeep doesn't take part in all the conjecturing, the jokes and perturbation. He knows that one double client equals two clients. Two customers come out of that strange wagon, and that's the only important thing. The devil does not enter into his calculations.

As for the wagon, that's a story in itself. Early one morning, the farmers saw it sitting on the communal lands. They could not explain how it got there, though they frankly didn't think much about it. Not that one often saw a wagon parked a league outside of town, but it was so humble—a golden, toast color like the earth itself—in those thistle-covered fields beneath an azure sky. It possessed a certain heraldic air that stirred some ancestral strain in the farmer's blood. Nobody objected to it. Not long afterward, however, the peculiarity of the wagon's inhabitant was discovered, and, at that point, the talk about witchcraft and fear started to spread through the streets of the town, and it was good to feel it breaking the tranquility. Distrust ran right alongside fear, but distrust was an old friend and really didn't disturb anyone.

*And now the second verse.*

Not even the best yarnspinner could hold his own against this story, simple as it is, and unpretentious.

She is María José and he is José María, two persons in one, each of them, if you think in terms of names, but absolutely unrelated to the idea the others have come up with that amalgamates the two of them into one being. Something profoundly religious. Unconfessable.

They are two, I repeat: José María and María José, born of the same womb on the same morning, perhaps a bit mixed up.

And the years went by for them, too, till they reached this point where a vast assortment of impossibilites began to weigh on them, over and above the desire to do as they wish. They can't just go on: they're stuck in the mud and out of gas. They can't even split up because the fear of one without the other becomes unbearable. At the same time, they can't sleep together for fear of that evil entanglement everybody knows about, the taboo of the species is contrary to the interest of the species.

He goes out at night, makes the darkness his own. She goes out in the daylight, as long as it lasts, and neither of the two cuts the cord, stays away any longer than necessary from the wagon, that womb on wheels. (And to think that they were so close, packed tightly together, when they began this life, and now they can't touch each other or even look at each other for that visceral fear of temptation.)

*(In those times before we were born, was yours the arm that clasped my body? From whom came that all-embracing pleasure, that placenta?)*

Now, without realizing it, he has begun to acquire the feline grace that is hers, and she has started to become firmer in her gesture and perhaps—who would deny it?—looks with longing at the women of the town, the only people who cross her diurnal path while the men are in the fields, eating up the earth with their tractors, or taking care of the cattle (work appropriate to this rough continent, with its feet and hands and even its soul in the earth). And he, by night, perhaps nearly despairs in his desire to reach out his own soft hand and touch one of those calloused hands that know of the knife and the raw flesh.

And every minute those hands pull farther away, and the town is more united against them, not letting them speak, not letting them explain.

It seems to me that in all of life's little dramas, it is useful to place the blame on somebody. Our scapegoat will be that longlost priest who named the two babies. The soutane, of course, distanced him from much sexual knowledge, but it really is unpardonable. He should have taken a better look: the one, María María, and the other José José, and that would have ruled out doubts. Not all such inquiries are salacious; sometimes they are scientific.

*Chorus*

"That man is a woman in drag. She is hiding something even without trying."

"That woman's a man, and he'll throw himself all over us if we give him half a chance."

No clear definition for them, poor things, and never a smile. It is all too much. After six days, on a Friday night, to be precise, José María can not gather the strength to move his body across the fields toward a comforting drink. He leaves María José almost the whole bed at first. But within a short time, things begin to get tangled: there it is, within the reach of a hand and of other anatomical parts, that long longed warmth. There: the caring and the hope, the return to the source, and so much more that it is best not to mention in case there are minors around. And there are: after the prescribed time a child was born, very beautiful and utterly sexless, absolutely smooth, though over the years it developed quite differently, with peaks and valleys, with an intriguing bulk and a dark cavity of notable depth.

Outside the wagon, no one ever knew which of the two had been the mother.

Did they know themselves?

Translated by Christopher Leland.

# Viennese Waltz

## Alicia Steimberg

Nilda was walking along a deserted street. She didn't know where she was going, how long she'd been walking, the name of the street, or the name of the city that street belonged to. She didn't know the day, the time, not even if it was morning or afternoon. She assumed it was summer since she was wearing light clothes. She knew, yes, that she was herself but didn't know if she had a home, a family, or a cook. She walked hesitantly, seeking some indication of something. The block seemed interminable; she stared ahead yet couldn't see the corner. She saw only the sidewalk, the houses with closed windows and doors, businesses with metal curtains lowered and signs that said "True Value," "Confidence," "New," but didn't specify what business they did. As she was examining a sign that said "Rose," in script, ending with a flourish, she sensed the presence of other people. In fact, in front of her were two very ugly women. She looked at them for a moment, then looked at her own dress. It was an old summer dress, completely faded and missing some buttons. Continuing with the examination of her own attire, she observed that she was wearing white slippers, all worn out, that were missing laces. She was wondering how she had gone out looking like that when one of the women asked her where Vienna Street was.

Vienna? Vienna? Is there a street named Vienna in this city? Haltingly she answered, "All I know about Vienna is waltzes."

The women kept looking at her as if they hadn't heard. She began to doubt she had actually said anything. Maybe she had only thought of that answer, and now she didn't remember what she had thought or what the women had asked. She sank into a reverie of Viennese waltzes and brightly illuminated palaces where ladies and gentlemen in formal dress spun around to the rhythm of music. She saw herself splendidly dressed, descending a staircase as the couples stopped dancing and formed facing double lines, creating a corridor for her to pass through. All of them took a deep bow. When she arrived at the foot of the staircase and smiled at the two nearest women, she noticed they were very ugly. In fact, they were the two women she had met on the street. Once more she was on the deserted street, and the women were looking at her angrily.

"If you don't tell me where Vienna Street is I'm going to faint," announced one of the women. She was so ugly it seemed impossible. She had an impossible face.

"It's impossible," thought Nilda.

"What do you mean it's impossible? I'm going to faint," insisted the woman. And Nilda realized that she hadn't only thought; she had spoken, too.

"Come on, come on, you're not going to faint," she answered sarcastically.

Then the woman's eyes went blank, which increased her ugliness by a few points, and Nilda was terrified not because she might faint but because she looked so awful. At that moment, she understood why that face was so abnormally ugly; it was twice the size of most faces. That, plus the loneliness of the street, the unending block, and her own ragged dress, finally overcame her with total terror. The woman was slowly fainting, and the other one, who was holding her up, also seemed about to faint.

What if they both faint? thought Nilda. What if they die right here? And she couldn't keep thinking anymore. She covered her mouth with her hand while the two women sank to the floor and screamed.

"Mommy! Mommy! Mommy!"

The third time it seemed that it wasn't she who had shouted and that the scream was not one of terror. It was just a cry. She listened hard to see if the cry would repeat. And indeed, it did.

"I'm coming, my love!" cried Nilda as she got out of bed and ran barefoot to the next bedroom. Standing in her crib, fresh and rosy-cheeked, the child cried, "Mommy, Mommy!"

It was 8 a.m. on Monday, March 18th, 1958, the temperature was twenty-two degrees centigrade, with a high percentage of humidity, the street was crowded and noisy, the sky partially cloudy. Nilda lifted the child from her crib. She found a toy for her to play with while she changed her diapers. The noise from the street was deafening. With the child in her arms, Nilda went to close the window. The city was Buenos Aires.

When the baby finishes her bottle, Nilda puts her on the floor to crawl and goes to the kitchen to heat up some coffee. She pours two cups and carries them to the bedroom. She awakens her husband, who sits up groggily in bed. The doorbell rings.

It's the baby sitter who comes in, places a bag of groceries on the kitchen table and picks up the baby.

"Good morning, Valentina."

"Good morning, Ma'am."

For a fleeting instant Valentina has the face of one of the women who fainted on the street. Nilda looks at Valentina worriedly for a moment and then goes to say goodbye to her husband, who's already at the door. Valentina has left the kitchen with the baby. Nilda unwraps a package of fish and sniffs it to see if it's fresh. In 1940, in a blackened kitchen, an old bent-over woman tests the smell of the fish.

"I went by La Plata Market," says a jovial, older man, leaning on the doorframe, "and I thought 'Let's get some fish for Clara.' "

Off in a corner, Nilda observes her grandmother, sticking her nose into the fish. The man stops smiling.

"What is it, Clara, the fish isn't. . ."

"Well, no, it's not spoiled. But. . ."

The man is hurt, near tears. He's so old, too. Though not as old as Grandma.

" That's odd," the man said. "I stopped at La Plata Market."

The grandmother keeps smelling the fish with a wrinkled nose. Nilda creeps up on her from behind, deals a blow to her neck, and pushes her face into the fish. The phone rings. Nilda puts down the fish that Valentina just bought and goes to answer it. On the other end of the line, a guttural voice asks, "Bank of Tokyo?"

"Wrong number." Nilda hangs up and leans back in the arm-chair by the phone. Valentina comes into the living room with the baby, ready for the morning walk.

Nilda is alone, straightening up the bedroom. She returns to the living room, tidies up the crowded desk. She puts a sheet of paper in the typewriter and types:

Monday, today is Monday.

She interrupts herself and looks through the window. In a build-ing across the street, a woman in a nightgown peers through the window. That woman spends her whole day in a nightgown, thought Nilda. I wonder why. She might be ill, she might be lazy, she might be one of those people who think you have to always wear a nightgown at home. That must be it. But how can I be sure. Nilda gets up, goes to the window, and gestures and shouts, asking the woman why she's always in a nightgown. The woman doesn't seem to move or to hear her. Nilda kneels at the windowsill. Below she sees a stream of vehicles advancing along the street. Nilda stands up on the sill, takes a leap that lands her on the window sill of the woman in the nightgown. Nilda goes into her room; the woman doesn't move from the window sill, nor does she seem to have noticed the leap and the arrival of Nilda, who clears her throat without results. She follows the direction of the woman's gaze, fixed on one of the upper story windows of Nilda's building, and discovers that it leads to a brightly illuminated room where several couples dance a Viennese waltz. Meanwhile, night has fallen;

it's a hot summer night. On one side of the lit room is a table set with wine goblets and bottles of champagne. In the darkness, Nilda turns to observe her neighbor and realizes she's crying.

"Let me guess," continues Nilda. "Did your boyfriend die? In the war?"

The woman stops crying for a moment and stares at the ceiling.

"You see? You see? Now it feels better" says Nilda, but the woman starts crying even harder.

"What war did he die in? In the first World War? The war against Paraguay? The battles of Vilcapugio and Ayohuma?"

The woman shakes her head negatively to each question, without ceasing to cry.

"Wait, be patient, I can guess. Let's see, what other war... But first tell me, what period do you belong to?"

For the first time the woman in the nightgown seems to calm down and looks straight at Nilda, who backs away in fear. The woman's face is incredibly old, infinitely consumed and wrinkled; there's a photo of a face like that in an issue of National Geographic, a hundred year old Indian lady of a tribe in...the Amazon, yes, in the Amazon. But do they dance Viennese waltzes there? There must be a mistake. Nilda, seated at her desk, takes a last look at the picture of an Amazon Indian in an issue of National Geographic, finishes the page she is typing and pulls it out of the machine. In the Amazon, the hundred year old Indian lady takes the cloth she's just finished weaving off the loom and shakes her hand. Behind her in the jungle, birds sing and monkeys screech. Nilda scans the page she has just written and shakes her head. She puts the paper in a folder and gets up to go to the bathroom.

Nilda looks at herself in the bathroom mirror. She smiles, throws her head back, turns to the side, then looks at herself again thoughtfully. From the mirror, a child's countenance, a round little face with inquisitive eyes and parted lips looks back at her. In a museum in Italy, they've preserved a sketch of Columbus when he was a child. Funny. The bathroom fills up with laughter, more and more delirious and strident. In the mirror, Nilda's face recedes until she can see herself full length, seated at a child's desk, coloring in a map where Columbus' voyages are represented by little dots. Nilda dips the pen in the inkwell, ready to write something on the map, but a big blob of ink drips out. Nilda cries and one of her tears falls on the stain.

The ink gets watery, the blue turns azure, the stain grows, turning into a puddle, a lake, a sea. The waves rise and break softly on the beach. Nilda deepens the well she was making in the sand. A wave washes up and erases the well. Nilda jumps up and runs to the beach umbrella. Under the umbrella, several people are huddled in the shade. It's noon. An uncle gives her a candy. He always has a candy for Nilda, even in the most unthinkable circumstances, for example when he made her go into grandmother's room shortly after the death of her grandmother, and her face and hair were so white they blended with the pillow.

"Say goodbye to Grandma," said her uncle, "she's gone for good."

Nilda rested her lips on that cold, hard cheek, drew back, and noticed that everyone around the bed was crying. When she opened her mouth to cry too, her uncle slipped in a candy.

There's still time, thought Nilda, seeing the adults go on with their conversation. She goes back to the shore with the flooded well. She looks into the bathroom mirror and sees her own eyes brimming with tears.

"Don't cry any more," said one of the women who fainted. "We'll find someone else to tell us where Vienna Street is."

Nilda gratefully dries her eyes and peers out the window to see if her daughter and the babysitter are returning from their walk. The traffic is more feverish than before, and the woman in the nightgown is slowly, ceremoniously airing out her sheets.

Translated by Lorraine Elena Roses.

# Garcia's Thousandth Day

## Alicia Steimberg

One Friday, for the fifth time that week, for the tenth time that month, for the hundredth time that year, for the thousandth time in her life, Ms. García appeared punctually at the office with all her makeup on: golden-tone foundation, black eye pencil, false eyelashes, turquoise eye shadow, coral blush and lipstick, sprayed hairdo, and nails covered with pearly polish. She went past the reception desk to office 212. As always, she sensed that the front office clerks were examining her and making comments.

For the thousandth time, García sat down at her desk and filled out forms till noon. Then she went out and ate lunch alone, as every day, seated on a high stool at a counter. She ordered a tuna sandwich, a diet soda, and tapioca pudding. She went back to the office. As always at that time, the coffee vendor was making his rounds. He followed García into the office and poured her coffee into a cardboard cup. García saw the black fingernails of the coffee vendor against the white of the cup and thought that the man's cleanliness was only superficial; underneath the standard starched cinnamon uniform, the tie and polished shoes he probably was wearing dirty rags. The coffee vendor smiled, as usual, as he covered the thermos and put away the money. When he left the office, García took out her rouge and a little mirror and touched up her makeup. She went back to the forms.

García wasn't supposed to get up from her seat before 6 p.m. At least she hadn't in the previous thousand working days. But ten minutes later, a terrible commotion came up from the street, and García went to look out the window. She saw her coffee vendor fighting with another coffee vendor. García didn't understand the reason for the fight. A few people passed by, paused at the scene and went on their way. García's coffee man punched the other one in the stomach; he screamed and tried to escape but fell on the ground and got punched many times more and couldn't hit back. García watched it all, covering her mouth with her hand. Some people went over and separated the two coffee men. The hairdresser from the ground floor and some clients with their heads full of curlers listened to the aggressor's explanation. His jurisdiction had been invaded. According to a previous agreement, the beauty parlor belonged to García's coffee man. The clients, who had just been sipping the invader's coffee, nodded in approbation and sympathy for the offended party.

The hairdresser and the head curlers disappeared into the beauty parlor. García's coffee man spent the rest of his anger smashing up the thermos; the loser lost no time, once he got up, in making for the corner. García went back to her desk and picked up her pen with a sweaty hand. A minute later she got up again and looked through the window. There was no one on the sidewalk and the only trace of what had happened was a puddle of coffee that wasn't steaming anymore. The thermos had rolled into the gutter. A woman holding a child's hand passed by. The child put one foot in the puddle. The mother pulled his arm to get him out of there and called him stupid. They kept walking and disappeared at the corner.

At six p.m., García finished the last form of the day, tidied everything up, collected her purse and took the elevator. The stale air made her nauseous. The elevator operator looked up from the comic book he was reading to greet her. García left the building and took a bus to return to her apartment in the Villa Urquiza. She stood for forty minutes and sat for ten. She walked two blocks and once again smelled something that made her nauseous. With the purse still hanging from her hand, she went directly to the bathroom, leaned over the toilet and threw up. She threw up the tuna sandwich, whole, the diet soda with bottle and all, the tapioca pudding topped with whipped cream, all of her makeup, including the lipstick. She threw up the mirror, the front office clerks' eyes, the number 212, the elevator man's comics, and the bus ticket. When she thought she had nothing left to vomit, she threw up the calendar page that marked her thousandth day as an office clerk, a dented coffee thermos and a kick in the stomach.

Translated by Lorraine Elena Roses.

# Segismundo's Better World

## Alicia Steimberg

I can't pinpoint the exact date when Segismundo departed for a better world. Nor can I be sure that his life after death was better than the one we knew him to lead on earth. Moreover, I can't state that Segismundo actually did go to another world, whether better or worse than the one we live in here below, assuming, as we've been accustomed to assuming since childhood, that one part of our existence happens here below and the other up there, in heaven.

What's certain is that Segismundo Linares did die. The proof can be had by requesting a special permit to open his tomb and see if the person buried there is really Segismundo. In my judgment, that would be the only authentic proof, since the remaining evidence of his life is all on paper, such as his death certificate or letters kept by his Aunt Margaret, who like all lonely old women had the habit of keeping everything. But paper, even with the signature and stamp of the municipality, is only paper and, therefore, easily adulterated.

Another piece of evidence (relatively) of Segismundo's death is

his absence, that is, his absence from the places he used to frequent in the period preceding his death.

About Segismundo's childhood no one knows anything, nor did
Segismundo himself because of a blow to the head sustained at
age fourteen, just when he was leaving childhood, that made him
forget everything before that time. When he regained consciousness, he found himself in a hospital ward. After a few days he could
speak, feed himself and get out of bed to go to the bathroom, and
he answered a series of questions posed to him by doctors. He
seemed to have no difficulty expressing himself; on the contrary,
he was talkative. But he didn't answer a single one of the questions meant to reconstruct his life before the blow to his head.
It was never learned where he lived, if he had attended school or
if he had been institutionalized. Nothing of that nature. He did,
though, speak of strange animals, mysterious rivers that flowed
through the mountains and of a village whose name he didn't
remember where one summer afternoon he'd seen a puppet show.

When Segismundo was brought unconscious to the hospital
emergency room he was wearing a brown suit, cheap but clean,
a white shirt, black shoes, no tie. He was three foot nine inches
tall, rather thin, and had regular features, no distinguishing marks,
and brown hair. The notice placed in the newspapers with a photograph taken in the hospital, brought no results. No one showed
up to claim him or identify him. After further investigations, not
worthwhile describing because they too produced no results, Segismundo was transferred to an establishment for abandoned minors
which for four years attempted to turn him into a useful member
of society.

There is no file on Segismundo's life in that home for minors,
which he left forever when he reached the age of eighteen once
they had found a job in a bar for him. Whether in the establishment for minors Segismundo suffered the unpleasant experience
typical of such places, if they played mean pranks on him when
he was new, if he joined one gang or another, engaged in homosexual activities or was a fink for the guard, no one knows. Nor
is it known whether he was taught any trade, unless cleaning the

kitchen and the bathroom or a bar can be considered a trade.

There are more unanswered questions. How long did Segismundo work as a janitor in that bar? When did he start working at the counter of the bakery across the street, thus suddenly moving up to a higher socioeconomic level? With whom did he associate during all those years besides his supervisors and fellow workers at the bar and the bakery? Was there a woman in Segismundo Linares' life (excepting, of course, his Aunt Margaret, who wasn't really his aunt but the owner of a boarding house where Linares lived for a while after his promotion from bar janitor to bakery counter boy)? From the point where Segismundo starts living at the boarding house, the circumstances of his life become somewhat clearer, though not a great deal.

It seems that Margaret, a childless widow, an industrious woman and a good cook, developed a great affection for Linares who, given the difference in their ages, could have been her son. But this was not, according to the good woman, the love of a mother for a son, but that of an aunt for a nephew. It was at her request that Linares began to call her "Aunt."

My conversations with the old woman, after the disappearance of Segismundo, were belabored and confusing. In the first place, I couldn't say exactly what moved me to return day after day, to the little house in the suburbs that Segismundo had bought with his savings and where he and Margaret went to live when she was too old and ailing to continue running the boarding house. But the fact is, I did keep returning, and the woman would talk to me about Segismundo. Actually she talked to me in reference to Segismundo, how she tended to him and prepared his favorite desserts. From there she'd go on to give me dessert recipes (I tried out a few; they were excellent), and it was impossible to get her back on the subject of Segismundo, at least that afternoon. Then, surrounded by the sad, suburban twilight and surfeited with the unending description of custards, syrups, and sponge cakes, I'd say goodbye to her. The woman would be left standing alone at the door of her house, and I'd usually turn around to see her small figure just one more time, before rounding the corner.

I don't know how many times I went to see that woman, nor how many facts she gave me on Segismundo's life. I also don't know what I was planning to do with those facts, once they were compiled. We—the old lady and I—were living here below and Segismundo was up there in a kind of blurry twilight fog in which no one knew what they were doing or why. Still, that wasn't awful, not even unfortunate. On the contrary, I remember that period as peaceful and infinitely sweet, compared with the terrible moments that followed, when the old lady was dead and the house, there being no heirs, became the property of the National Council of Education. One afternoon, like many others, I went out to the suburbs to see Margaret and I found her laid out and surrounded by four tapers, proudly watched over by neighbors. It would be superfluous to describe the house; it is easy to imagine that the rooms were simple but clean, that Segismundo's room was preserved just as it had been, the floor waxed and the bed made and that in Margaret's bedroom was a portrait of Segismundo, framed with black ribbon.

Except for the sad circumstances, there was nothing unusual about the house. The neighbors took up a collection for a decent burial, and I contributed as well.

Shortly after the burial, I went back to that house. How could I resist temptation? How could I not go back once more, in the shadow of twilight, to visit that place populated by vague memories, by shadows of shadows that nobody else wanted to remember? And how could I imagine that those walls held a terrible secret that deprived me of sleep for many nights as I sat on my bed, with all the lights on, waiting for that fateful call?

According to a manuscript found in the dresser drawer in the bedroom that had belonged to Segismundo, and that somehow escaped the judicial investigation (perhaps because the drawers were very deep, and the notebook was at the back; maybe because the looks of the notebook frightened the employee assigned to collecting the deceased's belongings), I was supposed to receive a telephone call, any night. The notebook was bound in black oilcloth, and the first pages were filled with tiny black script that could have belonged to a fourth grade student in 1942. It was a description, full of bizarre details, of the lives of some jungle animals. The animals lived like people, but the story didn't have the charm and innocence of those anthropomorphic tales for children. Those animals weren't animal-children, but animal-human beings-adults, and the incidents in their daily lives were filled with fear, hate, pretense and humiliations of all kinds, as if the author had been intent on collecting the most repellent aspects of human conduct, ignoring completely the best and most appealing. There was nothing humorous, and no one stopped thinking for a moment. Indeed, the thoughts of the snake, the hyena and the lion were frightening, as were their living conditions; they lived in close quarters, lacking food and water, and there were scenes in which they devoured each other. In any case, after three or four pages of such reading, the impact diminished. I stopped reading for a moment and remembered Segismundo's conversations with the hospital doctors. As I tried to make sense of my thoughts, I turned several pages without reading them. Then something horrible and unimaginable happened: my name was written in the notebook. In terror I devoured the message. After my name (which I hadn't even confided to Margaret, to whom I introduced myself as "a friend of Segismundo's") these words appeared:

"On page twelve you will find the name of the person who will phone you."

I looked at page twelve. It was blank.

I wish I could convey my horror at that discovery, what I felt seeing my own name in a strange or impossible context like seeing it chiseled on a mountain in China or tattooed on the chest of a mummy that's been buried six thousand years in the depths of a cave. What could all this have to do with two dull, humdrum lives, like Segismundo Linares' and mine? And how could I know, finally, whether his life had been dull?

I spent many sleepless, blank nights, as blank as that terrible notebook page. Finally, little by little, daily life began absorbing me. My husband couldn't sleep with the lights on, (besides, he never believed a word of this story; he attributed it to the influence of a medication I was taking at the time to combat a temporary depression); my children, perhaps influenced by my fears, developed a fear of light, instead of a fear of darkness like most children; and I had to acquiesce to a different medication to be able to fall asleep at night and let my family sleep.

I don't know what I did with the notebook after that chilling discovery. With it, I lost the only proof that it hadn't all been delirium. Little by little, with the new medication, the arrival of spring, daily obligations, and the disappearance of anything referring to Segismundo Linares, I began to calm down and think less about the matter. His story was forgotten for several years.

Segismundo reentered my life during a vacation in Cordoba we were spending at a place near Alta Gracia in a small hotel located in a valley. It was a very boring experience; the place lacked the attractions one expects in the province of Cordoba; the mountains were far away, a little brook that ran by the hotel was dried up most of the time, and part of it had turned into a swamp under a cloud of mosquitos. Now and then it would fill with water, and we could enjoy a swim. I discovered that it is perfectly possible to share a small supply of water with four or five large cows. So we spent our days hiking on plains not very different from those of the province of Buenos Aires, stuffed ourselves up at mealtime (the hotel owners were Hungarian and excellent cooks), and read a lot of detective novels.

The first night we spent at the hotel, I dreamed about Segismundo. I saw him standing in an empty room, smiling in a melancholy way and I went over to him with the excitement of a long-awaited meeting. He was wearing the brown suit and the white shirt from the picture that was printed in the newspapers. There were no greetings or introductions; Segismundo simply took my hand and led me to a door. That door opened by itself and led us into another equally empty room but with a telephone in the corner, on the floor, like when you are shown a condominium for sale or for rent and it comes with a telephone. Seeing the telephone gave me the chills. With that sudden realization that happens in dreams, I understood that I might receive the phone call announced in the black oilcloth notebook. Indeed, the telephone began to ring without Segismundo or I making any move to lift the receiver. I looked at the phone and then at Segismundo. He returned my gaze, smiling. Evidently he thought the call was for me. I lifted the receiver and said; "Hello." Silence at the other end of the line. I knew it was useless to repeat the hello. Segismundo kept smiling. I woke up panting. The room was dark, and there was total silence. I sat up for awhile, trying to chase away the ghosts; then I lay down and fell asleep.

"Last night I dreamed about Segismundo Linares," I told my husband the following morning.

I thought I saw a shadow of concern on his face, as if I were showing signs of a serious illness. I didn't go into it, and that day passed like any other. By nighttime, when I closed my detective novel and shut off the lamp, I no longer thought about Segismundo or my dream of the previous night.

The brook had no water, as usual. Anyway, I stepped into its muddy bed; my feet sank up to the ankles. I stumbled as far as some stones that jutted out of the mud and gazed into the distance. The sky was perfectly blue, like a cut-out above the distant mountains. I fixated on it like a person who suddenly encounters a supernatural being.

"Let's go," said a voice.

But it wasn't Segismundo speaking. His immense face drawn in the sky was tight-lipped, barely smiling. It was Segismundo's voice, separated from its owner. Curiously, none of this frightened me; the only problem was I couldn't lift my feet out of the mud. Suddenly I saw Segismundo, another Segismundo of human proportions, standing on a rock by my side. He took my hand to help me out of the mud. I stood comfortably next to him on the stone.

"Life is hard," continued Segismundo's voice.

I thought about his life and admitted, yes, that his life had been hard. Still holding his hand, standing on the rock, I began to cry and I woke up crying. That is, I thought I was crying, but my eyes were dry; the room was dark and completely silent, like the night before. This time I didn't try to stay awake.

"Let's go," said Segismundo, who now awaited me next to a hole in the floor of a dark grotto.

I looked through the hole—a narrow staircase descended from it to some place that I couldn't see. Segismundo gave me his hand to go down the first two steps, and then I continued alone. I arrived at a square room, lit by an open window. I didn't wonder where the light came from, though that basement seemed to be at the core of the earth; in dreams there are many things one doesn't question. On the contrary, one accepts the most unlikely situations and is only surprised when he notices that he's forgotten to get dressed and is standing stark naked on the street or maybe is frightened when he realizes he's gone up a steep, shaky staircase and is about to plummet down and break his neck.

Segismundo had disappeared. I was about to go up to the surface when I saw an object on the windowsill. It was the black oilcloth notebook. I turned the pages anxiously but couldn't find anything that had been in the original notebook. Not the animal stories, not my name, and not the message about the phone call. The whole notebook was blank. I looked out the window and saw the brook near the hotel. In the distance, above the mountains hovered the immobile face of Segismundo.

I'm dreaming, I thought. I have to find my pillow.

It's an old trick of mine. At times I dream a lot, and sometimes my dreams are upsetting. Once I discovered (in the course of a dream) that if I could feel the pillow with my head or my cheek, I could wake up. I had done the same with dreams whose content besides being upsetting was absurd or impossible. Of course, in order for this method to be successful, you must realize during the dream that it's a dream and that happens only rarely. But that time it did happen, and I regretted it, because that dream didn't upset me and did peak my curiosity. The fact is that I didn't dream about Segismundo any more that night.

I didn't tell my husbad about the new dream, so as not to worry him too much. The brook filled up with water, and we bathed in it. The cows only came by in the late afternoon.

After the sumptuous supper, with a luscious Hungarian torte

for dessert, my husband stayed to talk with the hotel owner, and I sat on the balcony to enjoy the cool evening air. I thought about Segismundo, who had become my constant companion. He was a secret companion who filled those summer days. A while later, the hoteliere said good night, and my husband went to our room; I explained that I wasn't sleepy yet ,and we stayed out on the porch a while longer. But not five minutes had passed when my eyelids felt heavy, and I went to our room. My husband lifted his eyes from the detective novel to look at me. He seemed to expect me to say something, but I only managed to smile. I lay down, or rather fell into bed and fell asleep immediately.

This time I wasn't motionless in the dream, like the spectator of a performance, but was running at high speed down the street shouting

"Segismundo! Segismundo! Segismundo!"

It was a residential street, and many heads appeared at the doors and windows, attracted by my shouts. It was the suburb where Margaret, Segismundo's adoptive aunt, had her house. When I realized that, I stopped, and I saw her in the doorway of her dwelling, just as when she would wait for me to tell me about Segismundo and give me dessert recipes. I stood in front of her, expecting her to say something, but she only looked at me sad and tight-lipped. Now the street was deserted.

"Segismundo's story must be written," said a voice that was Margaret's but didn't come from her mouth but seemed to descend from on high. I looked up and only saw the sky and the rooftops framed against it.

I looked at Margaret again and said, "Segismundo doesn't have a story."

The woman contemplated me, even more sadly, saying nothing. I pushed her aside and entered the house. In the middle of the empty room was a coffin and in it was Segismundo, alive and smiling.

Then I shouted, "When will you finally die, Segismundo?"

Segismundo seemed angry, and his face frightened me. This is a dream, I thought, and I sought the pillow with my cheek. When

I awoke, I realized that I had been crying. My cheek and the place where I had rested it on the pillow were damp with tears.

My husband wasn't sleeping. Holding up the detective novel in his hand, he regarded me with concern and said, "Tomorrow we're going back to Buenos Aires."

I didn't respond. Sometimes I think he knows things about me that I don't know, and I'm grateful that he takes care of me and makes decisions for me at certain points. I closed my eyes, but it took a while to fall asleep. In my mind, I told Segismundo not to worry, that it didn't matter because we'd meet again no matter where I was.

The following night, I didn't dream about Segismundo. We stayed in Cordoba because my husband didn't keep his promise about going back to Buenos Aires right away. It was all the same to me, and that was precisely what worried—and what worries—him about me.

My next encounter with Segismundo occurred after a very tiring day that we spent touring the area in the hotel owner's old car. My husband and he spent the whole time talking about the war years in Hungary and the rest of Europe; I abstained from participating in the conversation so I could think about Segismundo.

Our hotel room was on the ground floor and the window looked out onto a porch. Even though at night we left it open with the shade down, there was complete silence except for the song of a cricket and birds at dawn. Lying in bed I'd stare at the ceiling, white and monotonous as in all modern constructions, when I discovered that in each of its four corners was a design that looked like a flower bouquet. I sat up to see the designs more clearly, but it wasn't necessary because they began to grow until they covered the whole ceiling. Amazed, I observed that they weren't flowers but human figures in dazzling colors. In the center was God the Father seated on a throne and around him a chorus of angels blowing trumpets. One angel, much larger than the others with white outstretched wings, seemed to protect the figure of the Lord. That angel had Segismundo's face. I laughed and cried at the same time, and I turned to my husband to show him that my story and my dreams were real. But he wasn't there, nor was I in bed: I was seated on the floor of an empty room. I quickly looked up, afraid to lose the vision I'd had moments ago. But there they all were, translucent and resplendent: God, the angels, and Segismundo. I stood up and heard myself say, "It's true, it's true. Segismundo's gone to a better world."

Several days later we returned to Buenos Aires. I hadn't dreamed about Segismundo again, nor thought of him. Only a couple of weeks later I had the idea of looking for the black notebook. I didn't find it. I didn't try too hard, nor did I mourn the loss. Its disturbing contents no longer concerned me, not even its announcement of the telephone call or my name written in its pages. I regained, at least partially, my interest in everyday things and rarely am reminded of the life, the death, and the better world of Segismundo Linares.

Translated by Lorraine Elena Roses.

*Letters*

# The Perfect Married Woman

## Angélica Gorodischer

*In memory of Maria Varela Osorio*

If you meet her on the street, cross quickly to the other side and quicken your pace. She's a dangerous lady. She's about forty or forty-five, has one married daughter and a son working in San Nicolás; her husband's a sheet-metal worker. She rises very early, sweeps the sidewalk, sees her husband off, cleans, does the wash, shops, cooks. After lunch she watches television, sews or knits, irons twice a week, and at night goes to bed late. On Saturdays she does a general cleaning and washes windows and waxes the floors. On Sunday mornings she washes the clothes her son brings home—his name is Néstor Eduardo—she kneads dough for noo- dles or ravioli, and in the afternoon either her sister-in-law comes to visit or she goes to her daughter's house. It's been a long time since she's been to the movies, but she reads *TV Guide* and the police report in the newspaper. Her eyes are dark and her hands are rough and her hair is starting to go gray. She catches cold fre- quently and keeps a photo album in a dresser drawer along with a black crepe dress with lace collar and cuffs.

Her mother never hit her. But when she was six, she got a spanking for coloring on a door, and she had to wash it off with a wet rag. While she was doing it, she thought about doors, all doors, and decided that they were very dumb because they always led to the same places. And the one she was cleaning was definitely the dumbest of all, the one that led to her parents' bedroom. She opened the door and then it didn't go to her parents' bedroom but to the Gobi desert. She wasn't surprised that she knew it was the Gobi desert even though they hadn't even taught her in school where Mongolia was and neither she nor her mother nor her grandmother had ever heard of Nan Shan or Khangai Nuru.

She stepped through the door, bent over to scratch the yellowish grit and saw that there was no one, nothing, and the hot wind tousled her hair, so she went back through the open door, closed it and kept on cleaning. And when she finished, her mother grumbled a little more and told her to wash the rag and take the broom to sweep up that sand and clean her shoes. That day she modified her hasty judgment about doors, though not completely, at least not until she understood what was going on.

What had been going on all her life and up until today was that from time to time doors behaved satisfactorily, though in general they were still acting dumb and leading to dining rooms, kitchens, laundry rooms, bedrooms and offices even in the best of circumstances. But two months after the desert, for example, the door that every day led to the bath opened onto the workshop of a bearded man dressed in a long uniform, pointed shoes, and a cap that tilted on one side of his head. The old man's back was turned as he took something out of a highboy with many small drawers behind a very strange, large wooden machine with a giant steering wheel and screw, in the midst of cold air and an acrid smell. When he turned around and saw her he began to shout at her in a language she didn't understand.

She stuck out her tongue, dashed out the door, closed it, opened it again, went into the bathroom and washed her hands for lunch.

Again, after lunch, many years later, she opened the door of her room and walked into a battlefield. She dipped her hands in the blood of the wounded and dead and pulled from the neck of a cadaver a crucifix that she wore for a long time under high-necked blouses or dresses without plunging necklines. She now keeps it in a tin box underneath the nightgowns with a brooch, a pair of earrings and a broken wristwatch that used to belong to her mother-in-law. In the same way, involuntarily and by chance, she visited three monasteries, seven libraries, and the highest mountains in the world, and who knows how many theaters, cathedrals, jungles, refrigeration plants, dens of vice, universities, brothels, forests, stores, submarines, hotels, trenches, islands, factories, palaces, hovels, towers and hell.

She's lost count and doesn't care; any door could lead anywhere and that has the same value as the thickness of the ravioli dough, her mother's death, and the life crises that she sees on TV and reads about in *TV Guide*.

Not long ago she took her daughter to the doctor, and seeing the closed door of a bathroom in the clinic, she smiled. She wasn't sure because she can never be sure, but she got up and went to the bathroom. However, it was a bathroom; at least there was a nude man in a bathtub full of water. It was all very large, with a high ceiling, marble floor and decorations hanging from the closed windows. The man seemed to be asleep in his white bathtub, short but deep, and she saw a razor on a wrought iron table with feet decorated with iron flowers and leaves and ending in lion's paws, a razor, a mirror, a curling iron, towels, a box of talcum powder and an earthen bowl with water. She approached on tiptoe, retrieved the razor, tiptoed over to the sleeping man in the tub and beheaded him. She threw the razor on the floor and rinsed her hands in the lukewarm bathtub water. She turned around when she reached the clinic corridor and spied a girl going into the bathroom through the other door. Her daughter looked at her.

"That was quick."

"The toilet was broken," she answered.

A few days afterward, she beheaded another man in a blue tent at night. That man and a woman were sleeping mostly uncovered by the blankets of a low, king-size bed, and the wind beat around the tent and slanted the flames of the oil lamps. Beyond it there would be another camp, soldiers, animals, sweat, manure, orders and weapons. But inside there was a sword by the leather and metal uniforms, and with it she cut off the head of the bearded man. The woman stirred and opened her eyes as she went out the door on her way back to the patio that she had been mopping.

On Monday and Thursday afternoons, when she irons shirt collars, she thinks of the slit necks and the blood, and she waits. If it's summer she goes out to sweep a little after putting away the clothing and until her husband arrives. If it's windy she sits in the kitchen and knits. But she doesn't always find sleeping men or staring cadavers. One rainy morning, when she was twenty, she was at a prison, and she made fun of the chained prisoners; one night when the kids were kids and were all living at home, she saw in a square a disheveled woman looking at a gun but not daring to take it out of her open purse. She walked up to her, put the gun in the woman's hand and stayed there until a car parked at the corner, until the woman saw a man in gray get out and look for his keys in his pocket, until the woman aimed and fired. And another night while she was doing her sixth grade geography homework, she went to look for crayons in her room and stood next to a man who was crying on a balcony. The balcony was so high, so far above the street, that she had an urge to push him to hear the thud down below, but she remembered the orographic map of South America and was about to leave. Anyhow, since the man hadn't seen her, she did push him and saw him disappear and ran to color in the map so she didn't hear the thud, only the scream. And in an empty theater, she made a fire underneath the velvet curtain; in a riot she opened the cover to a basement hatchway; in a house, sitting on top of a desk, she shredded a 2000 page manuscript; in a clearing of a forest she buried the weapons of the sleeping men; in a river she opened the floodgates of a dike.

Her daughter's name is Laura Inés, her son has a fiancee in San Nicolás and he's promised to bring her over on Sunday so she and her husband can meet her. She has to remind herself to ask her sister-in-law for the recipe for orange cake, and Friday on TV is the first episode of a new soap opera. Again, she runs the iron over the front of the shirt and remembers the other side of the doors that are always carefully closed in her house, that other side where the things that happen are much less abominable than the ones we experience on this side, as you can easily understand.

Translated by Lorraine Elena Roses.

# Letters From an English Lady

## Angélica Gorodischer

*for Pam Dodds*

My dear Angélica,

I finally did what you had asked me and gave Mrs. Dodds your books. No, I did not go personally, so I did not have the chance to meet her. I simply did it through a messenger. You know, it is a long trip from my house to Muswell Hill, but it is not just that. I had so much to reorganize here in these days, and I did not want to continue being remiss with you.

Here it is cold already. London becomes gray and rainy, as in those old-fashioned novels in which there are retired colonels and punch and old ladies who write letters to the *Times*. However, it is still early, so early that I had not thought of resorting to my shutters, but Reggie pointed out a few days ago that it had become necessary to heat the rooms. As usual, he was right. Now I watch this unpleasant weather and the rains from indoors and feel much better. You would not like London now, I am sure, after having seen it when it was sunny. I must say that, in general, I do not share your opinion about London's beauty; there are many other cities that are more attractive, many warmer places. But I recognize there is a special moment, which you had the chance to witness, when all this gray ugliness disappears suddenly, one day in June, when it is necessary to go to Hyde Park and make sure it is real—the sun. Only because of that (not to mention the English are so English, as you say), I think I could not live in another part of the world, unless it was temporary, for a limited time, as it has occurred to me to do many times, knowing I will return.

I lead my usual life. I take care of the house, take my daily walks, go to the theater sometimes. I am sending you some newspaper clippings that I know will interest you, with the chronicle of the last shows I saw. Nothing important yet, excepting *Ivanov* where Gielgud dazzled me. They are going to show *Man and Superman*, which I hope to see, also *Portrait of a Queen* with Dorothy Tutin as Queen Victoria, a curious piece based on facts about the queen's life, from documents, letters and diaries. I will tell you about it.

Now that Stephen is not here, I have more free time. Do not think I do not regret it, or that I am trying to fool you or myself. But I have concluded that a man takes up much of our time. If I were inclined to melancholy (once again the old English novels, true?), I would tell you about the shelf that used to be occupied by Stephen's pipes, the tobacco, the pipe cleaners. Now, in its place is the china you liked so much and were scandalized to see kept in storage. And a crystal vase, yes, with flowers due to that melancholy I feel. Reggie laughs when I am sitting in that room and he comes in. He does not mock me, nor do I hear his laughter, but when I realize he has entered and lift my head, I know he has been smiling for a few seconds. I have rearranged the furniture in the master bedroom and even the color of the curtains—they are now bright yellow—a revolutionary color, like you wanted me to place in some corner of the house. Reggie's things are in the small bedroom, and at night I leave the two hallway doors open, in case he calls. The rest remains as you saw it. I hope someday you will visit me again. It is not easy, I know, but it is not so difficult that

I should deprive myself from thinking it will happen again. Reggie liked you very much, you know. And Reggie is not easy to please. Sometimes we talk about you and your visit, always with affection.

Write to me soon. I derive much pleasure from corresponding with you even if it is only to tell you these trivial happenings. I am also pleased to practice a language I used to speak and write as fluently as my own. I have started to read some books in Spanish again, I even bought one on Spanish contemporary theatre with the hope of making sure I do not commit too many crimes while writing. I await your letter.

Sincerely,
Sybil

My dear Angélica,

I find all you tell me splendid though I resist believing in that sun, that summer and those tanned skins from here where all is gray and we think, as you know, about a white Christmas. Talking about Christmas, today I received a gift from Stephen. He sent me a blue enamel clock from Paris, a semi-sphere, not too big— the size of a fist; it rests upon a bronzepedestal decorated with a relief of wreaths. Completely smooth, you wonder where the key is and even try to open a section of the enamel, and then you discover it is under the pedestal which is hollow and sits only on the edges. It chimes the hour, did I tell you? And also half and quarter hours, not like a cuckoo clock, more like a music box. I did not imagine Stephen was in Paris. He told me upon leaving that he wanted to spend some months on the continent, but I did not know why I assumed he would not leave, that he would remain in London. Some days later Reggie told me Stephen was abroad. I did not want to ask and tried not to think about it. You see, and now I receive this gift from Paris. I put it on the shelf of the ground floor room where Stephen used to place his pipes. Yes, maybe it is foolish, but I think it belongs there. It would be wiser to put it on the table by the window, but why should I be sensible?

Now I will have to buy Stephen a present, and that is a real problem. It is strange, but I never knew what to get Stephen: not during fifteen years of living together, nor now after four months of separation. Before I resigned myself always to a pipe, a cologne, a book. But now, I really don't know. What would you suggest? A precious and rare object like a clock? No. I know that even if I walked Portobello Road a million times I would not be able to choose. Clothes? I do not think it is appropriate. A pipe again? He has so many and has probably bought two or three more in Paris. Anyway, I am disoriented. I asked Reggie, but he did not answer. You know, no matter how tolerant Reggie has been (and I must confess Stephen was too, all he could be) he never felt much sympathy, or, needless to say, affection, for Stephen. Jealousy, I assume. Men are much more jealous than women. I always thought, and time has proven me right, that the traditional and somewhat ridiculous figure of the woman tormented by jealousy, crying all night and making life unbearable for all during the day would be replaced, at least among us, by that of the conventional man, attached to a job and happy, who treats his rival or his alleged rival with good humor or condescendingly and then some day does something surprising: commits a crime, for example, or in this case, something less drastic, thank God: leaves his own house.

Well, I am talking too much about myself. I become indiscreet when I write; it is like a fireside conversation and plenty of time ahead.

I go out for walks all wrapped up in jackets and coats and gloves. I have given up going out early in the mornings. It is too cold, too dark. I stay in bed until late, lazily and happily. And I only get up when I cannot stand another minute without breakfast. Then I become a housewife for a while and around noon I go out to buy groceries—that I do not do everyday. But those outings are not walks. I take my real walks after a light lunch. Sometimes it rains, but I go out anyway. London cannot be recognized and toured if not by foot (maybe before, in those tall buggies drawn by horses, on cobblestone streets, among the sizzling of gas lamps, and here I remember one of your stories) and I love to walk! Usually, at tea time, you can find me me out on the streets, having to choose a place when the desire to drink something warm makes for an expectation that I believe to be excruciating, and always has a happy ending. After tea, I come back home, sometimes on foot, usually by bus. And, if there is nothing interesting that night at the theatre, one can say my day is over. Last year, Stephen and I went out often. Reggie came with us only once and did not want to come again no matter how much I begged. I wished so much that we could be together in those days! And he too, do not think he did not, but noise and people perturbed him. This year, I do not know; I do not think we will go anywhere. We will stay home, and I will prepare small, intimate gifts for Reggie, which means no trouble to me; since I was young, I always knew what Reggie wanted or what he would like to have. Now, my only problem is a gift for Stephen.

I wish you a Merry Christmas, without snow, with lots of fun and a Happy New Year.

Affectionately,
Sybil

My dear Angélica,

So much time has passed without me writing that I feel really ashamed. I have no excuses, but will you be able to forgive me? Sometimes what we do is not really important or absorbing, but it takes time and we promise to do tomorrow what should be done, and we end up not doing it. For a month and a half I have told myself I would write to you tomorrow, until I decided today was tomorrow if I wanted you to receive this letter. I am writing before leaving for the theatre. I will eat upon my return; I have prepared some sandwiches and half an apple tart I cooked yesterday and, since it is still early, I sat down to write to you.

Now we are at season's peak. And still, I have only been to the theatre twice. I saw *Juno and the Paycock* and *Their Very Own and Golden City.* I liked them, especially *Juno*—I found Wesker's piece quite unequal (Does he copy himself? Is he trying to be loyal to something that no longer interests him?) But it has been weeks and now I want to distract myself a bit.

I have had no more news of Stephen, though I know he is in London because Reggie told me. Dear Reggie worries about me and accompanies me like no brother would for his older sister (so much older; I feel so much older though it is only nine years!) under any circumstances. I know he will be waiting for me tonight when I come back from the theatre, and I like so much to tell him what I have seen and analyze for him those little details that I feel are only important to me. People generally go to the theatre only to see the acting, or because other people are going and everybody is talking about the show. They would care equally about going to the movies or staying at home and watching TV or going to a party. I go to the theatre and cannot substitute it with anything else. All that I see and hear seems infectious and demands all my attention and memory.

You see—it is not a long letter or a very important one. I have no tidbit or small story to tell. I lead a life you already know of, only my walks are shorter than usual since Reggie does not accompany me, and I do not want to leave him alone for long. I know he misses me when I am not home, and it really is not a sacrifice to shorten a walk that never takes me anywhere if it makes him happy to see me come home. Sometimes I convince him to go out with me, but it is very rare, and we go to Regent's Park or some museum, places without crowds where we can share a tranquility similar to the one we have at home.

Thanks for your letters and the beautiful Christmas gift. I will remember you every time I use it and promise to use it often.

No, I have not thought of travelling. Yes, as you say, I could spend the rest of the winter in some interesting spot or travelling, but the prospect does not attract me excessively. Also, I do not think Reggie will want to move from London; he is so attached to home, and I would not leave without him or force him to follow me. I know he would come with me if I insisted; or if I left by myself he would join me at a later date wherever I am—but this time I have decided to stay.

I will let you go now because I must leave. Do not stop sending me letters.

Affectionately,
Sybil

My dear Angélica,

You see, now I write more often. Even though I don't know if this can be called a letter. I am sending you the program and critiques on *The Cherry Orchard*. I saw it last Tuesday and have not been out since then. I have not been to the theatre or anywhere else. Only one or two mornings to do the forced shopping of a housewife if I want to maintain a habitable house.

Reggie has changed; he is not well. He seems distracted, absent, indifferent to all. I worry and have asked him what is wrong, but he says nothing, he says it is nothing, and I have not insisted again. Sometimes it seems like he is not home, that he has left. I feel I am really alone and walk from room to room, go up and down stairs, I even go into the basement searching for him. Suddenly, I find him; he had been so still and quiet, sitting in a corner of his room or standing under the stairs or leaning against a wall in the parlor, that it seemed as if he had disappeared. I smile at him, I propose conversation topics or listening to music, and it is as though he does not hear me, as if he still were not there. That is why I do not have much time to write to you. I spend most of the day with him or near him.

Do not stop writing please. I always await your letters anxiously.

Affectionately,
Sybil

My dear Angélica,

Spring is coming, Reggie is better, and I feel much happier. He is not completely well yet, he is not like before, he is not my real Reggie, but all will be solved, you will see. We have spent many days, all the same, always home, together, talking sometimes, but silent most of the time. Some afternoons he would make a commentary (though one, only one, that made me hope he would be himself again soon) that would give me a chance to talk to him and that made both of us happy.

A week ago he suggested I go out again in the afternoons, but before yesterday I did not want to heed him. I went to Regent's Park, alone. It was late afternoon and becoming dark; it was very cold. I walked and walked and suddenly, I do not know how (Reggie and I were always closely linked, so acutely perceptive) I knew Reggie had followed me and was behind me. I was happy. I was about to turn around and run to him, but then—I do not know why—I thought maybe Reggie was not following me, but spying on me. I turned my head a bit knowing I would not see him, and I saw part of the empty road and the trees and nothing else. The noise of traffic came from further away on Marylebone Road. I went home rapidly. I felt I was losing Reggie's presence in the streets. When I arrived home he was waiting for me. I asked him if he had gone out and he said no.

However, he is better, happier, he is slowly returning to his old self. We talk more often, and we laugh together. He has asked me to go to the theatre again, because I like it so much, he says, and because he likes to hear me tell him everything.

I am glad about all you have told me and especially about your vacations having gone so well. No, I do not think I can return someday to Argentina, but if I do I promise to visit you.

I remember you with love. Reggie loves your letters as much as I do.

Affectionately,
Sybil

My dear Angélica,

Yes, I received both your letters, but could not answer them because I was so perturbed and worried about my problems that it would have been impossible to put togrther something comprehensible, trying to tell you about only one thing: Stephen. It is about Stephen. I remember telling you he was in Paris (he also told me he went to Italy) and then returned to London. I knew of his return through Reggie because the only news I had from Stephen was the Christmas gift he sent to me from Paris. After months without seeing him, without really missing him, I will be honest with you, I hardly thought of him anymore. And one day he came to visit. Yes, to our house, one afternoon; it was a real surprise, without Reggie even telling me. I opened the door when the bell rang, wondering who it could be, and there he was, as if he had just left, greeting me, smiling. I felt so confused I did not even invite him to come in until I realized we were both just standing there, like two teenagers that do not know what to say, on the porch, with an open door. I asked him to come in, and we sat down in the parlor, by the fire. I had the fire going because Reggie likes it so, and it makes the room more pleasant. I said I would make some tea and Stephen went with me to the kitchen. We talked, rather he talked while I took care of the water, the cups and the toast. He told me about his trips, his long vacation, he calls it. He spent five weeks in Paris and the rest visiting small towns in Italy, stopping here and there. He reached Sicily and thought of continuing south, crossing Africa, but he had spent so much money, though his affairs had gone well, and so much time that he decided to return. And he has been, I do not know how long, in London. He told me so many things, but only when we were sitting down, drinking tea, did he propose a most astonishing thing. I find it difficult to believe, but Stephen wanted us to forget the seperation, everything, and return to living together. I could not say anything, and I think it was better that way because I gave him a chance to go on and then he told me softly, so softly I did not understand at first, that it was necessary that I abandon Reggie and then we could start over. It was not the time to continue there, in front of him, without answering. I told him I would never, ever abandon Reggie. But that was the worst thing I could have done-telling him so categorically. He calmly said the most abominable things to me. I suffered then, believe me, like I had not suffered since the day Reggie died. He told me my relation with Reggie was abnormal, he reminded me of Mrs. Finton-Taylor—would you believe it?—whom I have not seen in so many years. I did not want to lose my head, but I am afraid I was about to cry, especially thinking that Stephen could so easily imagine that I was so uncaring as to abandon Reggie, leave him alone. But, I reminded him that Mrs. Finton-Taylor had done nothing but give me solace, a comfort nobody had been able to provide me with at the time, teaching me how to have Reggie always with me, like when we were children, as usual, like before. Stephen said many other things, always drinking tea, stirring it with the spoon, eating toast, as if it were a common conversation. Believe me, I was devastated. I explained to him. I tried to explain, but it was futile; he told me I had to go out, talk to people, travel, go to gatherings. He even suggested I visit a psychiatrist. It was horrible. I asked him to leave. I wanted to go upstairs, find Reggie and tell him, though I was sure he already knew. I felt he was so sad for me, not for himself, because he knows I will never leave him. Stephen left. I had not touched my tea. He told me to think about it and said he would call again. And he did call, many times, but I have not answered the phone; I have let it ring, sometimes for a long time. I have even reached the point of putting the phone in a drawer when it begins to ring. Stephen would be on the other end, listening to the humming and probably thinking that I was home and did not want to answer the phone. It was so, obviously. Some afternoons I have stayed home just to listen to the telephone ring. Reggie gave me courage and made me see how ridiculous the sound, which often made me nervous, was. We both laughed when it began to ring and I, laughing, would take the phone to a drawer and close it in. He also came here twice, Stephen. He rang the doorbell and stepped back to look through the windows, but Reggie and I went to the kitchen, without any worries at all. He stopped insisting two weeks ago; it has been two weeks since we returned to our peaceful life, our conversations by the fire. I do not go out any-more, and I am not sure if I will ever dare leave Reggie alone. He wanted me to start going out again, to the theatre, to walk at Regent's Park. He would not follow me anymore, he says, to see if Stephen is with me; he knows he is not. But I have said no, I will not go out. I order groceries on the phone and the theatre cannot, anyway, make up for these afternoons, these nights of taking care of him and talking like before. Do not worry if my next let-ters take awhile, if I space them out a lot. You see, I have so much to do. But you, please write, do not stop writing! You have so much to tell me! When I write I will let you know of the little things in our little lives, what we do, what we discuss, Reggie and I.

Affectionately,
Sybil

Translated by Mónica Bruno.

# Under the Flowering Juleps

## Angélica Gorodischer

In that era, the most famous men, the most admired heroes, were the discoverers of new worlds. Christopher Columbus discovered America in 1492, Roald Amundsen reached the South Pole in 1911, Vasco Nunez de Balboa discovered the Pacific Ocean in 1513, John and Sebastian Cabot discovered Newfoundland and Canada in 1497, Pedro Alvares Cabral discovered the coasts of Brazil in the year 1500. All this was repeated to children constantly, all the while reminding them of the vastness of the horizons now open to man's explorations.

\*     \*     \*

I entered the penitentiary Sweet Memory of Flowering Juleps barely an hour after setting foot on shore. Since I was the ship's Captain, I was accorded the most rigorous treatment. My men were taken away to another prison, one with more relaxed security as I understood it, and I never saw them again. It wasn't that we had committed a serious crime by disembarking there, or that all foreigners were automatically considered dangerous criminals; it was something much simpler and, to use the appropriate word, more infernal.

The Sweet Memory of Flowering Juleps was an enormous oddly-shaped building that loomed up in the middle of salt flats. When the sun was high, you couldn't look out because the reflection burned your eyes. I never got to see the whole establishment, though I can't say that it was for lack of time. But it was a totally senseless construction, made of wood and stone; it seemed to have begun with the central courtyard, paved, with cells all around. After that, I assumed, as I sat in a corner and looked around me, the other pavilions had been built, one on top of the other. A lot of them had shared walls or were interconnected, and the old cells had been turned into offices or storerooms. The result was a jumble of structures of different styles and sizes, stuck together every which way and randomly spaced, all truly disheartening to behold. There were windows that opened onto other windows, stairs in the middle of a bathroom, corridors that went around a corner and ended against a blank wall, balconies that perhaps had once looked out over a space that had later been filled by a new construction so that now there were hallways with verandas and railings, doors that didn't open or that opened right up against a wall, cupolas that had been transformed into rooms that could only be entered by bending over double, adjoining rooms that could be reached only by making a long detour.

But I am getting ahead of myself. They detained me just after I set foot on land, read me a long statement that listed all the charges, and took me to the Sweet Memory of Flowering Juleps. No one would answer my questions about the rest of the crew, or about whether there would be a trial, or about whether I could have a legal defender. No one would listen to my explanations. I was simply a prisoner. They raised the bars of the entrance to let us pass, and my custodians handed me over to the Director of the prison and read out the same statement as before. The Director said "Aha!" and looked at me, I think, with scorn; no, I don't just think it; I am sure. He pressed a buzzer and two uniformed jailers entered, with whips in their hands and pistols in their belts.

The Director said "Take him away," and they took me. That simple. They put me in a little room and told me to strip. I thought they were going to beat me, but I undressed. What could I do about it? But they didn't beat me. After hunting through my clothes and taking away papers, pencil, handkerchief, watch, money and everything, absolutely everything, they searched my mouth, ears, hair, navel, armpits, between my legs, making smiling gestures of approval and comments about the size, shape and possibilities of my genitals. They stretched me on the floor, not very gently, they pulled my buttocks apart and my toes, and they made me open my mouth again. Finally they let me stand up and they handed me pants and a shirt and nothing else, and said, "Get dressed." "And my clothes?" I asked. They threw everything in a corner, the money and documents, too, and shrugged their shoulders. "Hurry up," they said. That was the first time I got lost inside the building. But they didn't; they trod along with the sureness of a wise elephant, slamming doors and marching down passageways calmly. We came out into the courtyard, and there they let me go.

Barefoot on the uneven paving stones, aching all over but especially in the depths of my dignity, with a weight in my stomach and another on my spirit, I looked around me at what there was to look at. It was an oval courtyard, enormous as an amphitheater, full of men dressed like me. They were also looking at me. "And what do I do now?" I wondered, and I remembered blanket tossing, tar and feathers, and worse things for new initiates, and there I was with my bare hands. What could I do against so many? They left me alone for a good while. I tried to look like a hardened criminal, but I was tied in knots with fear. Finally one of them left the group and came over to me. He was very young, with curly hair and the left side of his face all swollen up.

"One of my most ardent desires at this moment," he told me, "together with a wish for liberty and the pardon of my elders, is that your god should afford you prosperous and tranquil hours, most amiable sir."

I should have answered something, but I could not. First I was astounded, then I thought it was the prologue to a cruel, collective joke, and later that he was a homosexual pursuing a curious strategy in order to insinuate himself. But that wasn't it at all. The boy smiled and waved his arm invitingly.

"The ancient Master has sent me to inquire whether you would like to join us."

"Gladly," I said, and began to walk.

But the boy stayed rooted in place and clapped his hands.

"Did you hear?" he yelled as loud as he could to all the prisoners in that enormous courtyard. "Did you hear? The foreign gentleman will gladly join us!"

I thought the trouble would begin here. Again I was mistaken, and pretty soon this turned into a habit. Everyone else ignored us once they had nodded their heads in approval, and the boy took me by the arm and led me to the most distant corner of the courtyard.

There were ten or twelve men sitting around a very old man, and we went up to them.

"They sent me over," said the boy, speaking with difficulty, "because I am the youngest and so can be expected to be indiscreet enough to address a question to someone, however illustrious he may be."

Well, I've learned something, I thought, at least I know that I shouldn't go around asking things.

"May you be welcome, most excellent sir." The very old man had raised his wrinkled face, showing a toothless mouth, speaking to me in contralto voice. "His god, as far as I can see, has accompanied him to this remote place."

I'll confess that I glanced around me looking for my god.

Those who were squatting got up and moved over to make room for me. When they were settled again, the boy waited for me to squat down too, so I bent down imitating the others, and only then did he take his place.

I didn't seem to have interrupted anything since they were all silent and continued to be so for a while. I wondered if they were waiting for me to say something, but what could I say if only questions occurred to me and I had already found out that I shouldn't ask them?

Pretty soon the very old man said that the amiable foreigner must surely be hungry, and since I was the amiable foreigner, I realized that the weight in my stomach was actually hunger. But the weight on my spirit was not, and I was not relieved of that until I left the Sweet Memory of Flowering Juleps, and not altogether even then. I said that yes, I was hungry, but that I didn't want to trouble anyone and that I would just like to know when meals were served. I hoped I had observed the approved style and that the last part of my sentence didn't sound like a question.

The very old man nodded in agreement and said, without addressing himself to anyone in particular, "Bring something with which to restore strength to the amiable gentleman and companion, if we may call him that from now on."

Trying hard to imitate the nods of the others, I assented with a slight smile. The calves of my legs ached, but I remained squatting.

One of the group got up and went off.

Then the very old man said, "Let us continue."

And one of the squatters began to speak, as if he were continuing a conversation that had just been interrupted: "In my opinion, there are two categories of numbers: those that serve to measure reality and those that serve to interpret the universe. The latter do not require any connection with reality because they are not made up of units but rather of meanings."

Two others spoke up at the same time. "Superficially it may seem that there are only two categories of numbers. But I think that the categories are infinite," said one.

"A number in itself does not exist, although it may be represented. But we should take into account that the representation of something is not the thing itself but rather the absence of the thing," said the other.

The very old man lifted one hand and said that it would be impossible to continue speaking if such disruptions occurred. And while I was trying to figure out what was expected of me, if I should say anything or not, or what I should say if I should say something, the one who had gone to get me some food returned and I ate it.

In a wooden bowl, there was a reddish, shiny paste floating in a thick broth. With the wooden spoon, I scooped up some of it and found that it had a slightly fishy taste, something like shellfish that had been cooked a long time in a mild sauce with a bitter aftertaste. The second mouthful seemed quite tasty, and the third, exquisite. By the time I had figured out that they were mantis embryos cooked in their juice, I had been eating them for quite a while and liked them, and it didn't matter. But that first day, I cleaned my bowl by scraping it, and they brought me water. I was satisfied, very satisfied, and I wondered whether or not I should belch. Nature resolved the question, what with the physical pressure and the squatting position I was in, and since everyone smiled, I was reassured. By then my feet had gone to sleep and my elbows were stuck into my thighs, but I managed to endure it. And they kept on talking about numbers. When someone said that numbers not only did not exist but that not even their representations existed, and that besides, they absolutely did not exist, someone else jumped in to cast doubt on the existence of any representation, and from there the existence of anything, of any being, and of the universe itself. I was sure that I existed, at any rate. And then it began to get dark and turn cold. But no one made a move until the very old man said that the day had come to an end: just so, as though he were God the Father himself. That reminded me of my personal god, and I began to wonder where he'd gone.

The very old man stood up and so did everyone else, including me. The other groups began to do the same thing. It was cold and I ached all over, especially my legs. We walked slowly over to a door and went through it. For the second time, I was disoriented. We walked far into the building, making very complicated turns, until we got to a great hall, with windows on one side, windows that at least looked out into an empty space at the top of which you could see the sky. Along the other shorter wall—I don't know if I said it was a vaguely hexagonal hall—there were windows that looked out onto a stone wall. There were mats on the floor, a big stove on one side, and doors, including one that was built into a corner. The very old man pointed out a place and told me that I would sleep there after having washed up in the bathroom. We all went in there and washed, dipping into basins attached to the floor and urinating into holes under which you could hear water running. When I returned to the hall, I discovered that I was sleepy and decided to postpone the problem of my future—that is my legal situation and eventually my escape—to the next day. But ever on the alert in regard to the prisoner's customs, I waited for the very old man to lie down first. Which he did all of a sudden, on the bare floorboards and not on any larger or softer mat, which I had been looking around for in vain. The others lay down too, and I did the same.

But it wasn't so easy to sleep. I was just a step away from sleep when I had to resign myself to a wait because all the others seemed to be speaking at the same time. It occurred to me that they must be talking about me, which would have been very understandable, and I opened my eyes a crack to watch their faces. I was wrong again. Like me, two others were stretched out and seemed to be asleep. But all the rest were debating some difficult question with the very old man as arbiter until one of the men asked him to designate three because that night there were so many of them. Many of what, I wondered, three for what? I closed my eyes. When I opened them again, the very old man had designated three prisoners who were silently stripping off their clothes. I began to stare, without worrying whether they saw me or not. One of the three was the young boy with the swollen face. The others looked over the three naked men, touched them, seemed to be choosing one and then stood over to one side, in lines, without hurry or anxiety. I watched how one after another, they lay down on them, took their pleasure with them, and passed them along to the next in line. The three let this be done to them with their eyes closed, without protest or enjoyment, while the very old man remained stretched out on the floor boards. When they were all satisfied, each one lay down on his mat and the young boy and the other two went into the bathroom and through the open door I could hear the water running. I fell asleep.

The next day, they woke me up with shouts. Not the prisoners, of course, but the jailers. They were in the corner doorway, whips

in their hands, pistols in their belts, yelling insults, get up you disgusting filthy garbage, sons of whoring bitches, revolting turds, but
they did not enter nor did they come close. The men got up pulling their clothes together; it was sweltering there inside with the
heat of the stove retained by the wood and the stones, and many
slept naked. I got up, too. The jailers left, and we took turns at
the ceremonies of bathing. I'd have given any- thing for a cup of
coffee, but guided by the very old man, we went out to the courtyard, to the same place where we had been the day before. Everyone squatted down around the very old man, and I decided to
see what would happen if I sat down on the ground with my legs
crossed. Nothing happened, and I stayed that way, dreaming of
a hot breakfast.

Before the very old man could say let us continue, and I'd have
bet anything that it was on the tip of his tongue, a man from
another group came over, and all faces in our group, mine too,
turned to stare at him.

"May the new day," said the new arrival, "be filled with pleasant
hours, meditation and repose."

The very old man smiled and said to someone, "Invite the amiable friend to come join us."

One of our group said, "Be it known that we would be extremely
pleased if you were to agree to join us, amiable friend."

"I have only come," answered the other, "sent by my Master who
begs for the authorization of the Ancient Master in order that one
of our group, desirous of expanding his vision of the world's knowledge, may spend a few hours with you, with it being understood
that we will provide for his alimentary and hygienic necessities."

"Tell your amiable friend," said the Ancient Master, "that we
would be pleased for him to do so."

The man in our group who had spoken before repeated the message, and the other went away. Shortly afterwards the invited guest
arrived and joined us. Once again a conversation about numbers
began which was incomprehensible to me. I tried to figure it out,
but it all seemed either totally pointless or extremely profound,
and besides, I was hungry.

I started thinking about my problem, not about my hunger, since that could wait, but about how to get out of there. It was very clear that I would have to ask how to set up an interview with the Director, but I didn't feel very eager to ask questions because of what the boy with the swollen face had said. And as I thought of him, I was conscious of two things: first, of what had happened in the dormitory, and second, of an idea to convert him into my ally and get him to help me when I needed it. I looked around for him and didn't find him. I half turned around and saw him squatting at my right, a little behind me and almost brushing against me. Splendid, I said to myself, and waited for one of the frequent silences in the con- versation about numbers. When everyone was silent, trying not to think about how he had been sprawled naked under the other men in the dormitory, I turned around and said to him:

"We should do something about that tooth that's bothering you."

He smiled at me just as he had the day before, as if nothing had happened to him in the meantime, and he answered that his god would decide the moment when the pain would come to an end. I decided to keep trying. I answered him that one could see that his god had determined that his pain should end because I was the instrument designated by his god to end it. He stared at me as though he didn't understand me, and I was afraid I'd made a mistake. But in a second his eyes gleamed, and he looked as though he could leap for joy.

"All you have to do," I told him, "is to find me a pair of pliers."

He assented with a nod and went over to kneel down in front of the Ancient Master. There was a long conversation in which the boy requested authorization and explained his reasons, and the very old man accepted and gave his authorization. The boy went off, and the guest stared at me in amazement as though I were a monster with three heads. The discussion about the num- bers and so forth ended completely. I continued to feel hungry, and the Ancient Master referred to that in parable.

"Long, long ago," he began his story, "there lived a poor man who was a woodcarver by trade. But very few people bought his carvings of human figurines, and the carver became poorer and poorer, so each carving was less beautiful than the last, and looked less and less like the original model. When several days had passed since the woodcarver had eaten, his carvings were grotesque and no longer resembled anything recognizeable. Then his god took pity on him and decided to make such a spectacle that people would come from far and wide to see it. So he caused the carved figure to come to life. The woodcarver was terrified by this at first, but then he thought: Curiosity seekers and wisemen and people from foreign lands will come to see this spectacle, and I will be rich and powerful. The beautiful animated carvings, which he had made in days of poverty and then of hunger, now greeted him and smiled at him. But the monstrous carvings menaced him and leered evilly at him, and the last one that he had fashioned began to drag itself along on its mishappen torso, trying to approach him to devour him. Horrified, the woodcarver pleaded for mercy so plaintively that his god took pity on him again and turned the monstrous figures into ashes while preserving the beautiful ones. And the woodcarver found among these a very beautiful woman whom he married and with whom he was happy for a time, and rich, too, exhibiting his animated figurines to the curious and the wise. But the woman, despite being of flesh, thanks to the transformation wrought by the woodcarver's god, still had a soul of wood, and she tyrannized him mercilessly for the rest of his life, causing him to frequently plead tearfully with his god to please transform the figures back into inanimate matter, since although he would lose his wealth, this would free him from his wife. But this time his god did not choose to listen to him."

I was left mulling over the significance of this and wondering what it had to do with the boy's tooth. Everyone else seemed to have understood because they smiled and nodded and looked at the Ancient Master and looked at me, but I couldn't make anything of it so I smiled without looking at anyone, and this seemed to be the right thing. We all, except for my stomach, seemed to be quite content.

Just then the boy returned with a pair of pliers. Made of wood. And offered them to me. I was going to have to make do with these, and I was sorry for his sake. I took hold of the pliers and said to him as gently as I could that in order to act as the instrument of his god, first I had to know his name. I'd gotten this idea that I had to know what his name was.

"Which of my names?" he asked.

Apparently there were questions one could ask. But the bad part was that I didn't know how to answer him.

"The name that I should use," I ventured.

I had guessed right again.

"Sadropersi," he said.

For me, he was always Percy.

"All right, Sadropersi, lie down on the ground and open your mouth."

I seemed to have stopped blundering, and I felt much surer of myself.

He lay down and opened his mouth, not without glancing over at the Ancient Master, and I indicated to some of the others that they should hold down his arms, legs and head. It was a terrible struggle, but I managed to pull out his tooth. I had it very slowly, moving it back and forth from one side to the other before pulling it so the pliers wouldn't break. And it must have hurt him more than the tortures of hell. But he didn't move or complain a single time. Tears were running down his face and blood filled his mouth; I was afraid he would choke, and every once in a while I lifted his head and made him spit. Finally I showed him the tooth held up in the pliers, and they all breathed great sighs as though I had pulled a tooth out of each of them.

The Ancient Master smiled and told us another parable:

"A woman was frying cakes in oil while she waited for her husband. But she ran out of oil while she still had dough left. She asked one of her neighbors for oil, but she was turned down. She went to one of her other neighbors who also refused her the oil to finish frying her cakes. Angry, the woman started to scream and yell insults at her neighbors, making those who passed by curious, until one of them yelled at her, 'Make your own oil and don't cause trouble!' Then the woman went out behind her house and cut the seeds of the plant called zyminia, ground them, and pressed them in cloth, thus extracting the oil that she needed. When her husband got home, she brought out the cakes on two platters, and told him, 'These are fried in the oil bought from the oil vendor, and these others are cooked in the oil I extracted from the plant called zyminia.' And her husband ate from both platters, and the cakes cooked in the oil extracted by his wife tasted better to him than the others."

Percy smiled more openly than the others, and I did, too, nodding. I'd prepared the ground now, and I just had to wait a little until I could ask the boy to tell me how to get to the Director. And while I was thinking about this and about my empty stomach, mealtime arrived. Nothing announced it, neither a bell nor a call nor jailers with whips, nothing. But the Ancient Master stood up, and after him everyone else, and we walked over to one of the doors and entered the warm interior of the prison. After crossing through some poorly marked areas where we blindly followed the lead of the very old man, we reached the big dining room on the first floor. We went up and down so many stairs that if I had been told I was on the sixth floor, I'd have believed it. But out the windows, we could see the main floor, the eaves and balconies of the other floors, and the white salt flats in the sunlight. Many men were cooking at stone hearths built into the floor, and as we entered, we divided ourselves into groups and headed for the hearths. We all squatted down around ours, the man who was cooking handed wooden bowls filled with the reddish paste and we ate.

I saw that others were doing what I wanted to do, which was to ask for more, and when I finished my bowl full, I asked for another. I drank a lot of water, and as on the day before, I felt satisfied.

The day went by without any other incident, and the night was peaceful. Percy seemed happy and looked at me gratefully. There was no other meal that day, but I was not hungry again. Having solved the problems of food and Percy's tooth, I had to think about how I would go about reaching the Director and what I would say when I had done so. But when I went to bed, I was so sleepy that I fell asleep before I could plan anything.

Again the next day, the morning began with the jailers' insults and shouts, which were received with the same indifference by the prisoners. Then the conversations in the courtyard, the meal, more conversations, always about numbers, and another night. I decided that I would talk to Percy:

"Sadropersi, esteemed friend," I was trying to learn, or at least imitate, the prisoners' way of speaking, "I would like to take a bath."

Percy got very worried; "Take a bath, amiable sir?" he asked, looking quickly all around him. "We are bathed by the gentlemen jailers."

"Don't tell me that those brutes scrub our backs with horsehair gloves?"

"The estimable gentlemen jailers," (it would seem that I should not have called them brutes), "fumigate, disinfect and bathe the prisoners periodically, excellent sir and companion."

"All right," I said. "When is the next time they will fumigate, disinfect and bathe us?"

But Percy didn't know. He thought that it might be soon because the last session had taken place a long time ago, and I had to content myself with washing with water from the basin.

This night was peaceful, too, and before going to sleep, I indulged a bit in feeling sorry for myself. Here I was, discoverer of worlds, shut up in a ridiculous prison with a ridiculous name, among people who spoke in a ridiculous way, humiliated and not victorious, demeaned and not exalted. And what would happen to my ship and my men? And more importantly, how was I going to get out of here? When I reached the end of this black train of thought, I fell asleep.

The next day, I again managed to draw Percy aside in the bathroom and explained my need to see the Director.

"The most distinguished director cannot be seen by anyone, amiable sir."

I suppressed the desire to speak loudly and inconsiderately of the Director's mother and Percy's mother.

"Tell me, amiable Sadropersi, what if someone stirs up a riot, don't they take him to see the Directr?"

I was asking questions, too many questions, but it wasn't this that caught Percy's attention.

"A riot, most excellent foreign sir and amiable companion! No one starts a riot."

"I know that, of course. But in the theoretical and highly improbable case in which I were to begin a fight in the courtyard, wouldn't they take me to the Director so he could punish me?"

He seemed to think this over.

"No one would fight with you, amiable companion," he finally said.

Damn you, Percy, I thought, and I gave him a wide smile:

"All right, all right, let's forget it. It was an academic question."

He smiled, too, and remarked, "There is much to be said in favor of the academies, most distinguished sir."

He had called me most distinguished, which was an honor, probably remembering the tooth business. Now that his jaw was not swollen, he was a handsome boy and it was understandable why they would choose him for lovemaking. I felt very uneasy. As for the enigmatic observation about academies, I let it pass; the last thing I'd want would be for them to exchange, in my honor, the topic of numbers, which I was getting used to, for that of the academies, about which I knew nothing. I didn't know anything about numbers either, of course, not anything that related to how they were discussing them at any rate.

We sat in the courtyard until mealtime, we ate and returned to the courtyard, and the Ancient Master recounted another parable.

"In the olden days, men were very unhappy because they lost their possessions, even the most insignificant and small of them, each time they moved from place to place. They took with them only their wives and children and relatives, at least those who were able to walk; the very old ones got left behind. And all this because they had not yet invented transport. Men traveled with their hands empty, lamenting the loss of the household goods and articles of clothing that stayed behind when they moved. But one man who needed to move to a distant city, had a wife he loved deeply. The woman was sick, she couldn't walk, and the man wept with grief, thinking that he would have to abandon her. He went up to the bed where she lay and embraced her so tightly that he lifted her up. Surprised, he took a few steps with the woman in his arms, and he took another few steps, and he walked out of his house carrying his wife and started out on the road. People came from everywhere to watch him go by, and pretty soon everyone understood that it was possible to carry whatever could be held from one place to another. Then great crowds could be seen going from one place to another carrying furniture, household goods, tapestries, books, jewels, and adornments. This went on for a long time, with people traveling in all directions and the roads and paths packed with happy people who showed each other what they were carrying, until everyone got used to this and no one was surprised any longer by the sight of a man carrying a sack in his arms."

Every time the very old man recounted a parable, I made an honest effort to understand its meaning. Needless to say, I never succeeded. This one about the invention of transport was no exception; it just seemed stupid to me, although once in a while I remember it and wonder again if there wasn't some important meaning hidden in it somewhere.

That infernal night the men assembled themselves again wanting to fornicate, and I didn't go to bed; I stayed with the group, and no one seemed to take notice. The Ancient Master designated Percy again, and two others who were not the same as the last time. The other two stripped off their clothes immediately, but Percy threw himself crying at the feet of the very old man, pleading with him to let him stay with the group and not be singled out again. I don't know what was going on in my mind. I felt sorry for the boy, and it seemed to me a dirty shame that he should be sacrificed twice in a row if he didn't want to be, but at the same time I was glad because I desired him, and I felt ashamed of both things, of desiring him and of being glad.

The Ancient Master told him in his soft contralto voice that he forgave him because he was too young to be able to distinguish between the convenient and the inconvenient, but he, Percy, already knew that questioning his commands was not allowed and that he should submit and obey as he had been ordered to do. Percy stopped crying then, and said yes. And the very old man told him that he, Percy, should plead, as a favor, that he should be allowed to be used by the others. Right there I hated the old man, but this seemed fine to everyone else, even to Percy, who smiled and said:

"Oh Ancient One, venerable and eminent Master, I beg you as a special and undeserved favor to my unworthy self that you should allow me to awaken the lust of my amiable companions."

The very old man allowed himself the disgusting comedy of pretending that he couldn't quite make up his mind, and Percy had to plead again. I stepped back, infuriated, and decided not to take part in such vileness. But when Percy stripped off his clothes and smiled at us, I went up to him although I was careful to stand behind him so that he wouldn't see my face. When it was all finished, I went off to sleep, tranquil and sad.

I was used to the routine of waking up, but that morning it seemed to me that the jailers insults were directed personally at me. I almost wished they would approach me with their whips and lash me. Not for having mounted Percy, but for feeling as happy as I did. Percy, on the other hand, treated me the same as always, and I had to make an effort to answer him naturally, and to look at him.

I had to distract myself; at all costs I had to think about something else and feel something else. In the courtyard, while the converstaion about numbers continued—here's a good question that I heard that morning: Is it possible to construct another universe using other numbers, or to change the universe by changing the numbers?—I thought again how to get out of there. Escape seemed to be the only possibility open to me, if I were to believe Percy, and there was no reason not to believe him, about how no one could get to the Director. But before that, I would try and speak openly with the Ancient Master, despite despising him for what he had done to Percy, since he did seem to be the most important of all the prisoners. I wondered why the very old man was there. For corrupting minors, probably. But what about Percy? And those were the sort of questions that could not be asked, surely.

After the meal, another man from another group came over to ask permission to greet the eminent foreigner. This was the second time I had been called eminent. With the usual formalities, the very old man granted permission, and we exchanged greetings and good wishes. What he wanted (though he didn't say so, I had to say it for him once I noticed) was that I should have a look at his mouth because he had a toothache. I found a huge ugly hole in one of his upper molars. I told him that I would take it out for him. There was another round of good wishes, and, inevitably, the Ancient Master told a parable.

"Once upon a time long ago, there was a man who had a plow with which he tilled his fields. Later he sowed them at the appropriate time and sat down to watch the young plants grow, and when the time was ready, harvested an abundant crop. But one terrible day the animal got sick, and seeing that it wasn't recovering, the man decided to kill it and sell its meat and its wool. Since he no longer had a work animal, he pulled the plow through the furrows himself, but the work went very slowly, and the sowing and harvesting were late and the yield not so great as before. When a neighbor saw him toiling away, he said to him, 'Miserable man, if you had been prudent and you had just waited, the animal probably would have recovered and now you wouldn't be worn out by work and impoverished by the lack of a good harvest.' And the man realized his neighbor was right, and he sat down at the end of his field and tearfully lamented for a long time."

Clear as a bell, I said to myself. If the man hadn't killed the animal, one of two things could have happened: either it would have recovered, in which case it would have kept pulling the plow for him, or it would have died, in which case he could still have sold the meat and the wool. But aside from a superficial condemnation of haste, I couldn't see that there was anything there of such importance that it should have provoked everyone's veneration. I put the question aside because the imminent extraction of another molar had put me on the spot, and the very old man was explaining the crime I had committed to my patient.

"The honorable foreign gentlemen disembarked on our shore

without previously transmitting any greeting with his ship lights and without going around in a circle three times," he was saying.

I felt obliged to defend myself when I saw the stricken face of the fellow with the decayed molar.

"In the first place," I said, "I didn't even know that this land was inhabited; and in the second place, even if I had known that, how could I possibly have been aware of the protocol which requires luminous greetings and circling around? Besides, I haven't been brought before any judge, nor have I been permitted to speak in my defense, all of which in my country would be considered an act of barbarism."

They were all very serious, and the Ancient Master told me that nature is the same everywhere, which I might or might not agree with but that's irrelevant, and that ignorance of a law is no excuse for not obeying it. I didn't smash him in the face because the arrival of Percy with the wooden pliers allowed me to think a little and remember that I needed the good will of the very old man. I spoke again about names, which of the names I should use, and the fellow with the decayed molar told me his name was Sematrodio. I had him lie down and began my work on him. It was difficult, more than in Percy's case, because the tooth wasn't as loose as Percy's rotten one, but to make up for that, there was less blood, and once again I was rousingly successful and called most distinguished.

Luckily, that day there were no more parables, but in the evening, the Ancient Master called me to him. After praising me he said that perhaps my sentence would be a short one due to my being a foreigner come from distant lands, surely no longer than twenty years. I think I almost passed out. Twenty years! I'm sure I closed my eyes and slumped to the ground.

"I understand your feeling," the very old man said to me, "I will probably die here inside, since I was accused, very justly, of improper use of two descriptive adjectives, two, mind you, during the course of an official banquet." He sighed. "That's why I want to give you, honorable foreigner and friend, a keepsake to take back to your foreign land when you return to it."

And from under his shirt he pulled a bundle of papers tied with a cord. My mind was filled by one thought: twenty years, twenty years, twenty years!

"Here you have," the very old man was telling me and I made myself listen, "a copy of the *Ordering That Which Is And Canon Of Appearances*. Keep it, eminent foreign sir, read it and meditate upon it; I know that it will serve you as consolation, illustration and guide."

I took the papers. Twenty years, how could that be possible? Twenty years! The very old man turned around and closed his eyes, and I went and lay down but hardly slept that night.

And at dawn, to try to forget about the twenty years, so appalling a thought it blocked my ability to plan an escape or a way of seeing the Director or anything that would allow me to leave there to look for my crew and get to my ship, I pulled out the papers and started leafing through them in the light reflected from the white salt flats outside. I understood about as much as I did of the numbers or of the very old man's parables. It was like a catalog with explanations, but it didn't make any sense at all. I remember, I read it so many times: "The System orders the world into three catagories: ante, proximate, and so. The first includes the forces, insects, numbers, music, water, and white minerals. The second includes men, fruit, drawing, liquor, temples, birds, red metals, predictions and sun-loving plants. The third includes foods, animals covered with fur or scales, the word, sacrifices, weapons, mirrors, black metals, shade-loving plants and keys." It went on this way, with lists and more lists, each seeming more ridiculous than the last. At the end, there were precepts and poems, and, on the last page, a sentence that spoke of a cord which tied together all the ideas, which I assumed was the cord around the bundle that the very old man had given me, in which case, the papers would be the ideas. And thinking about my sentence, with the bundle of papers tied by the cord put away under my shirt, I got up, went to the courtyard, ate and spent the rest of the day.

That night there was another council of men who clamored for someone to fornicate with, and I feared for Percy and for myself. But even though my fears for myself were justified, it was not a matter of the pleasure I'd have taken in seeing Percy chosen again, rather it was because it occurred to the evil old man to choose me, me, to be the female for the others, me. I was indignant, and I told him I couldn't care less what wasn't allowed, that I was a real man and no one was going to take advantage of me, no one. The very old man smiled and said a few pompous stupid things; it seemed that being selected was a show of deference, esteem and respect. I told him they could just start respecting others because I didn't plan to allow myself to be respected.

"Ah, honorable foreign sir and friend," said the very old man, "but in that case, who would give you food, who would provide you with asylum, who would receive you in his group, who would make your life bearable in the Sweet Memory of Flowering Juleps?"

Oh drop dead, I thought, and was just about to answer: "Percy would." But I didn't say it, of course, thinking of what the boy could expect if I did say it. The very old man waited, I suppose he was waiting for me to drop my pants, which I didn't do. Instead I stepped up and smashed him with my fist like I'd been waiting to do since that night when he had made Percy offer himself to everyone. Blood ran down his face, there was a heavy silence in the whole dormitory, and the very old man recounted a parable. He told a parable there, like that, with his split lips and bloody nose, and I listened to him waiting until he finished so I could go over and hit him again.

"Long, long ago," he said, "there was a boy who grew into a man. Once he had reached the age when he needed a woman, he latched on to a third cousin and wanted to marry her. But his father had chosen their neighbor's daughter for him in order to unite the two properties and commanded the son to obey him. The young man turned a deaf ear to his father's words, and one night he eloped with his cousin and fled with her to the forest. They lived happily eating fruit and small birds and drinking spring water until his father's servants found them and took them back home. There they celebrated, with pomp and ceremony, the wedding of the young man and the neighbor's daughter, and they shut the third cousin up in a cage where she was exposed to public scorn in the village square."

This parable I did understand. And since I understood it, instead of giving the very old man another blow, I grabbed him by the neck and twisted it until it broke. I left him there, thrown on the ground where he always slept, with his face bloody and his head at a right angle to his neck, and I yelled at them all:

"Get to sleep!"

And they all obeyed me and went to their mats. I fell asleep immediately and on the following morning I wasn't awakened by the jailers' insults but rather by a deafening shouting. Everyone was running back and forth yelling "disinfection, disinfection!" I saw a big group of jailers enter with whips in their hands. This time they used them: they lashed out blindly, and all the men raced naked around and around the bare dormitory trying to get away. I tried to get away, too, as ineffectively as the others. Suddenly the jailers lined up on either side of the corner door, and others came in with hoses. Icy water sprayed at us all; here was the bathing I had been wanting, splashing against our bodies, pinning us to the walls and the floor. Then I saw that the only one not moving was the Ancient Master and I remembered that I had killed him and why. The jailers must have seen him at the same time I did because a command was shouted out and the hoses stopped spurting icy water. One of the jailers went up to the old man's body, touched it, and the already blackened head wobbled from one side to the other.

"Who did this?," he yelled.

"I did," I said as I stepped forward.

I thought: if they condemned me to twenty years for not greeting them properly, for this they will shoot me down on the spot. I wasn't even afraid.

"Get dressed and follow us."

I put on my shirt and pants, and grabbed, who knows why, the bundle of papers the very old man had given me, looked over at Percy, and went with the jailers.

I'd gotten what I'd wanted, anyway: they took me to see the Director.

"I've heard about it," he said to me. "You've killed a Master."

"Yes," I responded.

"Take him away," he told the jailers.

They took me back to the room where they had stripped me and checked me over and dressed me as a prisoner, and they gave me back all my things. At least I was going to die as a Captain and not as a prisoner, as though it mattered. But I felt comforted. I put the *Ordering Of That Which Is And Canon Of Appearances* in the right pocket of my jacket. We returned to the Director's office.

"Foreign sir," he said to me, "you will be taken back to your ship and you are requested to return to your homeland as quickly as possible. The action you have committed has no precedence in our long history, and you will do us the favor of pardoning and understanding us when we say that it is impossible for us to keep a person like you in one of our public establishments any longer. Goodbye."

"And my men?" I asked.

"Goodbye," repeated the Director, and the jailers took me out of there.

They took me to the ship. Parked on a green slope, so different from the salt flats where the Sweet Memory of Flowering Juleps was built, she seemed to be waiting for me. I gave her a military salute, which astounded the jailers; I went over to her and opened the hatch.

"Goodbye," I said in my turn, but they didn't answer me, and it didn't matter to me because it wasn't to them I was saying goodbye.

I looked all around me to see if my personal god was coming along with me, and I set out straight for Earth, with the sun of Colatinus, as I myself had named the world I had discovered, shining directly on the fuselage and on the distant fields and mountains. Goodbye, I said again, and I began to read the *Ordering Of That Which Is And Canon Of Appearances* with some attention, to amuse myself on my solitary voyage home.

Translated by Mary G. Berg.

# The Resurrection of the Flesh

## Angélica Gorodischer

She was thirty-two her, name was Aurelia, and she had been married eleven years. One Saturday afternoon, she looked through the kitchen window at the garden and saw the four horsemen of the Apocalypse. Men of the world, those four horsemen of the Apocalypse. And good-looking. The first from the left was riding a sorrel horse with a dark mane. He was wearing white breeches, black boots, a crimson jacket, and a yellow fez with black pompoms. The second one had a sleeveless tunic overlaid with gold and violet and was barefoot. He was riding on the back of a plump dolphin. The third one had a respectable, black beard, trimmed at right angles. He had donned a gray Prince of Wales suit, white shirt, blue tie and carried a black leather portfolio. He was seated on a folding chair belted to the back of white-haired dromedary. The fourth one made Aurelia smile and realize that they were smiling at her. He was riding a black and gold Harley-Davidson 1200 and was wearing a white helmet and dark goggles and had long, straight, blond hair flying in the wind behind him. The four were riding in the garden without moving from the spot. They rode and smiled at her and she watched them through the kitchen window. In that manner, she finished washing the two teacups, took off her apron, arranged her hair and went to the living room.

"I saw the four horsemen of the Apocalypse in the garden," she told her husband.

"I'll bet," he said without raising his eyes from his paper.

"What are you reading?" Aurelia asked.

"Hmmm?"

"I said they were given a crown and a sword and a balance and power."

"Oh, right," said her husband.

And after that a week went by as all weeks do—very slowly at first and very quickly toward the end—and on Sunday morning, while she made the coffee, she again saw the four horsemen of the Apocalypse in the garden, but when she went back to the bedroom she didn't say anything to her husband.

The third time she saw them, one Wednesday, alone, in the afternoon, she stood looking at them for a half hour and finally, since she had always wanted to fly in a yellow and red dirigible; and since she had dreamed about being an opera singer, an emperor's lover, a co-pilot to Icarus; since she would have liked to scale black cliffs, laugh at cannibals, traverse the jungles on elephants with purple trappings, seize with her hands the diamonds that lay hidden in mines, preside in the nude over a parade of nocturnal monsters, live under water, domesticate spiders, torture the powerful of the earth, rob trains in the tunnels of the Alps, set palaces on fire, lie in the dark with beggars, climb on the bridges of all the ships in the world; finally—since it was sadly sterile to be a rational and healthy adult—finally, that Wednesday afternoon alone, she put on the long dress she had worn at the last New Year's party given by the company where her husband was assistant sales manager and went out to the garden. The four horsemen of the Apocalypse called her, the blond one on the Harley-Davidson gave her his hand and helped her up onto the seat behind him, and there they went, all five, raging into the storm and singing.

Two days later her husband gave in to family pressure and reported the disappearance of his wife.

"Moral: madness is a flower aflame," said the narrator. Or in other words, it's impossible to inflame the dead, cold, viscous, useless, and sinful ashes of common sense.

Translated by Lorraine Elena Roses.

# Annunciations

# When Everything Shines

## Liliana Hecker

Everything began with the wind. It all began when Daisy told her husband all about the wind. He hadn't even managed to shut the door to the house. He remained frozen in the position of shutting it, with his arm stretching toward the latch, and his eyes fixed on the eyes of his wife. It seemed like he was going to remain in this perpetual position, until finally, he howled. His reaction was surprising. For several seconds the two remained motionless, studying each other, as if they were trying to confirm in the presence of the other that which had just happened, that is, until Daisy broke the spell. With familiarity, almost with tenderness, as if nothing had happened, she leaned one hand against the arm of her husband in order to maintain her equilibrium while with the other, she pushed the door softly shut and then with her right foot and a felt slipper, removed from the floor the dust that had entered.

"How was your day, dear?" she asked.

And she asked it less out of curiosity (given the circumstances, she wasn't expecting an answer, nor did she receive one) than from a need to reestablish a ritual. She had to communicate with him succinctly by means of her habitual late afternoon question and transmit a message to him. *Be that as it may, everything is in order. Nothing has happened. Nothing new can happen.*

She finished cleaning the entrance and let go of her husband's arm. He withdrew suddenly toward the direction of the bedroom and left with the impression that a butterfly leaves behind in the fingers, when it frees itself quickly from the one who had held it by the wings. He hadn't used his slippers; this is how Daisy knew that her husband was furious. Without a doubt, he was exaggerating. When all is said and done, she had not asked him to hurl himself nude from the top of the obelisk. With her own slippers, she cleaned the shoe scuffs that he had left behind. However, she did not enter the bedroom: she knew that it was better not to add fuel to the fire. Right at the door, she changed her course and headed to the kitchen; later on she would find a more appropriate moment to talk to him about the wind.

She had just finished preparing supper (At first, so as to please him in spite of it being Wednesday, she had thought about having some steak with French fries, but she quickly changed her mind: vaporized grease saturates the cupboards, it saturates the walls, and even saturates the desire to live; if one leaves it floating around from Wednesday until Monday, which is the day of heavy duty cleaning, the grease has enough time to penetrate to the very pores of things and stay there forever. Therefore, Daisy took a frozen dinner from the freezer and put it in the oven.) and was setting the table when she heard her husband enter the bathroom. A minute later, like a good omen, the happy hum of the shower echoed through the house.

It was time to go to the bedroom. Daisy barely had entered when she verified that he had left everything in a state of disarray. She brushed his jacket and pants and hung them up, and then she made a little pile out of his shirt and socks and went to the bathroom and knocked on the door.

"I am going to enter, dear" she said sweetly.

He didn't answer but sang softly. Daisy took the undershirt and underwear and added them to the little pile. She washed enthusiastically. When she turned off the faucet, she heard him humming the waltz "Above the Waves" in the living room. The storm had subsided.

However, early the next morning, while they were eating breakfast and half-smiling so as to diminish the importance of the episode of the previous day, Daisy mentioned the thing about the wind. It was rather silly, she was ready to admit this, but it would cost so little; wasn't it true? He did not have to think about complicating his life in any way. All she simply asked was that when the wind blew from the north, he enter through the back door that faced south; and when it blew from the south, that he enter through the front door that faced north. A rather whimsical request, if that's how he wished to see it, but it would help her so much, he simply could not imagine. She had noticed that as much as she swept and polished, the floor of the vestibule always filled up with dirt whenever there was a north wind. Certainly, he could enter through anywhere he felt like when the wind blew from the east or from the west. And it wasn't even necessary to talk about the times when there was no wind at all.

"I know you don't think this is important enough to make such an issue over," she said, and then giggled.

He stood up and looked as if he were about to give a speech, cleared his throat loudly, almost with pleasure, and then gently stooped over, spit on the floor, recovered his earlier position, and left the kitchen with measured steps.

Daisy remained motionless, staring in vain at the circle of spittle shining in the light of the morning sun as though it were a tiny being from another planet on the floor of her kitchen. A door shut and opened, some walls rumbled, footsteps resounded through the house, another door shut with a clamoring noise. Daisy's mind barely detected the events Her entire being seemed to converge on the tiny spot on the floor. *An infectious spot.* A feeling of disgust lightly fluttered around in her head; it expanded like a wave and flooded her thoughts. On the bus when people cough, they spread invisible little drops of saliva, each droplet carrying thousands of germs, how many germs are there in... Thousands of millions of germs shook, jumped with joy and bounced about on the red tile. Mechanically, Daisy took the first thing that she had in her hand: a cloth napkin. Kneeling on the floor, she began to scrub the tile energetically. It was useless: the more she scrubbed, the more the sticky zone stood out like a stigma. *Flat germs creeping along like amoebas.* Daisy left the napkin on top of the table and went to soak a little sponge in detergent. She scrubbed the tile with the sponge and dumped a pail of water over it. She was about to dry the floor, when she came to a complete stop. Had she gone crazy? Hadn't she used a napkin for. . .? Good heavens, and to think how easy it is to raise a napkin to the lips. She picked it up with a pointed object and studied it with terror. What could she do now? Washing it did not seem to be very wise; therefore, she filled a pan with water, put it on the stove, and then tossed in the napkin.

She was rubbing the table with disinfectant (the napkin had been in contact with the table for a long time) when the telephone rang. She went to answer it and barely went beyond the door of the bedroom when she noticed something unusual, something that revealed itself to her like a weight hanging over her chest and whose reality she could not confirm until she hung up the phone and opened the closet door. Because it was not until then that she found out exactly what had happened; his clothing wasn't there. Very well, he had left, how marvelously fine, was she going to cry because of this? She was not going to cry. Was she going to pull out her hair and bang her head up against the walls? She was not going to pull out her hair, much less bang her head against the walls. Is the loss of a man something that should be lamented? As untidy as they are, so dirty—they cut bread on top of the table, they leave behind scuff marks from their dirty shoes, they open up doors against the wind, they spit on the floor and one can never keep her house clean, the body, one can never keep her body clean either, in the night they are like dribbling beasts, oh their breath and their sweat, oh their semen, the disgusting moisture of love, because my God, You who could do everything, why did You make love so unclean, the bodies of Your children so filled with filth, the world

You created so filled with rubbish? But never again. Never ever again in her house. Daisy pulled the sheets off the bed, removed the curtains from their rods, picked up the rugs, removed and dusted and brushed until her knuckles turned red and her arms began to cramp. She washed the walls, waxed the floors, polished the metal, got shimmering lusters from the pans, gave a diamond-like sparkle to the banisters, bathed bucolic porcelain shepardesses as if they were adored children, burnished wood, perfumed closets, whitened opaque surfaces, and polished alabaster figurines. And at seven in the evening, like a painter who puts his signature on a painting that he has dreamt about all his life, she shook the large broom into the garbage can.

She then breathed in deeply the wax-scented air and cast a rather long glance of satisfaction at her surroundings. She captured dazzling lights, savored the whiteness, tasted the transparencies, and noticed that a little bit of dust had fallen out of the garbage can while she was shaking the broom. She swept it up, gathered it with the dust pan and then emptied it into the can. She shook the broom again, but this time with greater care, so that not even a speck of dust would fall out of the can. She put it away in the closet where she was also going to put the pan when a thought suddenly worried her: people are usually careless when it comes to dust pans; they use them to pick up all sorts of garbage, but it never occurs to them that a little of that garbage must remain stuck to their surface. She decided to wash the pan. She covered it with detergent and scrubbed it with a brush while a dark liquid spilled into the sink. Although Daisy let the water run, a black stain still remained at the bottom of the basin. She cleaned it with a sudsy rag, rinsed out the basin, and then washed the rag. Then she remembered the brush. She washed it and dirtied the basin again. She scrubbed the sink with the rag and realized that if she now washed the rag in the sink again, this was going to be an endless business. The most reasonable thing to do was burn the rag. First she dried it with the hair dryer and then she took it out to the street where she set it on fire. Just as she entered the house, a blast of wind came in from the north and Daisy could not ignore the fact that some ashes had blown into the living room.

It was better not to use the big broom, which was now already clean. She used a small rag with a little bit of wax (because with rags it is always possible to set them on fire). But it was a mistake. The color remained uneven. She polished and spread the wax to an even wider territory; it was all useless!

At about five o'clock in the morning all the floors of the house were scrubbed, but a red dust still floated in the air, covered the furniture and stuck to the baseboards. Daisy opened the windows, she swept (later on she would find the time to clean the broom and in the worst scenario, she could throw it out) and was finishing the cleaning of the baseboards when she noticed that a little water had spilled. She looked at the water stains on the floor with dismay; she was getting tired and by the color of the sky it must have been almost seven in the morning. She decided to put this off until later; with luck she would not have to scrub all the floors again. She jumped into bed with her clothes on (later she must not forget to change the sheets again) and fell asleep immediately but the water stains expanded, softened and extended their tentacles. They had trapped her. They were a swamp in which Daisy was sinking fast and furious. She woke up frightened. She had not even slept half an hour. She got up and went to see the stains; they were already pretty dry but they had not disappeared. She scrubbed the area, but it never remained the same color. A light dizzy spell made her fall; she opened her eyes dreamily, vaguely glimpsed the streaks and sighed; she guessed she had not eaten anything in the last twenty four hours. She got up and went to the kitchen.

A warm meal would perhaps make her feel better, but maybe not—afterward she would have to wash the pots. She opened the refrigerator and was about to take out an apple when a wave of terror invaded her thoughts. She had not swept away the dust settlings and the windows were still open. She withdrew her hand brusquely from the refrigerator and knocked down a little basket of eggs. She watched the yellow viscous puddle spreading slowly. She thought she was going to cry. But there was no way she was going to do that; one thing at a time. Now she would sweep away the dust settlings; the kitchen floor would have its turn, nothing like a little bit of order. She looked for the big broom and the dust pan, she went to the living room, and when she was about to start sweeping, she noticed the soles of her shoes. Without a doubt, they were not clean; they had traced a discontinuous path of egg across the parquet floor. Seeing herself with the broom and pan almost made Daisy laugh. *Dust settlings* she murmured, *dust settlings.* She remembered, however, that she still hadn't eaten anything, so she left behind the broom and the pan and went to the kitchen.

The apple was in the center of the yellow puddle. Daisy picked it up avidly bit into it and suddenly realized that it was absurd not to prepare a warm meal, now that everything was a little dirty. She therefore put the pan over the fire, peeled potatoes (it was pleasant letting the long spiral potato peels sink lightly into the yolks and whites, now that everything had begun to get dirty and, in any event would have to be cleaned much later), put the steak on the grill and the oil in the skillet. The grease sizzled happily, the potatoes sputtered and Daisy realized that she had forgotten to open the kitchen window; be that as it may, it was too late to worry— the vaporized grease had already penetrated her pores and those of other things; it had permeated her clothing and hair and thickened the air as well. The smell of meat and of fried potatoes entered her nasal passages, overwhelmed her and made her go mad with delight.

Impatience can make people a little clumsy. Some oil fell on the floor as she removed the potatoes; she scattered it furtively with her foot, took out the steak, dropped it on the floor and while she picked it up the closeness, the contact, the marvelous aroma of broiled meat intoxicated her. She could not resist sinking her teeth into it before setting it on the plate.

She ate ferociously. She put the dirty things in the sink but didn't wash them; she was very sleepy, the moment to wash everything would soon arrive. She turned on the faucet so that the water would run and headed toward the bedroom, but she never made it there. Before leaving the kitchen, the oil on the soles of her shoes made her slip, and she fell to the floor. In any event, she felt very comfortable on the floor. She leaned her head against the tiles and fell asleep. The water awakened her. Slightly greasy, it slithered around the kitchen, broke off into subtle streams along the joints of the tiles and, thinning out but persistent, advanced toward the dining room. Daisy had a slight headache. She immersed her hand in the water and refreshed her temples. She turned her head, stuck out her tongue as far as she could, and managed to drink: Now she felt much better. Perhaps she was a little disheveled, but she lacked the energy to get up and go to the bathroom. Anyway everything was now quite dirty.

*She must not dirty her little dress.* Daisy was six years old and she better not dirty her little dress. Not even her knees. She had to be very careful and not get her knees dirty. That is until nightfall, when a voice would shout: time to take a bath! Then she would run frenetically to the back of the house, roll about in the dirt and fill her hair, fingernails and ears with it; she had to feel that she was dirty, that each little corner of her body was dirty in order to be able to later submerge herself in the purifying bath, the bath that would carry away all the filth and leave Daisy as white and as radiant as a flower bud. *Do daisies have flower buds, mommy?* She felt an indescribable sense of well being. She moved away a little from the place where she had been lying and felt like laughing. Her finger pointed to a place that was next to her on the ground. Poop, she said. Her finger then sunk voluptuously into the excrement, and she wrote her name on the ground. *Daisy.* But it wasn't very noticeable on the red tile. She now got up without much effort and wrote on the wall. *Shit.* Then she signed *Daisy* and drew a big heart around the inscription. A blast of air against her back made her shiver. The wind. It entered through the opened windows, dragged in the dust from the street, dragged in the world's garbage that stuck to the walls and to her name and heart; it mixed with the water that ran into the dining room, entered through her nose, her ears and her eyes and dirtied her little dress.

Five days later, on a luminous sunny day with a glorious blue sky and singing birds, Daisy's husband stopped before a flower stand.

"Daisies," said the vendor. "The whitest in the world. Many daisies."

With an enormous bunch of flowers, he walked toward his house. Before putting the key in the door, however, he performed a little charade, a roguish act that was filled with love and worthy of being viewed by a loving wife who would be spying behind the sheer window curtains: he sucked his index finger and raising it like a banner, analyzed the direction of the wind. It was coming from the north. The man, therefore, docily and happily relishing the unequaled taste of reconciliation, went around his house. Whistling a festive song, he opened the door, and a soft, gurgling splatter reached him from the kitchen.

Tranlated by Celeste Kostopulos-Cooperman.

# The Annunciation

## Cristina Peri Rossi

The Virgin Mary appeared while I was collecting stones from the water. I collect the big stones, not the little ones. She seemed to come from the sea, although I'm not really sure because the water is everywhere you look, and I was stooped over, my head down, collecting stones. I lift them out of the water, pick out the best, carry them in my arms and take them up to shore. At first I didn't think it was the Virgin.

*That morning it was gray and lead-colored like the sea.*

I had seen her only once before, in church, when we took her out for a procession. I never thought I'd see her walking down the beach with those special colored eyes and that sadness over the death of her son. I couldn't imagine it because I'm always alone and because she didn't have her crown, that Virgin's crown, but there she was, softly stamping down the sand under her feet. But then, I didn't doubt it for an instant. There's never anyone on this beach, hidden away as it is and somewhat far from the rest of the land. It's so remote, isolated, and only has the sea for company. I'm always alone, collecting stones. At first my hands freeze and my fingers slip; my fingers that want to grab onto the stones and hunt them as if they were sea animals. Whale stones, mountains from the sea. Straight ahead, down below, and to both sides, all you see is water, green and blue water, yellowish water, and enormous rocks stuck there like boats run aground. I plunge my hands in, and my fingers slip from the wet surfaces of the stones. The color of the stones changes when you take them out of the water. Sometimes they are full of moss and lichens, full of seaweed tangled up with sea urchins. But when your hands get used to it, they move through the water like fish. Then I rest them on the dark surface of a stone, take it between my fingers, and bring it up. Once the stones are hoisted up, I carry them to shore.

*We got here ten days ago, and since then we haven't seen anyone. Nobody has seen us.*

The fishermen's boats are tossed on the sand, abandoned. There are wildflowers growing up around the spongy boards of one of them, green stems and a white crown among the damp and splintered planks. It's dying slowly. It's dying, falling apart, lying there on the sand. A seagull flies overhead, its wings forming a cross, its chest dark, and it comes down lightly. It perches on the boat's useless oar, which is stuck, shaft first, into the sand. It used to be that when the fishermen went out to sea, in each boat there was a big lamp up front like an eye that lit up underwater secrets, the private life of the water and its fish, a round eye without lids, with a powerful and serene gaze. The fishermen used to clean it, scrub it, adjust its light, watch over it. Now their lamps rest caked with rust and drip their menstrual blood on to the sand.

*Just a little boy who plays in the water and collects stones.*

Sometimes a ship goes by in the distance. The sand invades the shore and climbs over the empty boats. I collect stones and carry them away from the water so that when the waves lick up the shore they don't find them. I work like this all morning. I often get tired of carting stones. My fingers are cold and cramping, the air is green, the trees roar with the wind, the waves howl, and I can tell there is some disturbance; the atmosphere, the elements are preparing something, something is developing in the sea's womb. But when

I look at the water and see so many stones beneath, I go back to my work right away without getting distracted, without stopping because there are so many more at the bottom. The water goes through my legs when I squat down, the water and some small fish, silvery, agile and uneasy. I don't know if they see me. I've never known what or how fish see, nor where they are looking, with those big, staring eyes. I don't know if they look through the water, if their glances are scattered among the stones and the seaweed at the bottom. I was never a fish. I didn't have fins on my side, I wasn't born in the sea, I didn't eat seaweed.

*In such a lonely place.*

There are stones of many colors, I'd say of all the known colors and of some others that only come from the sea and from living in the sea among lichens and plants. She didn't wear a crown; she was walking slowly, floating over the sand.

*As if he weren't alone, as if the water, the stones, and the sound of the wind were his companions. Totally absorbed in his work and some- how understanding the harmony of the universe. He found his role, his function in this routine task, and he took it on with dignity and respect, with conviction. Only the gulls have been able to see us.*

I collect stones every day, even if it rains or is windy. Sometimes the sea is calm when I go in, calm and still like an elephant lying on its side sleeping. The boats don't move, and their masts look like crosses. The water then is very heavy, as if it were made of stone. It's solid water, water made of cement. Nothing moves on its surface, nothing moves below. The sea's activity stops; it becomes dense and all water looks the same: heavy. Motionless, it marks everything with its peace; even the birds seem to fly more slowly so as not to disturb it. Other times, the wind blows hard and the gulls can't fly. They stay a long time hanging in the air, their wings tensed and open, unfolded, but unable to go forward. They cry and don't move, as if a string kept them prisoners. And the sea is full of waves, waves that disappear in the misty atmosphere. Then the boats get nervous and try to flee from the storm and find refuge in the beach huts; there are some that are so eager to get away that they pull on their ropes until they cut loose, and once freed,

get silly, like wanton and wild girls, going this way and that, losing their way, bumping up against each other and against the rocks,
hitting their hips on the stones. The wind roars, the waves splash
over the wall, the red buoys sink in this turbulent sea, and after
an instant pop up again, keeping their heads up as if they were
shipwrecked and trying with all their might to keep afloat until
someone rescues them. The sea roars and everything seems like
it's just about to break: the gray and mauve sky into thunder and
lightning, the gulls' tense wings, the little stone and wooden pier,
the boats' ropes, the lanterns and masts that list from one side
to another.

*How has he ended up here? Who could have brought him?*

There are white statues under the sea. I've seen them: sculptured
images of women, sometimes missing an arm, sometimes a leg,
others an entire head. They are not always there; they aren't always
visible. Sometimes the colors of the sea cover them up totally; at
other times its the long string of seaweed and its inhabitants, the
sea urchins, that hide their presence. Driven so deeply into the
bottom of the sea, they could be mistaken for it, if the bottom
were white, if it had a woman's hips. They never come to the surface. No current lifts them up, places them on a water pedestal.
No force from the bottom of the sea hoists them, raises them like
a banner. They don't come up to look at the sky or to lie down
in the sand like bathers. There is nothing that makes them want
to leave the water. They don't dream about the air or touching
land. Sunk into the bottom of the sea, sometimes they let a leg
or white arm be seen, and they hide their figures, their delicate
hands, their tilted necks. They hide their secrets, aloof, among the
folds of their gowns, and the oblivious fish pass by, touching them
lightly, nibbling their breasts, licking their white necks. They are
totally different from the mutilated bodies that the sea sometimes
brings up from the depths of war and throws on to shore, with
their panic-stricken eyes and hair streaked with seaweed. Decent
people, silently and without getting involved, gather them up—
they don't have teeth, ears, fingers, hands—and bury them up in
the mountain. Unhappy people hide them in silence, studding the

forest and fouling the land with their bodies.

*How has he ended up here? Who could have brought him?*

I was picking up a stone when I saw her coming from far away. Then I didn't know who was coming. The morning was green and the sea was murky. I only saw a gray figure that was coming with the wind. The stone was heavy, and I had to hold it with both hands. I stole it from the bottom of the sea when it was still golden; the air immediately darkened it and the water had taken little bites out of its surface, like so many eyes that now looked at me. I put it on the sand, far away from the sea's incessant drilling and layering, and I went back to shore, not without first looking at the gray figure that was coming with the wind and slowly getting closer.

*"Who is the boy?"*

*"He comes and goes from the water as if the sea were his domain. As if only he reigned over the entire area. But humbly. Like a worker. Concentrating hard on his tasks. Without stopping, I think he never rests.*

That morning everything was green, gray and green like under the water, like the color of the fish parading among the stones.

*I couldn't turn back then because he had seen me. Anyway he was very caught up in his work of carrying stones.*

I went back and forth. Back and forth. There were a lot of stones on the bottom; the bottom is always full of stones and seaweed. She was slowly coming closer. Like the waves, like the wind, she was coming closer, crunching the sand uder her feet. She walked slowly without moving her arms, and it seemed that her legs were barely moving. I don't know if she came out of the water or where she came from because I was very busy with the stones, which were giving me a lot to do. I didn't look anywhere but straight ahead. I didn't look back or off to one side.

*I was going to keep on my way, happy that I had not done anything to arouse his interest, when suddenly he looked straight at me, as if he recognized me, as if he had seen me before. He drove his eyes right into me and slowly, very slowly, as if he were identifying me feature by feature, as if his memory were bringing back marks, fingerprints, he straightened up right in front of me, now completely sure.*

I was going to keep at my work; I was going to go back to the water and bend down to get another stone when I saw her. I looked at her from up close and I recognized her. I was fixed to the spot.

*I hesitated a second.*

*He was in front of me.*

*I thought about running away. Fleeing.*

It's not every day you see the Virgin coming out of the water. It's not every day she comes walking down the beach. She didn't seem to be wet, and her clothes were completely dry. She had eyes the color of the sea just like I'd seen at church one time when they put her out in public and took her on a procession through the town. We children and the old people carried her around like a trophy from the sea, as if she were a gigantic exotic fish that was going to feed us all year long. We took her out of church and carried her through the town's cobbled streets, and everyone came out to look at her. The windows were opened and women and children threw flowers at her, old people left their beds to see her, and men who were standing at the bar turned around, put their drinks aside, and respectfully doffed their hats to greet her. Throughout the entire procession, I was afraid that she'd fall off her pedestal—the streets were cobbled after all—and roll on the ground, and that her black mourning cape would get all dirty and she'd lose the beautiful handkerchief that she held in her hands for drying her eyes at the death of her son. I was on the edge the whole time, watching her step by step, out of fear that she'd stumble and fall and that her delicate porcelain hands would get broken and that she'd lose her crown, and that tears would flood her eyes.

One time when we caught a very big fish, there was a holiday and procession and everybody came out to look at it. At night they put candles all around it, and some people made bonfires on the beach. All night the whales snored on the high seas.

And instead of running away, I ran toward her and once I was close, I bowed. I bowed formally for a moment. She looked at me calmly; then I raised my head and saw that her eyes were the color of water. I remembered those eyes well from the day of the procession, sad and undefinably tender eyes, the eyes of a woman whose son has been killed and who feels so much pain that she doesn't think about vengeance because her sadness is so great that it brings out more love than anger. That woman's son had been killed—his body was probably still floating in the water and one of these days would appear on shore, his throat cut and an eye gouged out, full of seaweed and lichens, full of mud—and now she was walking down the beach. You could tell she was suffering from her eyes although she looked serene enough. I handed her a fishbone cup to hold the water from her eyes, in case she wanted to cry. It was really a bowl made from a very big fish, just the right size to hold sea water, fruit juices, women's tears. It's also useful to dig in the sand, to make holes. She looked at the cup and took it into her hands. Bone gets white with time, white and dry, with little black holes. She seemed to like her present, but she didn't cry right away. She held it in her hands a long time, and she looked at herself in it as if it were a mirror. Right away, I set out to clean the sand so she could sit down. I picked a square space, sheltered from the sea and the wind, protected by some wild rush. The dunes there are as high as mountains, and they almost hide the woods. The mounds are so hard and compact that nothing can sweep them away, not a whipping wind, not even a drifting sea. I cleaned the space with wicker rods, taking off the ants, insects, pieces of wood, shells, and all the other things the sea had left behind. I swept the surface with great care and, stooped over, I smoothed it with my hands in order to have it flat and smooth, comfortable to sit on.

*I was surprised and didn't know what to do. He didn't ask any questions. He didn't say a word. Right away he brought me a bone cup, and he started to clean the sand behind a dune, taking off all its dirt and impurities. I looked right and left, looking for a way to disappear.*

Then I invited her to sit down. I invited her to sit down with a gesture; I put out my right arm so she could hold on to it and slowly bend over, taking a seat on the throne of clean sand that was nearby. She looked tired and who knows where she came from, following the shoreline, suffering, suffering, following the shore. Along the way, she had lost her crown or they had taken it from her, just like they killed her son. She had also lost that handkerchief that she always used to have in her hands to dry her tears, and the little light dress that covered her body was clearly not enough to keep out the cold. I invited her to sit down because she seemed tired, and the wind was blowing. At any moment, the tide would begin to come in, but she would be protected there.

*The enormous beach that we had all thought deserted lay as far as the eye could see. I wasn't familiar with this mountain; I didn't know where the sea ended. I could only turn back, exhausted and cold, turn back, but he would have seen me again in this vast empty space if I had decided to turn back. Then he probably would have asked me questions. I was vaguely unsettled as if waiting for a premonition. The gray and mauve sky suddenly opened up, making way for a round sun, the color of death and shining like metal. The outline of a distant forest, completely enveloped in mist, seemed to be suspended between the sea and the sky, as if it were ascending into the heavens. The air was damp, palpable, full of the tension of an upcoming storm. The sound of the water breaking and the wind blowing seemed to me like the death throes of some gigantic marine animal hidden among the waves. Everywhere there seemed to be a revelation in the making.*

Once she sat down, I gestured for her to wait and I ran off to the mountain to look for pine boughs, wild flowers and poppies. I know the mountain well, but I was so nervous and excited that I lost time going around in circles, dead ends that didn't take me anywhere. Like puppies that jump up into the air, turn about, and go back and forth like crazy when they see their master, I got lost among paths full of plants. I hurt my hands, grabbed flowers and boughs without thinking, pulled up roots, crushed stalks on account of my nerves, and squashed the ivy as I walked. My ears were attuned to the sound of the tide as it came in, they heard its ascent, its growth; I couldn't see it, but I could hear it. Like two enemies that know each other well, I lay in wait, and it was ready to take advantage of my smallest slip.

I ran down the mountain with my arms full of pine boughs and wild flowers, so fast that I lost some on the way. She was there, sitting in the square of sand I made for her, protected from the sea, the wind, and from the ants, melancholy, looking without seeing, and the breeze shook her fragile dress as if it were a sail. One by one, I placed the aromatic boughs at her feet, in a circle, taking care that they didn't touch her dress. There were gray boughs partly covered with lichen and with lighter covered bark; if you scratch them a little, right away the pine's true skin would appear, green and resinous. There were dry sticks, crackling with pointed ends, that are used to build a fire in winter. I thought that this smell would maybe help her bear her sadness. She didn't look at me; she looked far away, and the water in her eyes was as deep as a day of fog and storms. There were some little pine nuts, just come out, very tight on the bough, with a hard shell and bright color. And there were white starling nests among the pine boughs, soft and silky like cotton balls. They were lightly woven nests that the birds embroidered with care; I thought that their softness and smooth surface would provide her with some nice sensations, welcoming and warm. Surrounded by boughs and plants, wild flowers and rush, she looked like a mountain virgin who had come down to the beach to look at the sea for a moment.

Right away I went to look for the piece of wood in the shape of a wolf that the water had dragged up the day before. Sometimes the water does this: brings things then leaves them on the shore and goes away as if it had traveled so far, as if it had walked days and nights just to bring that one thing, just to nudge up onto the sand those things it has collected on its journey. They are the sea's humble gifts; after thinking for hours and hours, after going back and forth from the depths to the surface, it hurls up a dead fish, a rotted piece of wood, a handful of seaweed or an open and empty shell. They are its wet, humble tributes. It had brought the piece of wood the day before; I found it not far from there, on the shore, wet from the waves, and I took it out of the water. That was hard because it had absorbed a lot of water and had become heavy. It was the shape and color of a sea wolf, so I grabbed it again by the head and dragged it over the beach to place it beside the Virgin. I left it next to her, but facing the sea so it wouldn't miss the world from which it came, in which it had been born and lived. He lay down to rest, tame, but he kept his head erect, overseeing the coast and its dangers. Watched over by the sea wolf like this, her throne seemed less forsaken, her realm more guarded. Surrounded by pine boughs, reeds, and flowers, having the stately figure of the wolf in front of her, she seemed more like the Virgin that I had seen that time in church, dressed in a black robe and carried around on a moveable pedestal. As I did then, I gave her lots of white flowers, yellow flowers, lilac and celestial blue flowers picked on the mountain. I hurried down the mountain and placed them, one by one, on her dress. Sometimes she looked back—her dead son—and her eyes were infinitely sad. With a gesture, I showed her that the mountain was full of flowers, that there were many more, but that I couldn't bring them all; I had other things to do for her. The tide advanced, serious, step by step, and each time it got closer to us. It left its damp stain on the ground, a little bit of foam floated by and later left, innocently, as if it hadn't moved forward, as if it wanted to hide its progress. I looked at the sea and then looked at her. There was considerable distance separating them, but I started to build a small sand wall anyway, to keep the odd stream of water from wetting her feet. I am very fast when I work, and I'm used to fighting the sea. I quickly built a sand barrier, a moist sea wall a few centimeters high that would act as a fortress against the water's penetration. I made it this size so she could look over it at the sea without having to get up or even raise her head.

On the other hand, the sea could see her only with great difficulty.

*He brought me small gifts. Things from the sea and forest. I don't know why he did it, but I thought I couldn't stop him. Whatever it was that he imagined, I didn't understand. His gestures were full of kindness and appreciation, and I was too tired to reject these gifts no matter how crazy they were. Although numb with cold, tired and without energy, I thought that I couldn't spend much more time there. Clearly it was dangerous to stay out in the open, defenseless on the enormous beach, exposed. As dangerous was to turn back, have the boy look for me and go around shouting to find me, alerting everyone to my presence. I stayed still, without knowing what to do, without deciding, letting myself be more tired than cautious. Meanwhile, he kept coming and going, bringing little presents with each trip.*

I went to look for an old oar half buried in the sand. It had stayed sunken there, part of the remains of a fishing boat—eaten by the salt, dampness, and water—whose broken skeleton served some birds as a stronghold. I had sometimes played inside the boat, full of stagnant water. I had touched its wooden planks, its crossed masts, felt its surfaces, skimmed its hollows. And the oar was hidden in the sand, sticking out its widest end, useless and full of holes. I brandished it in the air like a sword, shaking off all the sand that had stuck on it and, whirling it above my head, I ran along the deserted beach until I came to the dune where the Virgin was resting. I was very happy when I offered it to her, showing her what to do with it. First, I made all the gestures necessary to row. Then with rapid movements, I showed her how it could be used, if necessary, as a defensive weapon. She didn't pay much attention to my lessons. She was worried and looked behind her constantly. I left the oar at her side, like a queen's sceptre. I remembered the hole in the rock where I was saving things that I rescued from the sea. I was happy to have been collecting things every day so that I could now go find them and give them to her. She didn't say anything, but she waited. Just like a sailor who returns from each one of his trips loaded with presents and happy to be home; just as he affectionately and smugly displays his cloth from China, textiles from Holland, and jewels from Egypt; I too came and went, fervently, happy to go, happy to return. But her sad eyes looked backward, without seeing. The whole time I was afraid she would fall. They picked us, the old and the children, to carry her, to bring her through the crowds, to guide her through the town. It was my job to push the pedestal from one side. We left the church enveloped in a majestic silence, fitting for a procession. The old men and women went up ahead; we children followed.

*We were hidden for ten days without anyone seeing us, without one of us being recognized. Only a little boy found one of us walking on the beach.*

Stumbling, we pushed the cart, which was hitting against the cob-bled street and shaking. She was in mourning, wearing a long black velvet robe that hung from her head to her feet because they had killed her son. And she was very sa;, a great sorrow came through her wet eyes, the color of water. The robe was black and soft, a very deep black, very moving. I touched just the edge of her robe and trembled. Now she wasn't dressed in mourning, surely because a lot of time had passed since her son's death, but the sorrow didn't change. Now she wasn't dressed in black, but she suffered just the same. And her hands—the hands that showed were very slender and very white—under the black velvet robe held a lace handker- chief, surely to dry the tears when all the water she carried in her eyes overflowed at her son's death. The robe had a golden border, a small design in thread that I couldn't bring myself to touch. She still hadn't cried because the handkerchief was dry, but her expression was that of someone who would start crying at any moment, not screaming like the women of the town when they cry, but sadly and gently because the weeping from dis- covering that they've killed her only son is not one of shouting; it's one of deep sorrow. All the torches were lit when we set off from the church. And the old people's faces were full of wrinkles that got deeper in the candlelight. I was afraid that she would fall walking through the cobbled streets.

"She can fall," I said to one of the townsmen who was pushing along with me.

"If we walk carefully, she won't fall," he replied, but I didn't feel reassured.

If one of the others, for instance, were just a little less careful, she could fall to the ground instantly and hurt herself and dirty her robe and lose her beautiful handkerchief and scratch her hands. It was easier for us to protect her from the soldiers (from those soldiers who had killed her son) than to keep her from falling.

"Someone might be careless," I told him, nervously.

"She won't fall," he answered. All of us together will support her.

I had saved many things in the hole: old rusty fish hooks that still kept their sharp points, menacing creatures; parts of line that had fallen off fishing rods; pieces of net that used to trap fishes and had become moldy; huge shells to hear the sea when you're far away and can't see it; a gigantic fishbone whitened by the sun;

a burro's jaw; many pieces of sea glass, multicolored and polished by the water; tree bark with lichens still clinging to them; ropes from the boats; sailor's knots; big twisted nails; and a dark wooden box that floated in from a sunken ship. I stuck my hand into the hole and took out everything, one by one. I ran with my hands full to where she was—looking backwards—and I kept putting things in her lap. The tide kept coming in, each time a little bit closer, licking the edge of the sand wall. I drove the fishbone into the top of the wall like watch tower, a silent warning beacon, a light in the night that tells the traveller of a nearby danger: a sandbank or a sunken ship. I spread the piece of net at her feet, a majestic carpet for her to walk on; it was a smooth and delicate net, and with it, I outlined a map of the country where we would have liked to live, before the war. I planted the sea glass all around her like towers, like so many bishops and pawns, a purple horse head, a steel sword, a golden lantern, a mistletoe cathedral, an emerald fish eye. I placed the knots next to her hair so that it would not blow away, to fasten it to the sand if it wanted to run, if it wanted to go away to cry out its grief somewhere else. And I fastened the ropes around her waist, to tie her up like the boats are tied to the pier against the wind and the swaying tide. Surrounded by so many trophies, she seemes to be a water virgin, a marine statue, the figurehead of a ship I had seen once in a Maritime Museum. I had made a crown out of a long tendril of vines and placed it on her head; it was dark with very green leaves growing out of each side of a supple stem. Slowly, ceremoniously, I put it on her head. Now she seemed just right, finished and perfect, like the Virgin in church. Some bright wet seaweed on her dress became her robe.

*He came and went, from the sea to shore, from shore to me, but always distant, never coming to close to me. A bird flew over, and he threw a stone at it. Harsh, he frightened away the ants and the mollusks. Cautious, he watched over the advancing tide and was always moving, very busy, bringing things.*

Then I heard a noise. A different noise that didn't come from the sea or the sand. I know beach noises well, the noises of the birds, of rough sea, of underground currents. I know the noise of the faraway wind and of clouds charged with electricity. I heard a noise, and I got up immediately. I looked from one side of the beach to the other. The tide, coming up, was licking the edge of the sand wall that I had made. The fishbone, erect as a lighthouse, was aiming at the gruff sky. The tide, going back, was leaving sea-weed on the shore. And the sea wolf, lying down with its head raised, was watching, expectantly, close to us.

*I had to make a decision. Speak to him or flee, return to the place I had come from, even at the risk of his following me, even at the risk of his starting out on my same path.*

The noise came from the mountain, and neither the trees nor the wind made it, neither the birds nor the branches caused it; it was much more muffled and metallic sounding, it was a human noise. I got to my feet and on guard; she kept sitting, looking backward.

"Where are the men who killed her son?" I had asked when we took the Virgin from the church.

"I don't know," my friend answered. "Pay attention to pushing the cart."

Most likely now they are looking for her. All this time I had been playing without realizing that they were probably closing in. I know the sounds of the sea and the mountain well. I know when it sounds like a storm is brewing, when the wind is coming up and when the fish are snoring. They crucified him, after making him drag a heavy cross for the entire way, they made fun of his pain. And they wouldn't hesitate to do it again if they found her. And now the tide was climbing up the wall, licking the fishbone.

*Then I heard a noise. Not just one, but one that lasted a long time and was followed by others. A noise that filled me with fear and anxi-ety. I am not familiar with the noises of the mountain or of the sea. I always lived in the city.*

They were advancing, without doubt. They were advancing through the mountain, and they had the resolute steps of men who are armed and ready for anything. The steps of Roman sold-iers, with their heavy swords, and their crowns of thorns and their summary judgments, and their slow crucifixitions.

*The gulls were crying, and the sea was getting higher. So too the wind blowing among the pines was making the branches rattle and I heard sounds of something breaking. I heard wood groaning and stones hammering.*

I ran to the top of the mountain and saw them coming. They had pistols and guns.

*Then I decided and started to run back in the direction I came from. I started to run, and I stepped on the flowers. I heard the crackling of the shells, and a piece of glass stuck into my foot. I started to run without looking behind me, suspicious of the sound of the sea, the sound of the wind, and the shrieking of the birds.*

They had pistols and guns, dogs, knives, and lanterns. From the top of the mountain, I saw them coming. There were many Roman soldiers and their officials, their hirelings, their vassels and servants.

*I ran without thinking, I ran without knowing, I ran between the water, the birds, and the wind. Then I saw him. He was holding some big wooden oars which he spun around his head to frighten the soldiers. He probably took them by surprise, protected by the afternoon shadows. He knocked down two or three in this way, running with the oars in his hands and spinning them around in a circle, like a windmill's vanes. At first he probably caused confusion. It was dark, and he was very agile; he moved around very quickly from one place to another, without letting go of the oars.*

I ran without thinking, I ran without knowing, I ran between the water, the birds, and the wind to stop them.

*But then I didn't see anything more. I had to turn around to keep running. Until I recognized the sound of shots. The only sound you hear in the city.*

Translated by Mary Jane Tracy.

# Selections from Silendra

## Elizabeth Subercaseaux

### Tapihue

It never appeared in the press; not even when the River, La Toribia, flooded and the waters rose to the second floor of the house of the parish priest washing away three of the four filing cabinets that Don Francisco kept and leaving half of the town, as a result, without baptismal records and certificates of birth and death.

In those days, the newspapers were occupied with other things.

The nation never found out what Enedina's last words were when she kissed her children for the first time. No one learned that Ramon Chandia had returned from the dead. Actually, he didn't return for a long time... He came as Fulgencio, but no one ever found this out.

The people who lived in the important cities never learned about what happened far away at the cattle ranch in Peral; they didn't hear about the glass bird that terrorized the ranch by opening its womb and rising heavier than before, filled with the bodies of piled up peasants, until it disappeared from sight.

Who investigated the case of Juana? No one. How could they

investigate it if the neighbors didn't even know her name. Gilberto was the one who said that people without baptismal records are called Juan.

Adela's place hasn't changed. Adela died many years ago, but not her voice.

Filuca has probably forgotten a large part of her childhood, but she still remembers the moment when she entered the room on tiptoe with the chamber pot in her hand, calling out to them: "little mice, little mice" and then discovered the old woman in the corner.

Gilberto's coffins were made of oak. Neither kings nor leaders nor dictators have slept in beds as beautiful as these coffins of Tapihue: a town that didn't appear in the newspapers and that is not designated on the maps of the nation because the Captain ordered that it be erased.

That colorful land where Enedina and las Melanias lived for years amid helplessness, resignation and death, however, did not die.

# Enedina

She looked rather reserved and sad. She would spend a long time in front of the hearth waiting for the water to boil. But that wasn't what she was really waiting for. When the kettle, trembling from the steam and heat, began to totter, she continued doing the same thing.

She didn't know how to read or to write. She was naturally wise. One day she said, "I am tired of infinities." Actually, she didn't say this, but it was as if she had.

Her face was pale, her hair black, and her eyes, like mirrors of water, seemed to be looking for people in other dimensions. She was not looking at them. What I think that she was doing was reading their thoughts.

She spoke very little, and when she did, it was to say some short remark that apparently wasn't related to anything, but when spoken acquired a different dimension of meaning. "Today is Thursday just like yesterday."

She was as poor as an onion and closed. She didn't know it, or perhaps it didn't matter to her.

She had five children that glided along the hallway of the house silently like cats. They were extensions of herself. One knew this merely by seeing: the destinies of Vitoco, Ramon, Nora, Francisca and Eduvina were tied to the destiny of that other, like a torrent of blood is bound to the fate of its heart.

No one ever saw them near her. No one heard her name them nor did they hear them call her "mom." Nevertheless, they were stuck together. They formed a tree. They were like branches that never lower themselves in order to talk to the roots. . .this is how they were.

Her name was Enedina.

One morning she said, "My face hurts." She really said this. She also said "When the face hurts, the body is transformed into living sponges and it is not possible to know if the hunger felt is real or if it is a desire to die; time continues being time, but without hours. Noises arrive as if they were coming from afar, and death becomes unattainable because when the face hurts one knows that it will not come."

In the afternoon, she kissed her children for the first time. "I am going into the woods to look for water," she said. From there, she never again returned.

The next day at dawn, her body appeared in the branches of a tree, swaying with the sweetness of a flag without a country, forgotten throughout all the lands.

## Juana

She walked slowly, supported by a cane. Her legs could not have been weaker. Her ragged skirt barely managed to cover her knees. Her chest was deep-set and her waistcoat unbuttoned.

Raul saw her from the window.

"An old woman is coming!" he shouted.

"This hen refuses to eat; why did you name her Carmela?" asked

Melania from the backyard, as she looked furiously at Carmela: "Even though you have a name, tomorrow I am going to wring your neck, you fiendish hen!" she pronounced, hurling her away.

"To whom do you think the old woman belongs? She has to be someone's grandmother, although she is walking around alone without a child," Raul reflected.

The woman was closer. He could now see her face. Her eyes were green and her skin was so thin that her pointed chin looked like a bone sticking out in the air.

"She is a witch," thought the little boy, and he hid behind the gate, only drawing one of his eyes toward the narrow opening. At that instant, a dog appeared. He came running. He stopped in front of the old woman. She also stopped. The dog began licking her ankles, and the old woman raised her head; she rested her hands on the cane and remained motionless, looking at the sky.

Raul opened the gate a little. "She stands like a statue. No part of her is moving. The dog is licking her legs."

The woman was smiling, but barely. Her face was overcome with sorrow and tears.

"Now she is crying!" shouted the boy.

"You will also end up crying when I give you a spanking for having named the hen," said Melania from the backyard. "Why is it so difficult to twist Carmela's neck? There is no stew! Although it is the Feast Day of Saint Gilberto, there is no stew. We will just have potatoes with cornmeal and pork sausage," she decided.

At that instant, the dog stood erect and fixed his eyes on those of the old woman. It was then that she fell to the ground, lightly and slowly as if gravity no longer existed.

"Mom!" The woman collapsed like a piece of wire, the woman...

Melania arrived at the spot running, to get a look.

"A dead woman... A dead woman in the street! Why didn't you inform me sooner? Go tell the priest and your father to come here."

The priest knelt on the ground. While he took her pulse, he placed his ear over her heart.

"She is dead."

"We must inform her relatives," Estela said.

The neighbors had gathered around the body. Everyone spoke at the same time: "Someone must go find out where her relatives live." "This woman is not from Sauzal or Puyehue." "Her shoes are worn." "Her waistcoat is mended." "Poor thing, look at her face: she died crying."

"I wonder what her name is," speculated Raul.

"It is Juan," responded Gilberto with his eyes fixed on the lean body. "Those who don't have a name are called Juan."

"But she was a woman," insisted Raul.

"Then she will be called Juana," said the priest.

The dog wagged his tail and stretched out next to the dead woman.

## Silendra

When Juvenal disappeared, Silendra went crazy. She refused to open the door.

"Put on the chain and lock the padlock with a key. We shall never leave here again," she told her two daughters who looked at her in terror.

Silendra had been an ordinary woman. She had even been happy. She was Melania's friend and was the one who dressed her before the others put her in the coffin. She also consoled Gilberto and convinced Juvenal to give him the pig.

"Do it to console him," she said.

"Having a pig is not like having Melania," he replied.

"Something is better than nothing. Remember that when someone who is loved dies, hunger comes."

"Don Francisco says that is anxiety."

"That is probably what it is, but hunger comes nonetheless."

Silendra's madness started on the day that the sergeant told her "your Juvenal does not appear on the list of the prisoners" and Gilberto told her that he had seen the sergeant take the prisoners away in a wagon. That night Estella had been awakened by the sound of the shot, and that day, Silendra's madness began.

"We are going to eat corn," she informed her daughters who looked at her again in terror.

"She went crazy," Aida said looking at her sister.

"Yes," intervened their mother, "from grief."

One day she ordered them to make sweet tamales, the next day, corn bread and then corn soup. When she tired of warm corn, she ordered them to give it to her cold: corn salad, corn juice and cold turnovers made of corn. Everything was very salty, but later, when she tired of the salt, she ordered her meals with sugar.

"What are we going to do when our provisions run out? We are low on sugar and she adds four spoonfuls to each dish. And very little corn is left."

"You will plant corn, and you will harvest it. When the sugar runs out, I will eat the corn with salt like before."

In October, her teeth began to fall out.

"She eats too much corn," observed Fidelina, the younger of the two sisters.

By January she was toothless. From then on, she ordered them to give her broth.

The sisters sighed from relief. "We won't have to continue with the corn," they said, but their mother heard them.

"You will plant it as before, but you will also drink broth like me. I do not want to see a single ear of corn in this house. As soon as you harvest it, you will throw it into the river."

This is why the hen learned how to swim: to reach some of the thousands of grains that were being carried off downstream. Fidelina had seen the hen dive into the water and a subterranean fear prevented her from sleeping one night; if their mother had noticed the boldness of their hen, she would probably punish them for having permitted it. But she quieted down. Ever since the madness began, Silendra did not move from the rocking chair.

This situation persisted for a long time. Aida and Fidelina got thinner by the day, and Silendra got crazier.

"From grief," she repeated, "from grief."

The sisters didn't dare contradict her. They did not even dare remove the padlock key that Silendra kept in her apron pocket.

They were also weak, but to avoid falling into the throes of despair, they invented little amusements in the yard and in the orchard. In the yard, they parcelled out large cement tiles, and they competed over who would sweep her own tiles best. In the orchard, they played with the corn stalks, which they had given names. One was called Abel. The stalks were their children and they played house. The sisters became so fond of Abel that he began to acquire human characteristics. They would listen to him complain in the evenings and they would see him smiling in the morning.

"How did you sleep?" they would ask him.

The corn stalk didn't say anything, but they would hear "better than yesterday."

When March arrived, they were filled with grief. They would have to shell Abel and throw him into the river together with the others. This time, however, they did not pay attention to their mother, and they buried him alive in a corner of the yard.

A few days later, Fidelina could not get out of bed, and a week later, Aida got sick. The sisters were ill and couldn't speak, but Silendra thought that they still were meeting in the orchard and working in the cornfield.

One night Silendra burst into sobs. She called her daughters, but they didn't respond. She called again, "Aida, Fidelina, wake up. We have to look for Juvenal."

There was a thick silence and a smell of dead storks floating in the room. Silendra abandoned the rocking chair for the first time.

She appraoched the bed of the dead girls.

And she cried.

## Francisco

"Father, I killed my children."

"Silendra! Where have you been all these months?"

"In my home, Father, where I killed my children."

The priest left the confessional and took Silendra by the hand. "You are all skin and bones. What has happened to you? You look as if you were at death's door."

"I killed my daughters. I killed them by starving them, and from grief as well. For these reasons," she told him as she gave him a piece of paper. It was an old piece of paper. The words could barely be read.

"Juvenal and I wrote this on our wedding day. Read it. Read it aloud."

The priest started to read: "You will not abandon me. If it is my destiny to die before you, it doesn't matter because I will take with me the bag of tenderness that you gave me, and there, over the fresh earth of my grave, the men will scatter the earth of your love. Then my bones will not get cold, and I will not be frightened as I listen to how the worms talk, and my eternal bed will not be a niche that is icy and silent. My bed will be a different space with your eye in mine, your hands on my face, your laughter and your silence, will live forever submerged in my motionless body. I will not abandon you," the priest continued reading. "If everything is the other way and it has been written that you are the one who will abandon me forever, I will arrange things so that the men will scatter my affection over the fresh earth of your grave. This way I will prevent your bones from getting cold, and you will not listen, terrified at how the worms talk. Then your eternal bed will not be a niche that is icy and silent. Your bed will be a different space with my eyes in yours, my hands on your face, my laughter and my silence will live forever submerged in your motionless body."

Further down were the two signatures: Silendra and Juvenal.

"I don't know where his grave is. I don't know where to go to throw earth over it," stammered Silendra. Then she told him how Aida and Fidelina had died.

"I got the madness of corn. I got the madness of seclusion. Later I became obsessed with the broth, and when I wanted to leave and look for him, the girls were embraced on the bed and dead."

Don Francisco observed her. He couldn't believe that it was true. But it doesn't matter that he didn't believe it, because it was.

"I believe you, I believe you, I believe you," he continued repeating unable to convince himself. Quickly, he brought her to her home.

"Eat a little bread. It will make you feel better."

Silendra ate eagerly.

"Eat more. I will also give you a cup of tea. Now tell me what happened."

"Juvenal doesn't have a grave. That is what happened."

"We will make him one tomorrow right away."

"Without his bones?"

"The bones don't matter. The soul is what matters."

"But the soul does not turn cold nor does it get scared when the worms talk. The body is what matters. How am I going to bury my loved one if I don't know where his bones are?"

"But you have the bodies of Aida and Fidelina," said the priest remembering at that moment that the girls were still on the bed.

"Let's get them out of the house. We must notify the people of Tapihue and inform them. The mass will be given today. The burial will be tomorrow, with flowers and hymns."

The woman looked at him as one looks at people from the other side of a lake, almost without recognizing him. Her eyes went astray and suddenly she doubled over like a piece of cord and fell to the ground so sweetly that it was as if she had fallen while flying.

"Silendra!" the priest called out.

She didn't say anything, and a tear that was beginning to slide down her cheek began to cool on her skin.

Translated by Celeste Kostopulos-Cooperman.

# Two Words

## Isabel Allende

Her name was Belisa Crepusculario, not through baptism or because of her mother's insight, but because she herself sought it out until she found it, and dressed herself in it. Her occupation consisted of selling words. She travelled through the country, from the highest and coldest regions to the scorching coast, setting up in markets and fairs four sticks with a cloth awning, under which she protected herself from the sun and the rain to see her customers. She had no need to call out her wares, because with so much walking here and there everybody knew her. There were those who waited for her year in, year out, and when she appeared in the village with her bundle under her arm they would line up in front of her stall. Her prices were fair. For five cents she would give out poems learned by heart; for seven she would improve the quality of dreams; for nine she would write love letters; for twelve she would make up insults for irreconcilable enemies. She also sold stories; not fantastical tales but long, true chronicles which she would recite from beginning to end, without skipping a word. That is how she would carry the news from one village to the next. People would pay her to add a few lines: a child was born, so-and-so died, our children were married, the harvest caught fire. In each place people would sit around her to listen to her when she began to speak, and that is how they would learn about the lives of others, of faraway relatives, the ins and outs of the civil war. To anyone who bought fifty cents' worth she'd give as a gift a secret word to frighten melancholy away. Of course, it wasn't the same word for all—that would have been collective deception. Each one received his own, certain that no one, in the entire universe and beyond, would use that word to that specific end.

Belisa Crepusculario was born into a poor family, so poor that they did not even have names to call their children. She came into the world and grew up in the most inhospitable of regions and until her twelfth birth- day she had no virtue or occupation other than surviving the hunger and thirst of centuries. During an interminable drought she was forced to bury four younger brothers, and when she understood that her turn had come she decided to set forth across the plains towards the sea, wondering whether on the road she might be able to trick death. She was so stubborn that she succeeded, and not only did she save her own life but also, by chance, she discovered the art of writing. As she reached a village near the coast, the wind dropped at her feet a newspaper page. She lifted the yellow and brittle piece of paper and stood there a long while staring at it, unable to guess its use, until her curiosity overcame her shyness. She approached a man washing his horse in the same muddy waters where she had quenched her thirst.

"What is this?" she asked.

"The sports page of a newspaper," the man answered, not at all surprised at her ignorance.

The answer left the girl astonished, but she didn't want to seem impudent, so she simply enquired about the meaning of the tiny fly legs drawn on the paper.

"They are words, child. Here it says Fulgencio Barba knocked out Tiznao the Black in the third round."

That day Belisa Crepusculario found out that words fly about loose, with no master, and that anyone with a little cunning can catch them and start a trade. She reflected on her own situation, and realized that, other than becoming a prostitute or a servant in a rich man's kitchen, there were few jobs that she could do. Selling words seemed to her a decent alternative. From that moment she worked at that profession and never took on another. At first she offered her wares without suspecting that words could be written in other places than newspapers. When she became aware of this, she worked out the infinite projections of her business, paid a priest twenty pesos to teach her to read and write, and with the three pesos left over from her savings bought herself a dictionary. She perused it from A to Z, and then threw it into the sea, because she had no intention of swindling her clients with prepackaged words.

One August morning Belisa Crepusculario was sitting under her awning, selling words of justice to an old man who for twenty years had been requesting his pension, when a group of horsemen burst into the marketplace. They were the Colonel's men led by the Mulatto who was known throughout the area for the quickness of his knife and his loyalty towards his chief. Both men, the Colonel and the Mulatto, had spent their lives busy with the civil war, and their names were irremediably linked to calamity and plunder. The warriors arrived in a cloak of noise and dust and as they advanced the terror of a hurricane spread across the marketplace. The chickens escaped in a flutter, the dogs bolted, the women ran away with their children, and there was not a single soul left in the marketplace, except for Belisa Crepusculario, who had never before seen the Mulatto, and who was therefore surprised when he addressed her.

"It is you I'm after," he shouted, pointing at her with his rolled-up whip, and even before he finished saying so two men fell upon Belisa Crepusculario, trampling her tent and breaking her inkwell, tied her hands and feet, and lay her like a sailor's sack across the rump of the Mulatto's mount. They set off southwards at a gallop.

Hours later, when Belisa Crepusculario felt she was on the point of dying with her heart turned to sand by the shaking of the horse, she realized that they were stopping and that four powerful hands were placing her on the ground. She tried to stand up and raise her head with dignity, but her strength failed her and she collapsed with a sigh, sinking into a dazzling sleep. She awoke several hours afterwards to the murmurs of the night, but she had no time to decipher the sounds because as she opened her eyes she was met by the impatient eyes of the Mulatto, kneeling by her side.

"You're awake at last, woman," he said, offering his canteen for her to drink a sip of firewater mixed with gunpowder to jolt her back to life.

She wanted to know why she had been so mistreated, and he explained that the Colonel required her services. He allowed her to wet her face, and immediately led her to the far end of the camp where the man most feared in the entire land lay resting in a ham-mock suspended between two trees. She couldn't see his face because it lay hidden in the uncertain shade of the foilage and the ineffaceable shadow of many years living as an outlaw, but she imagined that it must be terrible if the Mulatto addressed him in such humble tones. She was taken aback by his voice, soft and mellifluous like that of a scholar.

"Are you the one who sells words?"

"At your service," she mumbled, screwing up her eyes to see him better in the gloom.

The Colonel rose to his feet and the light in the Mulatto's torch hit him full in the face. She saw his dark skin and his fierce puma eyes, and realized at once she was facing the loneliest man in the world.

"I want to be President," he said.

He was tired of roaming this cursed land fighting useless wars and suffering defeats that no trick could turn into victories. For many years now he had slept in the open, bitten by mosquitoes, feeding on iguanas and rattlesnake soup, but these minor inconveniences were not reason enough to change his fate. What really bothered him was the terror in other men's eyes. He wanted to enter villages under arcs of triumph, among coloured banners and flowers, with crowds cheering him and bringing him gifts of fresh eggs and freshly baked bread. He was fed up with seeing how men fled from his approach, how women aborted in fright and children trembled. Because of this, he wanted to become President. The Mulatto had suggested they ride to the capital and gallop into the Palace to take over the government, in the same way that they took so many other things without asking anyone's permission. But the Colonel had no wish to become simply another dictator, because there had been quite enough of those and anyhow that was no way to coax affection from the people. His idea was to be chosen by popular vote in the December elections.

"For that I need to speak like a candidate. Can you sell me the words for a speech?" the Colonel asked Belisa Corpusculario.

She had accepted many different requests, but none like this one, and yet, she felt like she could not refuse, for fear that the Mulatto would shoot her between the eyes, or even worse, that the Colonel would burst into tears. Also, she felt an urge to help him, because she became aware of a tingling heat on her skin, a powerful desire to touch this man, go over him with her hands, hold him in her arms.

All night long and much of the following day Belisa Corpusculario rummaged through her stock for words that would suit a presidential oration, while the Mulatto kept a close watch on her, unable to tear his eyes away from her strong walker's legs and untouched breasts. She cast aside words that were dry and harsh, words that were too flowery, too faded through much use, words that made improbable promises, words lacking truth, muddled words, and was left with only those that were able to reach unerringly men's thoughts and women's intuitions. Making use of the skills bought from the priest for twenty pesos, she wrote out the speech on a sheet of paper and signalled the Mulatto for him to untie the rope that held her by the ankles to a tree. She was brought once more into the Colonel's presence, and seeing him again, again she felt the tingling anxiety she had felt at their first meeting. She gave him the sheet of paper and waited, while he stared at it, holding it with only the tips of his fingers.

"What in the Hell's name does it say here?" he asked at last. "Can't you read?"

"What I know is how to make war," he answered.

She read him the speech out loud. She read it three times, so that he would be able to learn it by heart. When she finished, she saw the emotion drawn on the faces of his soldiers who had assembled to listen to her, and noticed that the Colonel's yellow eyes were shining with excitement, certain that with these words the presidential seat would be his.

"If after hearing it three times, the boys still have their mouths open, then this stuff works, my Colonel," approved the Mulatto.

"How much do I owe you for your job, woman?" the chief asked.

"One peso, my Colonel."

"That's not expensive," he said, opening the pouch which hung from his belt with the leftovers from the latest booty.

"And you also have a right to a bonus. You can have two secret words, for free," said Belisa Corpuscolario.

"How's that?"

She explained to him that for every fifty cents a customer spent, she gave away one word for his exclusive use. The chief shrugged, because he had no interest in her offer, but he didn't want to seem impolite with one who had served him so well. Slowly she approached the leather stool on which he was sitting and leaned over to give him his two words. Then the man caught a whiff of the mountain smell on her skin, the fiery heat of her lips, the terrible brushing of her hair against him, the wild mint breath whispering into his ear the two secret words that were his by right.

"They're yours, my Colonel," she said drawing back. "You may use them as much as you wish."

The Mulatto escorted Belisa to the edge of the road, never taking his begging mongrel eyes off her, but when he stretched out his hand to touch her she stopped him with a gush of made up words that dampened his desire, because he believed they were some sort of irrevocable curse.

During the months of September, October and November the Colonel delivered his speech so many times that, had it not been composed out of long-lasting and glittering words, the constant use would have turned the speech to ashes. He travelled across the country in all directions, riding into cities with a triumphant air, but stopping also in forgotten hamlets where only traces of garbage signalled a human presence, in order to convince the citizens to vote for him. While he spoke, standing on a platform in the middle of the marketplace, the Mulatto and his men distributed sweets and painted his name with scarlet frost on the walls. After the speech was over, the troops would light firecrackers, and when at last they would ride away, a trail of hope remained for many days in midair, like the memory of a comet. Very soon the Colonel became the most popular candidate. It was something never seen before—this man sprung from the civil war, crisscrossed with scars and speaking like a scholar, whose renown spread across the nation moving the very heart of the country. The press began to take notice. Journalists travelled from far to interview him and repeat his words and the number of his followers grew, as well as the number of his enemies.

"We're doing fine, my Colonel," said the Mulatto after twelve weeks of success.

But the candidate did not hear him. He was repeating his two secret words, as he now did more and more frequently. He would repeat them when nostalgia made him soft, he would murmur them in his sleep, he would carry them with him on horseback, he would think of them just before pronouncing his celebrated speech, and he would surprise himself savouring them at careless moments. And every time these two words sprang to his mind, he would sense the mountain perfume, the fiery heat, the terrible brushing and the wild mint breath, until he began to roam around like a sleepwalker, and his very own men realized that his life would come to an end before he reached the presidential seat.

"What's happening to you, my Colonel?" the Mulatto asked many times, until one day the chief could bear it no longer and confessed that the two words he carried embedded in his gut were to blame for his mood.

"Tell them to me, to see if that way they lose their power," his faithful assistant begged him.

"I won't, they belong to me alone," the Colonel answered.

Tired of seeing his chief weaken like a man condemned to death, the Mulatto slung his rifle over his shoulder and set off in search of Belisa Crepusculario. He followed her traces throughout the vastness of the land, until he found her beneath her awning, telling her rosary of tales. He stood in front of her, legs spread out and weapon in hand.

"You're coming with me," he ordered.

She was waiting for him. She picked up her inkwell, folded her awning, draped her shawl over her shoulders and without saying a word climbed on the back of his horse. During the whole journey they never even motioned to one another, because the Mulatto's lust for her had turned to anger and only the fear of her tongue stopped him from whipping her to shreds, as he would have done with anyone else in a similar situation; nor was he willing to tell her how the Colonel went about in a daze, and how what had not been achieved by many years of battling had suddenly been wrought by a charm whispered in his ear. Two days later they reached the camp, and he immediately took the prisoner to the candidate, in front of all the troops.

"I've brought you this witch so that you can give her back her words, my Colonel, and she can give you back your manhood," he said pointing the rifle's muzzle at the woman's neck.

The Colonel and Belisa Crepusculario gazed at one another for a long moment, measuring one another at a distance. The men understood that their chief would never be able to rid himself of the charm of those two cursed words, because as they looked on, they saw how the bloodthirsty eyes of the puma softened as the woman now stepped forward and held him by the hand.

Translated by Alberto Manguel.

# The Authors

ISABEL ALLENDE was born in Lima, Perú, in 1942 but considers Chile to be her native country. One of Latin America's best-known and most distinguished writers, her work includes the international best-seller *The House of the Spirits*. She has written many plays and short stories and has been a journalist since the age of seventeen.

Long a strong supporter of human rights and democracy in Chile, where she lived until her uncle, Salvador Allende, was overthrown by a coup d'état, she has also given strong support to women's rights issues. She presently resides in California.

Translations of her work into English include:
*The House of the Spirits*. New York: Knopf, 1985.
*Of Love and Shadows*. New York: Bantam, 1987.
*Eva Luna*. New York: Bantam, 1989.

MARÍA LUISA BOMBAL was born in 1907 in Viña del Mar, Chile, to an upper-class family of landowners. She traveled at an early age to France where she was schooled and completed her university training.

Upon her return to Chile, she associated herself with the Bohemian literary figures of the time, including Humberto Díaz Casanvera. Throughout the thirties, she lived in Buenos Aires and participated in the activities of the journal *Sur*.

Bombal's novels and a few collections of her short stories are characterized by a surrealistic prose as well as a universe filled with magical undertakings. Her themes of erotic frustration, social marginality, and cosmic transcendence are profound in expressing women's predicament from a female perspective.

She has been widely translated into English, and her work appears in:

*New Islands*. New York: Farrar, Strauss and Giroux, 1988.

Her work in Spanish can be found in:

*Última Niebla*. Seix Barral: Barcelona, 1988. This collection includes her complete works.

María Luisa Bombal died in Santiago in 1982.

ALINA DIACONÚ was born in Bucharest in 1951 and at age 12 migrated with her family to Buenos Aires.

Among her works:

*La señora*, 1984.

*Buenas noches profesor*, 1986.

*Enamorado del muro*, 1987.

MAROSA DI GIORGIO, born in 1941, lives in Montevideo but rarely appears in literary circles. Her work, "Los papeles salvajes," is one of the most intriguing prose poems to be published in Uruguay, where genre classifications of language are abolished.

Among her works:

*Historias de las violetas*. Arca, 1967.

*Magnolias*. Arca, 1970.

*La liebre de marzo*. Montevideo: Arca, 1971.

SARA GALLARDO was born in Buenos Aires in 1931. She worked as a journalist in the 1950s and began traveling extensively in Latin America, Europe, and the Orient, sending articles to the most prestigious newspapers in Buenos Aires.

Gallardo wrote several novels and short stories yet she was not a known figure in Argentine literary life. Her work deals with marginal areas in Southern Argentina and the Patagonia. In her narrative, the landscape acquires a new, mythical element as do the people who live on it.

She died in 1988.

Among her works:

*Enero.* Buenos Aires: Editorial Sudamericana, 1958.

*El país del humo.* Buenos Aires: Editorial Celetia, 1987.

*Páginas de Sara Gallardo.* Buenos Aires: Editorial Celetia, 1987.

ANGÉLICA GORODISCHER is one of the most original science fiction writers in Argentina and the most well-known in Latin America.

She was born in Buenos Aires in 1941 and later moved with her family to the city of Rosario where she began writing her stories. All of them deal with science fiction themes and the achievement of feminine utopias.

Among her works:

*Trafalgar,* 1967.

*Casta luna electrónica,* 1975.

*Las pelucas,* 1970.

*Bajo las jubeas en Flor,* 1988.

LILIANA HECKER was born in Buenos Aires in1943. The winner of many important literary prizes she, along with Alicia Steimberg and Ana María Shua, is considered to be one of the most exciting writers of today. Hecker has dedicated herself to writing and works as a journalist.

Among her works:

*Los que vieron la zarza,* 1966.

*Las peras del mal,* 1982.

Her work has appeared in English in the collection *Other Fires, Short Fiction by Latin American Women,* edited by Alberto Manguel.

LUISA MERCEDES LEVINSON was born in Buenos Aires in 1912 and died in the same city in 1987. Considered to be one of the most exciting and intriguing figures in the Argentine world of letters in the 1940s, she was a good friend of Jorge Luis Borges and Adolfo Bioy Casares.

Levinson writes primarily short stories, using the themes of people versus the land, fantasy, and human relations. She is regarded as a serious writer in that she has broken away from the traditional role of the Argentine woman writer by transcending her own experiences and projecting them into the world of ideas.

Luisa Mercedes Levinson has been translated and anthologized in French, German and Greek. Her stories and novels have yet to be translated into English, and her work in Spanish is now out of print.

Among her works:

*A la sombra del buho.* Buenos Aires: Losada, 1972.

*Las tejedoras de hombre.* Buenos Aires: Losada, 1972.

*El estigma del tiempo.* Barcelona: Seix Barral, 1977.

*La isla de los organilleros.* Buenos Aires: Losada, 1964.

SILVINA OCAMPO was born in Buenos Aires in 1903 where she still lives today and where she was declared "illustrious citizen" in 1990. Ocampo is one of the least-known members of the distinguished generation of writers that published in Sur, a journal founded and directed by her sister, Victoria.

She studied painting in Paris and exhibited her work in both Paris and Buenos Aires. She has also published award-winning collections of poetry but is more widely-known for her short stories.

The numerous collections of her short stories deal with themes of the fantastic where ordinary events unfold in an extraordinary manner. Women and children often appear as protagonists. The stories take place in a familiar and ordinary social order, thus conveying an ambiance of normality to the lives of protagonists surrounded by the unusual, the magical, and the unreal.

Ocampo married another fantastic story-writer and novelist, Adolfo Bioy Casares, and was a long-time collaborator of Jorge Luis

Borges. The three of them edited the only major anthology of fantastic literature ever to be published in Spanish and also translated into English.

Among her works:

*Los días de la noche*. Buenos Aires: Sudamericana, 1970.

*La furia y otros cuentos*. Buenos Aires: Sur, 1959.

*Las invitadas*. Buenos Aires: Losada, 1961.

Her only collection of short stories published in English is *Leopoldina's Dream*, (New York: Penguin, 1988) translated by Daniel Balderston.

Her latest works include:

*Y así sucesivamente*. Barcelona: Tusquets Editores, 1987.

*Cornelia Frente al espejo*. Barcelona: Tusquets Editores, 1988.

Her work has been anthologized in French, German, Hebrew and Italian.

ELVIRA ORPHEÉ was born in Tucumán in 1930 and lives in the city of Buenos Aires where she has dedicated herself to writing fiction as well as journalistic articles. Orpheé studied philosophy and letters at the University of Buenos Aires and took courses in literature at the Sorbonne. She has published novels, short stories and articles and she has won several important literary prizes in Argentina.

Her work deals mostly with life in her native Tucumán.

Her narrative is unusual for the lyrical quality of language used to describe the harsh landscapes and resentful people who inhabit them.

Orpheé has two collections of short stories where the principal themes deal with the fantastic, possession by demons, envy, and misery, as well as domestic life in the provinces. Elements of magic give these short stories an aura of mythical tales.

Among her works:

*Aire tan dulce*. Buenos Aires: Sudamericana 1966.

*Su demonio preferido*. Buenos Aires: Emece 1973.

*Las viejas fantasiosas*. Buenos Aires: Emece 1981.

She has had a novel published in English, *The Angel's Last Conquest*, translated by Magda Bogin.

OLGA OROZCO was born in Toay, a small city in the Argentine Pampa, in 1920. She later moved to Bahiá Blanca and then to Buenos Aires.

She is one of Argentina's most distinguished poets, yet her work is virtually unknown in the United States. Orozco's poetry is characterized by a surrealistic and almost cosmic sense of anguish as well as what she often calls an essential search for God.

Among her works:

*La oscuridad es otro sol*. Buenos Aires: Losada, 1967.

*Obra poética*. Buenos Aires: Corregidor, 1979.

*En el revés del cielo*. Buenos Aires: Sudamericana, 1987.

ALEJANDRA PIZARNIK, born in 1936, lived both in Argentina and France and is considered to be one of the most prolific and original poets of her generation.

Her poetry, always centered on the fantastic, includes a collection of prose poems of short narratives based on Valentine Penrosi's *Erzebeth Bathory: La Contesse Sangrante* (Paris, 1963) which tells the story of the murder of 600 girls due to the sexual perversion of the Countess Bathory.

Pizarnik's poetry is obssesed with the theme of death and with the creation of a poetic language as a means of transcending life. She committed suicide in 1972.

Among her works in English:

*Alejandra Pizarnik: A Profile*, edited and with an introduction by Frank Graziano. Durango: Logbridge-Rhodes, 1987.

CRISTINA PERI ROSSI was born in Montevideo in 1941 and studied literature at the University of Montevideo. Due to her resistance to the military takeover in Uruguay, she was forced to flee to Barcelona, Spain in 1972. She still resides there.

Her work is multifaceted and includes collections of short stories, journalistic essays and poems.

Rossi's collection of short stories is innovative. Political events masquerade in several of her allegories without direct reference to the political situation of her native country.

Among her works:

*Indicios pánicos*. Montevideo: Nuestra América, 1970.

*La rebelión de los niños*. Caracas: Monte Avila, 1980.

*El museo de los esfuerzos inútiles*. Barcelona: Seix Barral, 1983. Her novel, *The Ship's Fool*, was published by Reader's International in London in 1989.

ANA MARÍA SHUA was born in 1952 in Buenos Aires. After studying journalism and working for several newspapers, she has decided to dedicate herself to writing full-time.

Her work is receiving important recognition in Argentina, and her novels and short stories have been on the bestsellers list in Buenos Aires. The collection *La Suerena* is of extreme innovation and poetic quality.

Among her works:

*Soy paciente*. Buenos Aires: Losada, 1980.

*Los amores de Laurita*. Buenos Aires: Editorial Sudamericana, 1983.

*Viajando se conoce gente*. Buenos Aires: Sudamericana, 1984.

*Los diás de pesca*. Buenos Aires: Corregidor, 1987.

*La sueñera*, 1989.

MARCELA SOLÁ was born in Buenos Aires in1936. She began writing late in life and has published one of the most exciting collections of short stories that deal with fantastic themes and political expression.

Her style is lyrical but at the same time shows a cruel human nature, similar to the style of Silvina Ocampo. Sola's language is refined, poetic, and often touches on the magical and mysterious.

Sola was awarded a visiting writers grant at the University of Iowa in 1984 and has taught at the University of Montreal.

Among her works:

*Los condenados visten de blanco*, 1983.

*Mis propios ojos no dan abasto,* 1984.
*Manual de situaciones imposibles,* 1990.

ALICIA STEIMBERG, born in Buenos Aires in 1945, is considered to be one of the most exciting Argentine writers living today. She devotes her entire time to writing and is the author of several collections of short stories and novels. Her book, *Amatista,* has been on the bestsellers list in Argentina and was a finalist in the prestigious contest of the *Sonrisa Vertical* sponsored by Tusquets Publishing House.

Her stories have the ability to speak of the unreal through the humor, irony, and detachment of her protagonists.

Among her works:

*De músicos y relojeros.* Buenos Aires: Grijalbo, 1967.

*La loca 101.* Buenos Aires: Ediciones de la Flor, 1971.

*Su espíritu inocente.* Buenos Aires: Pormarie, 1981.

*El árbol del placer.* Buenos Aires: Emece, 1986.

ELIZABETH SUBERCASEAUX was a very outspoken journalist during the Pinochet regime, and is one of the most outstanding Chilean writers of the younger generation. She has dedicated her life to journalism and wrote for various newspapers which were against the military dictatorship.

Among her works:

*Silendra,* 1987.

*Canto de la raíz lejana,* 1989.

LUISA VALENZUELA, daughter of the well-known writer Luisa Mercedes Levinson, was born in Buenos Aires in 1938 and grew up surrounded by important literary figures. She began working as a journalist and wrote for the prestigious newspaper *La Nación.* She also published in the United States. Her themes range from the personal and the erotic to the political context of Latin America. The latter is prominently reflected in her recent work, which deals with political tyranny. She is one of the most prolific writers of her generation as well as one of the most translated.

Among her published works in English:
*Other Weapons.* Hanover, New Hampshire: Ediciones del Norte, 1975.
*The Lizard's Tail.* New York: Farrar, Strauss, Giroux, 1983.
*Open Door.* San Francisco: North Point Press, 1988.

# The Translators

MARY BERG is an assistant professor of Spanish at Wheaton College and a fellow at the Institute for Literary Studies at Harvard University.

MONICA BRUNO was born in Costa Rica. A graduate of Wellesley College, she is presently a graduate student at Columbia University. She has completed an English translation of a collection of short stories by Costa Rican women writers.

SHAUN T. GRIFFIN, a poet and translator, lives in Reno, Nevada. He is the author of several publications dealing with Nevada authors.

REGINA HARRISON is an associate professor of Spanish at Bates College in Maine. She has written many articles dealing with Latin American women writers as well as anthropological studies of Perú and Ecuador. She is the author of *Sing Song and Memory: Quechua Songs*.

ELAINE DOROUGH JOHNSON is an assistant professor of Spanish at Augustana College. She is presently translating a collection of stories by María Brunei.

CELESTE KOSTOPULOS-COOPERMAN is an assistant professor of Humanities and Modern Language at Suffolk University. She is author of *The Lyrical Vision of María Luisa Bombal* and many essays on Latin American writers.

CHRISTOPHER LELAND is a professor of creative writing at Wayne State University and the author of *Mrs. Randall and The Book of Marvels.*

SUZANNE JILL LEVINE is one of the most distinguished translators of Latin American literature. Her translations include *A House in the Country* by José Donoso and *A Plan for Escape* by Adolfo Bioy Casares. She is a professor of Spanish at the University of California at Santa Barbara.

ALBERTO MANGUEL is an Argentinian translator who now resides in Canada. He is the editor of *Other Fires*, a collection of short fiction by Latin American women.

JANICE MALLOY is an editor and translator presently working at D.C. Heath in Boston. She has translated the work of Marjorie Agosín.

EMMA SEPULVEDA-PULVIRENTI is a poet, literary critic, and associate professor of Spanish at the University of Nevada, Reno. She is the author of two collections of poetry.

ELIZABETH RHODES is associate professor of Spanish at Boston College and a specialist in medieval and golden age Spanish literature.

LORRAINE ELENA ROSES is a professor of Spanish at Wellesley College and a specialist in Cuban literature. She is the author of *Voices of A Storyteller: Cuba's Lino Novas Calvo*.

RICHARD SCHAAF is a distinguished translator especially well-known for his translations of poetry. His most recent work is a translation of *The Black Heralds* by César Vallejo. He lives in Washington, D.C.

NINA M. SCOTT is a professor of Spanish at the University of Massachusetts. She is the editor of *Breaking Boundries*, a collection of essays on contemporary Hispanic women writers.

MARY JANE TREACY is a professor of Spanish at Simmons College and has published essays on the writing of Latin American women writers.

ALISON WEBER is a professor at the University of Virgina and the author of works on Latin American writers.